PRAISE FOR *FULL COVERAGE*

'As someone who has been engorged or eviscerated by music journalism for decades (and has lied about being so affected by it for just as long), being asked to read a history of this country's music press tickled me pinkish. For me, growing feverish with the need to know more about the facts and fantasies of music during the '80s and the '90s and ever since, publications like *Juke* or *RAM* then street press were essentials, above eating or whatever other things folks do to sustain themselves. By charting the rise of *Go-Set* and its aftermath, the big mags like local *Rolling Stone* and *Juice* and the lesser-heralded *Roadrunner*, Sam has given enthusiasts like this old nerd a sensational history not only of music journalism but also a cultural history – how our population, our cultural cringe and our flickering, sputtering spotlight on the world stage created heroes and villains of unique character. *Full Coverage* is affectionate, often tough, yet lacking the braggadacio of similar tomes from other regions that herald the writer as the only hero of the story. There are heroic, foolhardy, cruel and noble stories here, and I'll be reading again after I scour the dusty stores of this land for copies of *Roadrunner*.'

Singer-songwriter and guitarist Tim Rogers (You Am I)

FULL COVERAGE

A HISTORY OF ROCK JOURNALISM IN AUSTRALIA

SAMUEL J. FELL

MONASH UNIVERSITY PUBLISHING

Published by Monash University Publishing
Matheson Library Annexe
40 Exhibition Walk
Monash University
Clayton, Victoria 3800, Australia
publishing.monash.edu/

Monash University Publishing: the discussion starts here

ISBN: 9781922633934 (paperback)
ISBN: 9781922633958 (epub)

NATIONAL LIBRARY OF AUSTRALIA

A catalogue record for this book is available from the National Library of Australia

Cover and typesetting by Peter Long
Author photograph by Claire McGarry

Printed in Australia by Griffin Press

CONTENTS

PREFACE

It's Easter Monday 2005 and I'm leaning against the doorframe of a converted shipping container. Dusk has long since descended and it's chilly. I'm wearing a jacket, jeans and an old black beanie.

Inside the container, which is acting as a dressing room of sorts, are a crew of musical vagabonds lit in fluro candescence, in various states of repose, barely visible through thick, cloying smoke. The colourfully clad woman next to me passes along a smoking number as a figure across the space yells over at me, 'Thirsty, man?'

I nod yes and he bends from his considerable height, fishes about in a tub of melted ice at his feet and reefs out a can of beer, which he tosses to me with a toothy grin. I manage to catch it with one hand while smoking with the other.

I stand there and I take it all in. I resist the urge to pull the cheap plastic biro from behind my ear, the small notebook from the back pocket of my jeans. Definitely not the Dictaphone tucked somewhere in the worn green canvas bag slung over my shoulder.

My photographer is in here somewhere too, lost in the haze on the other side of the room.

There's a commotion behind me and I turn and come face to face with American musician George Clinton, pink, purple and grey dreadlocks heaped upon his head, his face a mess of curled beard, dressed in all colours of the rainbow and more, the colours of psychedelic funk … he looks at me askance before stepping past into the smoky light and rousing his gang of reprobates, for they are indeed Parliament-Funkadelic and they were due on stage to close out the Byron Bay Bluesfest some twenty minutes ago.

They all laugh and stretch and pat me on the back as they stamp out joints and upend beer cans and stride out to play their music to 10,000 people like it ain't no thing. They've been doing this for decades.

And then it's just me and my photographer. If it wasn't for the dissipating smoke and crumpled cans, chairs left askew, I wouldn't be sure any of it had actually happened. I had a strange, lingering feeling that this was, if only for a short time, a glimpse into another world, one I couldn't find again if I searched a lifetime.

And I searched for a long time. Not specifically for the world inhabited by P-Funk (for there are precious few who find that world, and then their way out again), but for worlds inhabited by musicians of all stripes, musicians who I admired and who talked to me through song, worlds I then felt duty-bound to share with as many people as possible, no matter the detrimental effect on my own mental stability.

Such is the lot of the music writer, the music critic, the rock journo – 'the enemy' as we were termed in the Cameron Crowe movie *Almost Famous*, a slur directed at me in real life on more than one occasion. But it mattered little, that tag. The only thing that *did* matter was the collecting of music, the listening to music, the dissecting of music and the sharing of music and the worlds from which it emerged with anyone who would read what I wrote via the pages of whichever magazine or newspaper would pay me to write about it.

I searched for these worlds but never really found them, not in their entirety, anyway. I'd be invited in for a glimpse – via tag-alongs, ride-alongs, drink-alongs and sing-alongs – and I'd do my best to capture them, or at least remember them, so I could write about them in such a way as to make these worlds seem like places others were inspired to seek out too.

Rock critics have been attempting the same thing for decades, and not just in the musical hotbeds of America and England, but in Australia as well. For Australia is the only southern hemisphere country to support a dedicated rock 'n' roll press for any decent length of time, and this press has existed alongside an equally vigorous music scene for over fifty years.

It began in the mid-1960s with *Go-Set*; it morphed, in the 1970s, into a serious enterprise via the pages of *RAM* and *Juke*; it proliferated through the 1980s and 1990s with the almost uniquely Australian medium that was street press; and it's since transformed into the online music and culture hubs that exist today. As it developed, it spawned the careers of countless writers, editors, photographers, publishers and commentators. They prodded and dissected and promoted and encouraged the music, and rock journalism and Australian music grew together.

Australian music has been well documented, but the press that existed alongside it all hasn't. It's a small yet colourful slice of Australian popular culture which boomed, which quickly became an integral part of the music industry itself and which is, in a digital era, evolving faster than it ever has done before. The technology is different, but the possibilities remain endless.

In the music and the culture these publications have covered, there is a unique splendour. The communication of passion through words, the recording of history, the capturing of a time and place – all this is beautiful in its own tangled way.

In speaking to scores of people in order to piece this story together (there were also a handful who declined to talk, for one reason or another), it was obvious that most felt similarly. They were proud to have lent themselves to the subculture of Australia's rock 'n' roll press.

PART ONE

The Beginning

The Birth of Australia's Rock Press and the Rise of the Counterculture (1966–1975)

1

FRIDAY NIGHT IN MELBOURNE

'It was an awakening.'

Ian 'Molly' Meldrum

Back in the mid-1960s, David Pepperell would cover a lot of ground on a Friday night in Melbourne. As roadie for a slew of local acts, Pepperell had become adept at navigating the southern capital, criss-crossing the Yarra numerous times in between packing and unpacking vans, loading and unloading onto various stages, often multiple times a night.

'I remember one night we did five,' he recalls. 'We could get them on and off the stage in about seven minutes. Because you had no PA [system], they were provided, and you used the house band's equipment. So you'd run on with your guitars and snare, set up, play and get off. That's all you were carrying.

'It was big distances, from the Coburg Swinger to, say, Kew Town Hall – you had to work it out,' he adds with a laugh. 'But you could make $2500 on a Friday night, it was massive, absolutely massive. And that was between the band and one or two roadies – six guys – so you figure how much money that is. And that's when wages were about $20 a week.'

From the Swinger to Kew, across the river to the St Kilda Town Hall, perhaps back to Prahran or Moorabbin, maybe even out east to Box Hill, venues capable of holding up to 1000 people, swelling audiences adding their young voices to the cacophony, to the sound of the times themselves. Five bands a night (a couple of audition bands who weren't paid, a couple of local bands and a headliner), plus bands playing spot gigs – slots reserved for those with a hit single, usually half an hour or so – all to packed houses.

This was Melbourne's suburban town hall scene, running strong from the early 1960s and getting bigger as Pepperell worked his magic off-stage and behind the wheel as the decade hit its halfway mark. 'It was huge,' he emphasises.

Now a respected journalist and writer, and former owner of seminal Melbourne record shop Archie & Jugheads, Pepperell in the early 1960s was merely twenty, a mad music fan with his finger on the pulse of all that was happening in his vibrant southern city. And it was *happening*. Pop and rock 'n' roll were alive, filled with youthful energy, a new music for a newly awakened group of kids. Melbourne was the epicentre of it all.

'Melbourne was probably more like [swinging] London than any other city in the world,' remembers iconic Australian performer Normie Rowe, who cut his teeth on suburban Melbourne stages through 1961 and 1962. 'That's where that popular music culture, or teenage culture (which was spearheaded by the music), I think that's where it was born, it was moulded.'

This culture had been in the making for some time. Over in America, Elvis Presley, Chuck Berry and Bill Haley were in full swing. In Australia, Johnny O'Keefe (inspired by Haley and his Comets) was forging a rock 'n' roll career on the fledgling medium that was television. Programs such as the ABC's *Six O'Clock Rock* (which featured O'Keefe and his band the Dee Jays) and TCN-9's *Bandstand* were making tentative forays into capturing this burgeoning youth market.

The first half of the twentieth century had hardly been easy. Rowe points out: 'People [were] having to deal with stuff over which they had no control, so we're talking about World War I, the Great Depression, World War II and even leading into Korea … these were big fucking social issues. Issues that personally affected people's lives, family members getting killed, dynamically powerful social issues. And then all of a sudden, after the Korean War there was none of that, there was this sort of lifting of a blanket. At the same time, somebody had developed pressing vinyl records, and then somebody had come up with the idea of pressing a seven-inch vinyl record, with a track on each side. And that was the first time in history [that] music was wrested from the head of the household and laid in the hands of young people.'

Inspired in part by this new music, young people began looking beyond what their parents had taught them. The music struck new chords and heralded new times; it enabled the youth to move and think outside of convention. While television shows such as *Six O'Clock Rock* and *Bandstand* were conduits into this musical world, in early 1960s Melbourne the tried and tested medium of radio was many young people's greatest influence. The powers that be in Sydney tended to be conservative and loath to embrace the cultural change that music was heralding; Melbourne was vivid and vivacious by comparison, lead in part by 3KZ DJ Stan 'The Man' Rofe, who became for many the guide into this exciting, cacophonous world.

'Stan was up with every trend in music,' remembers Billy Pinnell, these days regarded as the doyen of community radio in Australia. At the time he was a young man, fresh into the medium, in what was still a fledgling music industry in Australia. 'Before the Beatles and the Stones broke in '62 or '63, there was always Elvis. Elvis was the man.

Even when the Stones and whoever became popular, Stan would have this contest, Elvis versus the Beatles, and Elvis would wipe everyone off. This was [via] phone calls, so there'd be fifty phone calls to ten or something [in favour of Elvis], so Stan would play a lot of that kind of music – Little Richard, Chuck Berry, all the rock pioneers. And that's all you had to play until the Beatles and the Stones opened the doors for the English bands. But Stan was on top of all that as well. He was so influential.'

Journalist Jeff Jenkins recalls Rofe being like a record-company A&R (artists and repertoire) guy. 'He had a deal with Qantas and they would fly records in for him. He knew what was happening way before any record company,' Jenkins says.

'Stan didn't do it privately, 3KZ used to import [the records],' Pinnell clarifies, 'because they gave Stan total freedom to program his own show. No one else on the station had that freedom except for Stan.'

Rofe's love of rock 'n' roll helped to grow this scene in Melbourne. Suburban town hall dances popped up everywhere, becoming meeting places, places of discovery, of a new kind of freedom. And to be fair, it wasn't only Melbourne where rock 'n' roll was taking hold – Sydney's music scene was growing too, despite the city's more conservative bent, due largely to its hosting of variety television show *Bandstand*, which went national as Channel 9 expanded its reach in the early 1960s. Adelaide, Brisbane and Perth were soon throbbing too.

Ian 'Molly' Meldrum, younger than Pepperell and Pinnell but still very much alive to what was happening around him, cites the 1964 Beatles tour as a galvanising force in Australia's youth music scene. While the country had already seen tours by jazz greats Louis Armstrong (1954), Gene Krupa (1954), and the Dave Brubeck Quartet (1960); Welsh singer Shirley Bassey (1957); and crooners like Nat King Cole (1955) and Sammy Davis Jr (1959), never before in Australia had a group toured that incited the excitement and fervour the Beatles did, truly heralding the arrival of the new rock 'n' roll.

'After the Beatles, no doubt, it really started getting bigger and bigger,' Meldrum says. 'Because the Beatles happened ... and then there was a flow of artists coming to Australia through the amazing contacts and enthusiasm that Kenn Brodziack had with a great organisation in England; he signed up all these bands that came and toured Australia.' The Beatles' tour would have birthed countless bands in lounge rooms and garages around the country, which spilled into the town halls and beyond. 'Obviously in Sydney,' Meldrum says. 'And over in Adelaide, [things were] thriving in Adelaide – The Twilights, Masters, they were very active and creating their own music. And they had an influence – their influence was from their English heritage and things like that – they brought that to Australia.'

But Melbourne remained the hub. Rofe had been broadcasting rock 'n' roll from his booth at 3KZ since 1958. The Beatles played six of their eighteen shows in Melbourne in mid-1964. By the mid-1960s discotheques sprung up in the CBD, throbbing with myriad sounds from across the world.

'That was the golden age of bands,' Pepperell recalls. 'The scene was absolutely jumping. Everybody was out all night, particularly in the summer. And then you had The Catcher open in 1967 – it was this gigantic warehouse up in Flinders Lane, it was huge. And that went all night. And you could have breakfast there in the morning – there was a café on site.'

Pepperell is telling me this some fifty years after it happened. He's animated, waving his arms around a lot, letting his coffee go cold. He regularly interrupts my questions as he remembers another detail. He retells these stories with no small amount of nostalgia for a time that, even as it was happening, would have seemed momentous. 'It was insane,' he confides.

As the 1960s continued, youth culture exploded and it became obvious that being a rock 'n' roll musician was no longer a pipe dream but an actual possibility. The scene grew. Discos like Sebastian's, Bertie's and The Thumpin' Tum popped up in the city and immediately became popular.

Around the late 1960s, Melbourne (again, leading the Australian charge) played host to the beginnings of a blues boom. A clutch of bands based out of the Victorian capital were reinventing this old sound. It was grungy, working-class Australian blues, blues with swathes of boogie, blues with touches of psychedelia, even. Bands like Carson, Billy Thorpe, Buffalo, Madder Lake and perhaps the granddaddy of them all, Chain, were at the vanguard. Many would go on to sign with a young Michael Gudinski and his management company, Consolidated Rock.

Chain's roadie was Jiva Lawler, a thinking man's rock 'n' roller who later went on to edit Gudinski's short-lived rock paper *Daily Planet*. In the waning months of the 1960s though, he was the man who drove the van, who carried the gear, who sorted the shit for one of Australia's premier bands of the time.

'A typical Friday night started at two in the afternoon,' Lawler recalls of Chain's tenure. 'At the Village Green Hotel, I forget the suburb. Two 'til five or something there. And then we'd go and do an early spot at, say, Sebastian's in the city, that was the major disco. And Bertie's – Bertie's and Sebastian's had the same ownership … So I would do four carry-ins and carry-outs on a Friday, and finish at 3.00 am at the Tum, the late spot. And it was just all good, all exciting. Fans loved it, it was really a high time. Probably the peak, the peak of going to clubs in Melbourne, packed out everywhere. Good money, amazing money. In those days, I collected money from the owners of the places we worked for, and I'd have $1500 in my pocket when we went home, which in those days … and we paid $300 for a pound of Durban Poison, the best.' He pauses, remembering. '[That] didn't last long.' He laughs.

Chain's music, over the early years, became synonymous with the smoking of pot, and it certainly wasn't just them. The scene was 'very much dope-fuelled, everyone was smoking', Lawler says. 'Every band. Not just blues bands, pop bands too, everyone was smoking ... Sydney, we did a lot of gigs in Sydney, and all the bands there [smoked].'

Lawler calls it 'an amazing time', and it was. Australia's music scene, led by Melbourne, was becoming a force in its own right – the place was thumping.

And yet, among all this action there was something missing. It wasn't just the lack of a magazine or newspaper to pull this scene together. There was a movement afoot, a revolution. This wasn't yet the counterculture – that was still a little way off – but it was the foundation of the counterculture, the beginnings. And right at the centre of this movement was music. Rock 'n' roll and pop, and its rabid ingestion, was a key motif of youth culture, a way in which young people touted their freedom, revealing this burgeoning insurgency.

And so the advent of a dedicated musical press wasn't just about music and the live scene in various cities, but about giving the youth who were championing it a voice. On 2 February 1966, that voice was first heard: *Go-Set*, the paper that Australia's youth needed, that sought to capture this time, effectively began what became an Australian rock press.

2

GO-SET AND THE BIRTH OF THE AUSTRALIAN ROCK PRESS

'It unified a whole generation of people.'

Lily Brett

Tom Jones, black-and-white, a little grainy, adorned the first issue of *Go-Set*. Jones looked youthful and clean-cut, having not yet developed the hip look he went on to cultivate.

The publication itself, though, was hip. *GO-SET* was splashed across the cover, with the straplines 'Weekly A-Go-Go' and 'The Teens and Twenties Newspaper' in smaller type beneath. No one had seen anything quite like this before: a paper aimed squarely at a youth market, focused on music.

The editor, listed on the small masthead, was Tony Schauble, a young Monash University student who had been a co-editor of the student paper, *Lot's Wife*. His editorial ran on the first inside page. It heralded the beginning of half a century of the Australian music press – a rock press:

You'll find where there's a demand someone will eventually make the effort to cater for it. For years it's been obvious that Melbourne was lacking a good journal that would cater solely for the tastes of the active teens and twenties set.

Now look here! Something just had to be done about this. And finally something has been. Go-Set is Going Going for you and everything you want. Going all out to capture the imagination of the Movers.

Go-Set is nothing like kinky magazines that have hit the stands in the past. To begin with, it's not a magazine at all – but a live-wire newspaper keeping a watch on the fast-moving pulse of the *Go Set*.

You see, that's where we got our name. And that's who we're aiming to reach. But we want you to be in it. After all, it's even more your paper than it is ours. We exist – femmes and fellas – to be at your service.

You let us know what you want (if we don't already have it in this issue of Go-Set and the chances are we have). If it is within our limited powers – whoever started that rumour about the power of the Press? – we'll run it in the next issue.

If you've got any questions or problems in any field, then drop us a line. Music, fashion, surfing, skiing, motoring, skindiving, sailing, electronics or anything – you ask and we'll supply an answer by an expert. If you have personal or career problems we'll do our best to help you.

Now sit down and listen a minute! How often is it that you've had something bugging you that you just wanted to break out of but couldn't find the place? Every one of you cats has felt the lash of the Oldies kicking back and screaming 'No sonny, you're not grown up yet junior, save those big words till you get a little older'. Now's the time to really break loose.

Let's hear of it right from the bottom of your inhibitions. This is one time the Oldies don't have any say in it. Go-Set is **your** paper and what you want to say is what Go-Set prints. Get it?

> Right! We'll get Go-Set and go … go … go with the trendsetters.
> Make your mark in the world and shout it out loud: Go-Set!

With those 392 words, an ethos was unveiled, an agenda set. This wasn't just a throwaway pamphlet, a cobbled-together magazine or even, as Schauble writes, a live-wire newspaper – it was a platform from which to shout, for a generation who were beginning to realise there was more out there than their parents were letting on. Phrases like 'Every one of you cats has felt the lash of the Oldies', 'Going all out to capture the imagination of the Movers', 'Make your mark in the world' and 'Now's the time to really break loose' were rallying cries. They are all the more powerful today knowing what happened throughout the end of the 1960s and the early 1970s, how the counterculture movement changed the world. This first editorial loudly proclaimed *Go-Set*'s motives, as both Schauble and his co-founder, Phillip Frazer, who would take over editorial duties from the second issue, made it plain that this was a magazine that was about change, about defining a generation and giving them a sense of belonging.

'There was nowhere else to bind a whole generation of kids who were my age … [or] two or three years either side,' recalls Lily Brett, an early contributor to *Go-Set*, now a novelist based in New York. 'There was nothing that bound them together, that reflected them. [*Go-Set*] showed them they were a generation with their own voice.'

From that first issue – hastily thrown together in a house in the inner-east suburb of Malvern and unleashed upon the public on 2 February 1966 for the reasonable price of 15 cents – *Go-Set* began to grow. The inaugural issue was sold only in Melbourne, but from the magazine's second issue, which featured Herman's Hermits on the cover, it had a wider reach. Distribution into Sydney began via Bill Robinson, a friend of staff photographer Colin Beard who ran a book-distribution network. From there, the sky was the limit.

'The peak would have been 70,000, maybe 75,000 copies [a week],' says Frazer, who was at the time a Monash student involved with *Lot's Wife*, just like Schauble. 'Within seven months of our first issue, we were outselling *TIME* magazine in Australia,' he says, adding with a laugh, 'it was a good thing to say, wasn't it?'

Go-Set didn't just fill a niche, it filled a need.

In the two decades that followed World War II – in which the western world was forced to question many ideas and values previously taken for granted – the youth mindset had begun to change, as young people became fuelled by a restlessness, a wanderlust, a curiosity about the world around them. These kids weren't seeing this world as their parents had. They were seeing possibility and, as a result, began to hanker after something different.

In the early 1960s, a handful of youth-oriented music magazines popped up around the country. These small publications, none of which ran for more than a few years, were the first to tap into the emerging youth market, but the audience was not yet there. It was *Go-Set* that arrived at the right time, in the right place, and established itself quickly as the voice the youth wanted. Schauble and Frazer had realised that youth culture was changing, and that music was at the forefront of this change.

Radio had played an important role in the growth of the youth music industry in Australia to this point; along with flyers stapled to telegraph poles and posted in shop windows, it was where teens heard about the dances and gigs happening in town halls out in the suburbs, as more and more bands popped up every weekend, and more and more teens started going. Yet unlike even Stan 'The Man' Rofe's rock 'n' roll music program on 3KZ, *Go-Set* was produced exclusively for teens. Schauble was in his early twenties, Frazer was nineteen – if they were older than most of their readers, it wasn't by much.

'We were aiming at the age group between thirteen and nineteen, [and] as I was nineteen, it wasn't that hard,' Frazer says with a laugh. 'We could see what was hot, but also the attitude. Being the same age of the kids in school, we'd be cheeky in the same way, we'd be rebellious in the same way; the jokes, they got our jokes, we weren't talking down to them. That was the crucial thing … the entire staff of *Go-Set*, from day one, was of that age group. We had no grown-ups.'

'This was something so different – there was nothing else that spoke to a young generation in their own language,' says Brett. '*Go-Set* was speaking to its readers with writing that was largely written by people more or less their own age.'

This quickly became a huge part of *Go-Set*'s appeal to its readers. When in early 1967 the magazine expanded into Sydney, establishing an office in the New South Wales capital, David Elfick was deemed the man to run it and staff it. But 'while I was the Sydney editor, an enormous amount of credit goes to my assistant, Cleo [Calvo],' Elfick explains. 'Because she *was* the paper, she was the fan that got a job in the paper. So when nine girls jammed into a phone box after school ringing up *Go-Set*, saying, "Is that *Go-Set*?", all giggling and carrying on, if I got that call, what a waste of fucking time, you know? Cleo always had the patience with everybody, as one fan to another. And I think that was a massive cornerstone, or piece in the puzzle of the success [of the magazine].'

The staff had varying degrees of knowledge of the subject matter. Photographer Colin Beard, who was part of the *Go-Set* team from the beginning and who went on to forge a career as a fashion photographer, credits some of the magazine's early success to the fact that he and journalist Doug Panther were not music fans. 'I was never a rock 'n' roll enthusiast, and neither was Doug,' he says. 'And that was a good thing, because we were dispassionate about it, and I think it's much better to be dispassionate about it, because if you're not, you go off on all sorts of biased tangents. We were learning, and as we were learning, we discovered all sorts of things … and as a result we dug into things – we didn't make any assumptions, we dug deep to find out about it, because we were learning, which often resulted in much more interesting coverage.'

* * *

Given rebellion was a large part of the new cultural shift and that taking 'advice' from 'the oldies' wasn't high on the agenda, it's little wonder the youth of the time embraced *Go-Set* so fervently. As well, the magazine initially looked to cover a wide variety of subjects close to the hearts of its readers. Music, yes, but also, as Schauble notes in his editorial, surfing, motoring and fashion.

The first issue included columns on women's fashion and surfing, and a short article entitled 'How to Buy a Second-hand Sports Car'. It also featured a double-page spread under the heading 'The Scene, the Seen' ('*Go-Set*'s Weekly Go-Go Guide'), which consisted of photos taken by Beard at gigs held the previous week, a society page of sorts. And an article, complete with pictures, on a new dance, The Thump – 'the best thing since The Twist'. (David Pepperell claims to have pioneered this dance with his first band, The Boys, prior to becoming a roadie.)

The advertising, too, was aimed at a youth market. Local venue The Thumpin' Tum had a full-page ad; a Young Breed Photography Competition took a half-page. Pop music television show *Kommotion* had a quarter-page, as did Olympus Motor Trimmers and sportscar specialists Pitstop. The back page was taken up by a 3UZ ad featuring local DJ Jimmy Hannan.

But the music took centre stage. The Tom Jones feature in the first issue, headlined 'The Wailing Welshman Talks to *Go-Set*', begins earnestly but demonstrates a passion for and interest in music and its makers that would come to define the magazine's style: 'Thomas Jones Woodward projects a strange kind of image, that of a man who, with a little more experience in spheres other than pop singing, could become one of the best all-round entertainers we've seen in quite a long while.' *Go-Set* was not hard-hitting journalism, perhaps, but it was certainly fuelled by an enthusiasm for the music that so enamoured its readers.

There was a feature on the band The Groop, tagged as 'Melbourne's answer both to overseas artists and interstate talent'; a column by 3UZ DJ Ken Sparkes, consisting of 'titillating morsels of miscellaneous gossip'; a short article on Melbourne singer Pat Carroll, who'd been entertaining troops in Vietnam; and one of the first printed versions of a local Top 40 chart, which became a staple of *Go-Set*'s makeup. At number 1 was The Seekers with 'The Carnival Is Over', followed by the Beatles, The Yardbirds and Tom Jones, with Australians Billy Thorpe and Normie Rowe getting a look in too.

Journalist Christie Eliezer, who began writing for *Go-Set* in the magazine's later years while he was still at school, refers to *Go-Set*'s early incarnation as a 'frothy pop magazine' ('Fashion and girls and all the rest'), a characterisation Frazer doesn't deny. 'I think it was that, but it changed,' he says. 'So frothy pop, sure. But if you're going to describe it in any more than two words, then, you know, it gets more complex.'

What wasn't complex was how it all unfolded. *Go-Set* not only became a hit almost straight out of the gate, but it managed to sustain that success, eventually becoming tagged as the 'pop music bible'. It was the epitome of cool, a voice for a generation. This reputation was not to be taken lightly, as Lily Brett notes. 'I do know that Phillip and Tony were really conscious of the influence. And I don't know if at the time they were conscious that this was providing … a cohesive element for my generation. They gave a cohesion to that generation of kids. It was very clear that we belonged there.'

* * *

Contrary to popular belief, *Go-Set* was not Australia's first music paper. That honour goes to *Australian Dance Band News*, a jazz-inspired trade paper that first appeared on 1 June 1932, changing its name in April the following year to *The Australian Music Maker & Dance Band News* (*Music Maker* for short). Edited in its early years by Eric J. Sheldon[1] and George Hart, it continued quietly right through until the early 1970s, shortly after it merged with Sydney street paper *Sound Blast*.

The publication was launched at a time when jazz was popular, and became a resource for local musicians looking to keep abreast of what was happening in the genre's homeland of America, and over in Europe. It appeared monthly and, as well as reporting on overseas happenings, was a trusted chronicle of Australia's small music scene, which focused primarily on classical music and jazz.

During the late 1960s and early 1970s, the magazine made attempts to cover the new musical scene that was building around it. Yet its readership was older, and it never made a sustained effort to appeal to a younger generation. It failed to capture what it was the kids were after post-Beatles. The merger with *Sound Blast* was an attempt to do this, but it proved fatal for both magazines. After four decades, it ceased to be.

'Jazz was kinda big still, because it was dance music,' says music journalist and author Clinton Walker of *Music Maker*'s early times. 'That's what my mother grew up with in Melbourne, going to see traditional New Orleans jazz bands in order to dance. There was another one at that time too, *Tempo*, [that] dated from the pre-war … *Tempo* was more oriented towards brass marching bands, which was a big thing. But *Music Maker*, that was a bit more modern, so they did modern American jazz, pop, radio music ... *Music Maker* was an incredibly impactful publication that went for a really long time.'

As well as jazz and classical music – with a bit of brass band thrown in for good measure – country (or hillbilly, as some term it) was popular. The country music scene was chronicled in a publication called *Spurs*, which was owned for most of its life by Slim Dusty, who bought the publication with his wife, Joy McKean, in 1956. 'He bought it off whoever started it. Hillbilly music in Australia at the time was a huge thing,' Walker tells me. 'And I don't know what the numbers are, but those sorts of people would have been selling tens of thousands of records with every release in the fifties. Because there wasn't anything else, there was no other entertainment, there wasn't even TV.'

After taking control of *Spurs*, Dusty and McKean moved the magazine's operations to Sydney, where it was run by McKean and her sister, Heather. Yet touring commitments made it hard to manage, and so the day-to-day running of the publication was taken over by the McKean's mother, Millie, who ran *Spurs* until it closed in 1960. Country music was beginning to decline in popularity around this time as the rock 'n' roll juggernaut picked up steam.

At the turn of the decade, as the staunchly conservative 1950s petered to a close and the 1960s reared its shaggy head, a handful of teen-oriented papers began appearing all over the country. These papers were looking to tap into youth culture, as opposed to music culture, which was not yet large enough to warrant much attention from independent publications, let alone the mainstream media. Magazines like *Teen Topics*, *Teens Today*, *Australian Rock 'n' Pop* and *Hep Cats* were marketing to teenagers, whether as stand-alones or as inserts within popular publications such as *Woman's Weekly*, but as these teens were only just starting to come out from under the shade of the parental umbrella, they failed to build significant readerships.

Perhaps the best-known and most successful of these publications was the Consolidated Press–owned *Everybody's*, a glossy that first appeared in 1961, evolving from the merger of long-running magazines *The Australian Woman's Mirror* and *Weekend*. *Everybody's* was, in its early years, a 'women's' magazine, catering in the main to younger women. Pop culture historian Jeffrey Turnbull notes, 'It covered everything from Australian lifestyle to views on current issues, as well as fashion. Its format was colourful and bold and, at times, it wasn't afraid to feature the more insalubrious aspects of the new teen culture.' However, '*Everybody's* was not effectively targeting the teen market as such, but aimed itself more towards the young adult profile and was a quality pictorial, although at times it delved into the sort of stories that the lower quality tabloids liked to feature.'[2]

As youth culture began to crystallise, *Everybody*'s focused more on pop music, to the extent that at least for a short while it was viewed as a key competitor to *Go-Set*. Turnbull observes: 'From about 1964, it incorporated *Disc* magazine – an insert specially dedicated to pop music [–] and this was only really superseded when *Go-Set* came along.' The specialist pop section was edited by Maggy McKeig, a journalist with her finger on the pulse of what was 'happening'. It was largely due to her influence that *Everybody's* managed to remain relevant as the times changed rapidly around it.

Being backed by Frank Packer's Consolidated Press didn't hurt *Everybody's*, either. The magazine's production values far exceeded those of *Go-Set*, designed to catch the eye as well as the mind. However, it wasn't as hip as its newer rival, and folded in 1968, only two years after *Go-Set* first appeared.

There was another notable exception: *Young Modern*, an independent magazine published out of Adelaide. It not only lasted a few years (as opposed to a few issues), but captured what *Go-Set* ended up embodying.

In an article he wrote for rock paper *Roadrunner* (also Adelaide-based) in their July 1978 issue, music writer Stuart Coupe delved briefly into *Young Modern*'s history, shedding light on a paper that was ahead of its time. First appearing on 15 February 1962, *Young Modern* made its motives clear from the start:

> Hi there! Hi! We're making history in Australia this week. For the first time in the Commonwealth teenagers and young people everywhere in South Australia now have their very own magazine produced exclusively for them and not linked in any way with anything published for 'squares'. For YOUNG MODERN has been designed, edited and produced by a staff of young moderns who really know what young moderns want to read … the things they're interested in doing, seeing and hearing. If you expect YOUNG MODERN to be a 'sensational' magazine, we're afraid you'll be disappointed for our aim is to present young people's news and views in a sober and factual fashion. But if you have held fears that our features and reports might be a little 'old hat', tinged perhaps with a little too much adult moralising, you'll be pleasantly surprised.

This maiden editorial, penned by editor John Carroll, showed clearly that the point of the magazine was to capture a new type of pop culture, which was blossoming largely under the radar and away from the monotony of 'square life'. At the same time, the publication was in its own way fairly square. According to Coupe, it pushed a 'fairly definite moral code through numerous articles about social behaviour'. Not a terrible surprise given the Swinging Sixties had only just begun.

The magazine wasn't purely music-focused. It aimed to capture the hearts and minds of a generation in a general way, as reflected in its regular content categories: Features, Clothes, Beauty and Grooming,

TV and Movies, Records and Music, and Cars, along with extras such as Faces and Places (essentially a society page), Your Problems Solved (an advice column) and Top 40. These were topics the editorial team deemed to be important to young people who weren't squares. And while they perhaps didn't realise it at the time, it was a solid formula, one which would come to define *Go-Set* in its early incarnation.

Clinton Walker agrees with Molly Meldrum that the Beatles' June 1964 tour (two and a half years after the first issue of *Young Modern* appeared) spurred the development of a dedicated Australian rock press. 'The whole difference is just the Beatles, isn't it,' Walker emphasises. 'All those *Everybody's* and all them, it's all the pre-Beatles stuff, and as soon as the Beatles came along, publishers would recognise that there's enough – well, it probably took a little while, but then they go "This is sustainable," and then they'll get involved.' This tour showed that music, both as an industry and as a journalistic subject, was viable. 'I've looked at a lot of the papers [from the early '60s] and no, it wasn't ever taken seriously,' Walker says of music having mainstream cultural relevance. 'Blanche d'Alpuget will claim she covered the Beatles, which she did, but it was all on the front page of [*The Daily Mirror*], all about girls screaming and stuff like that. So the music [itself] was not a serious issue at all.'

Young Modern appeared fortnightly and produced an impressive eighty-seven issues, finally pulling the pin in early 1965, just before it was due to become a weekly. There was even a brief foray into the Melbourne market, which didn't produce the results its editors were after. *Young Modern*, while ahead of its time, couldn't adjust quickly enough to a post-Beatles-tour world. It had the formula right, but its readers weren't quite ready to embrace something this 'radical'.

Across the border to the east though, as people like David Pepperell and Jiva Lawler clocked up the kilometres and soaked in the sounds, history was being created. It was becoming very obvious to some that there was a gap to be filled in the newspaper market. Tony Schauble's first *Go-Set* editorial gave voice to it all. And the almost immediate popularity of the publication confirmed beyond a doubt – Australia's rock press was here to stay.

3

THE MECHANICS OF A MUSIC MAGAZINE

'Rock 'n' roll, the pill, offset printing, all at once.
That's what we got.'

Phillip Frazer

The origins of *Go-Set* can be traced back to Monash University's student newspaper, *Lot's Wife*. Both Tony Schauble and Phillip Frazer were co-editors of the paper (Schauble from the very first issue), and it was there that they gained experience in all things editorial and the finer points of magazine production. Perhaps more importantly, by working on *Lot's Wife* at a university becoming known for its student activism, they were privy to this stirring youth movement and the music that was driving it.

Lot's Wife was a fledgling publication. First appearing in 1964, it was started as a complete retool of existing student paper *Chaos*, which was deemed to be 'somewhat lacklustre'.[3] Through the editorial vision of Schauble, John Blakeley and Damien Broderick, it quickly became a far more respected publication – as *Lot's Wife*'s maiden editorial noted, '*Chaos* is in an unhappy state, and unhappy are the students who must perforce be twice-monthly associated with it.' It was named for the biblical story in the Old Testament in which Lot's wife, upon fleeing a disgraced Sodom with her family, looked back at her people and was turned into a pillar of salt. Hence its tagline 'Don't Look Back', which also signalled its progressive politics to a new generation.[4]

Lot's Wife effectively replaced *Chaos* and through the 1960s and 1970s became a powerhouse in student publishing. Over the years it has been edited by or featured a number of prominent Australians, including former treasurer Peter Costello, lawyer Julian Burnside, actor Rachel Griffiths and cartoonist Michael Leunig. It was a hotbed of intellectual and radical thought, a petri dish for the burgeoning youth culture, and a key influence for these two young, fresh thinkers.

There were two things that Schauble and Frazer were exposed to by working on *Lot's Wife* that were relevant to *Go-Set* – the power of music as cultural fuel, and the advent of offset printing, both of which were revolutionary in their own regard.

'Monash was a hip young uni – it was where everything groovy was supposed to be happening if you were a uni student,' Frazer remembers. 'They had bands that came and played ... local bands doing the union nights, as they called them, the socials, the dance events, the happenings. And even though I was only moderately interested in the music scene, I got the point that the local music scene was growing, that there were more bands popping up every day. And just hanging out and talking to friends, anyone who had their eyes open could see there were bands playing every Saturday night at about thirty different town halls around the suburbs of Melbourne.'

Ian 'Molly' Meldrum also noticed that although the Australian music scene was relatively young, it was growing at a rapid rate. 'It was starting to move, you know?' says the behatted commentator, who was one of *Go-Set*'s earliest contributors. 'And, you know, it wasn't only in

Melbourne, it was happening everywhere – obviously in Sydney and over in Adelaide … the Battle of the Sounds was so big, groups from everywhere, Perth, Brisbane, all making their mark.'

'[Tony] had a general idea that this was a hot subject, the culture was gonna catch on,' notes Frazer. The scene was primed for a paper like *Go-Set*. The seed, via *Lot's Wife*, had already been planted.

Prior to the mid-1960s, newspapers in Australia were printed on linotype presses, where hot metal was poured into differently shaped moulds and the resulting slugs were used to press the ink onto paper. This was a time-consuming process that limited the economical use of colour and the printing of pictures. '[Tony] was somewhat of a tech-oriented dude, and he'd figured out that the new rotary offset printing presses were a whole new ballgame, and they were. That was really the beginning of newspapers being printed off photographic processing,' explains Frazer. With offset printing, 'you weren't in a grid anymore'. 'For the first time ever, a picture was cheaper than a thousand words – you could actually print a mag full of … creative graphics.'

Tony Schauble confirms: 'On the technical side, it is true that the possibility of launching *Go-Set* was [aided by] the advent of web-fed offset printing and phototypesetting.' Web-fed offset printing involves feeding a roll of paper through a press, as opposed to printing pages individually. 'These processes were adopted quickly by suburban newspaper publishers and it made a significant change to the economics of newspaper publishing – it was now as cheap to publish photographs as it was to publish print, and to use a multitude of fonts for headlines. It was also now economical to use colour – all things that were vital to the appeal and success of *Go-Set*. At the same time, *Go-Set* was fortunate to have two extremely talented photographers [Colin Beard and Vera Kaas-Jager], both of whom went on to significant careers, and who produced the extremely high-quality photographs for which the paper was noted.

The offset printing revolution made possible all the subsequent music and political publications Phillip developed. The computer and digital age has obviously made publication easier today, but it was a significant development in accessibility of communication at the time.'

Schauble located what was probably the only rotary offset press in Melbourne, out in Glen Waverley – Waverley Offset Press, a family-owned business who he approached to print *Lot's Wife*. As Frazer recalls, with a laugh, 'They were kinda straight types, but they thought, you know, what could go wrong?'[5]

'Tony knew more about the potential of offset printing than they did,' he continues. 'And then he told me, and I'm a quick study and I know tech stuff reasonably well, and I could see even more than what Tony was talking about, that the potential was enormous. So we learned, and when we had the idea to do a rock 'n' roll paper, [that's what we used] … well, a pop paper, let's be real. I mean, the term "rock 'n' roll" was around, of course, but we were pretty commercially oriented.'

So the idea to create a music publication was directly inspired by the potential that offset printing demonstrated. Armed with the ability to produce quality pictorial cheaply, the pair saw a new publication as a way to make money.

'We weren't doing this because we were in love with it, we were doing it because we thought we might be able to make a living out of it,' Frazer says. 'I could see immediately how much you could do with the graphic look, and that's what we took advantage of. The real base sales [of *Go-Set*] were twofold at the beginning – one was the gig guide, and the other was printing up big photos, like full-page photos, of some guy who was hot, or some gal for that matter, who was on kids' radars.' This focus on pictorial played a pivotal role in *Go-Set*'s early development, laying a foundation from which it would build – more rapidly than anyone could have thought.

* * *

The concept for what became *Go-Set* was developed with little fuss. Frazer says, 'We didn't think for very long, we acted very quickly.' Indeed, the timeline from the initial idea to the publication of the first issue on 2 February 1966 was a little over a month.

'The day Tony and I came up with the idea, we kicked it around for half an hour, and I told him to come back in an hour while I typed something up, a single page is about what it was,' Frazer recalls. 'We gave it a name, and then I said, "Let's ring up 3UZ and see if they're interested." So *that day* we were in to see the boss of 3UZ, told him what we were doing, and he said, "All right … we'll put an ad on the back page of every issue, you'll run one of our top DJs in a column every issue, and that's the way it'll be, a trade-out – we'll do ads on radio for whatever we think it's worth." So great, a good deal.'

The next concern for Schauble and Frazer, two youngsters with a big idea, a way to produce it and a little backing from a popular local radio station, was finding people to fill pages with content that would resonate with their intended audience – and not just once, but weekly. The aim was to make money, but as is true today, it's quality content that drives sales. 'We thought we would cover fashion as well as pop. There was a kinda craze at the time for slot-car racing, so we had a column on that. Surfing,' Frazer muses. They managed to make the initial issue work – ads were sold, content was generated, staff were found. Frazer came back to the Malvern house one day to see a brand-new pink Cadillac pulling away. The young driver had offered to work for free, and had offered the use of her car. That woman was Lily Brett. On another occasion, a couple of months in, Frazer lobbed up to the Malvern house to find a stranger sweeping the kitchen floor. That stranger was Ian Meldrum.

It had all started to come together – a pop paper designed to hook in the kids with stories on their musical idols, full-colour pictures and all manner of other morsels affecting the lives of these young men and women looking for their place in the world, their own ideals. And this last was perhaps most important of all, the real *raison d'etre* of *Go-Set* – among the dross and the teenybopper motifs was something more substantial, something that truly drove the magazine as it grew in those early years.

'I was somewhat of the view that most of this was trivial,' Frazer confesses, 'but nevertheless, it was a culture, I could see that. I got the feel that this was going somewhere further. A massive feedback that I took notice of was that the voice, the culture – we were all in it together, we were trying to reinvent a decent culture that made sense. Because our parents, whether we loved them or hated them, were still hanging onto pre-war England as where reality was invented – "We kind of make our best out here and we're second-class" and "The old standards and values, we still need to protect them, otherwise we'll be lost at sea." We didn't believe all that shit. Plus, the pill arrived and changed the world, bingo, right at the same time all this was going on.' He laughs. 'Rock 'n' roll, the pill, offset printing, all at once. That's what we got.'

The first issue was distributed throughout Melbourne, but from issue 2, thanks to Bill Anderson, the book distributor who had a list of all the newsagents, it went further afield. 'Bill knew what the fundamentals were,' Frazer explains. 'He just needed some person power, so we got all our mates at Monash to come out once a week for a few weeks, until he got set up and found a trucking company that would do it for him.'

Advertising was hard to come by at first. For the initial issue, Schauble and Frazer managed to fill the allocated space with ads that 'may or may not have been paid for', Frazer says. After a few issues, it became easier.

In part, this was due to Terry Cleary coming on board. 'Terry was selling advertising, and he did it really well, very charming man,' remembers Colin Beard. The sentiment was echoed by Jen Brown, who contributed to a number of Phillip Frazer's later publications: 'Terry … was always able to get a lot of ads from the venues, record companies. Sometimes they'd get cross if there was a bad review, there'd be controversy,' she says. But 'he was a genius ad-man, and a real sparkler of a man, an incredible person'. Cleary remained with the paper as its ad-man for years.

It was also because the magazine's audience grew so fast. 'With big-time advertisers, like airlines and Levi's, it was clear to them we had the market, so that was easy,' Frazer explains. 'Not easy, but it should have been easy and some of it was. And that was decent money.'

Not that money was ever plentiful, especially in the early days. 'In those first months,' recalls Beard, 'I used to have to ration. We'd get thirty-six exposures, and I used to ration them to twelve frames per group or artist, and if someone got thirteen, then the next one only got eleven. It was that tight, it really was.'

'There was very little money,' Lily Brett concurs with a laugh. 'We'd have to drive to the printers – it was so unwieldy and amateurish in many, many ways, but there clearly was just a huge need.'

The paper now had a semblance of order, it was attracting advertisers, it had a skeleton staff and people were taking notice. *Go-Set* had found its niche, embraced by the youth population as well as by the music scene itself. All three were set to grow together steadily for many years to come.

'I think Phillip and Tony and the others who were working with them at that stage to start it all were visionaries,' says Meldrum. 'It didn't take too long for them to create what became an official music paper for Australia.'

4

A TIME AND PLACE

'You try to put out a special Monkees anything ...
Fuck you, we'll kill you.'

Phillip Frazer

By 1967, as *Go-Set* was cementing itself as the paper of choice among the music-loving youth, Melbourne's music scene was changing. While town hall dances were still swinging out in the suburbs, the inner city became an alternate stomping ground, with myriad venues offering space to the same music and bands as the town halls but in a central location.

It really started through an act of youthful rebellion. Or, perhaps, necessity. Michael Browning, then an eighteen-year-old with time on his hands, inadvertently began what became Melbourne's discotheque scene, along with a group of mates.[6] It commenced in a St Kilda penthouse on the seedy side of town – in hindsight, the perfect birthplace.

'I was friendly with a family, the Knight family, who lived in Sunbury,' Browning recalls, 'and we were pretty bored living out there. My friend's father owned a block of flats in Beaconsfield Parade in St Kilda, which had a gigantic penthouse on the top with a huge patio – it was beyond huge. Quite incredible. It was so big, he wanted too much money to rent it, and because it was in Beaconsfield Parade in St Kilda – in those days, nobody wanted to live there – we just stayed there for nothing. And we had a party one night and it was just extraordinary, overrun with people, and we looked at each other the next day and said, "That was amazing. Why don't we do this every Saturday night and we'll charge [punters] to get in?"' He laughs at the absurdity of it all. 'And there was no approval from anyone, we just did it. And out of total naivety; [we were] a couple of country boys, really.

'And a family friend's brother was an antique dealer – he was an amazing interior decorator too – and he set it up for us with some sort of Edwardian vibe, which was really all the go coming out of England in those days, everyone got dressed up in that style, that was the fashion. So it was enormously popular.'

It wasn't to last. 'Suffice to say, after about two months the police discovered us, and the liquor licencing discovered us, and closed us down,' he says ruefully. Such was their drive though, their realisation that this was *something*, they knew they had to take advantage, and so the inner city seemed an ideal place to relocate.

'We quickly found a building in the city, and my friend's father, because we'd made such a success with the St Kilda one, he financed it for us,' explains Browning. 'It was a three-storey building in Exhibition Street and we called it Sebastian's, and that became enormously popular in the day. Alongside another club in La Trobe Street called The Thumpin' Tum, which was a really cool discotheque, and then the Catcher and several others just popped up everywhere. It was obvious there was a market for it.'

The live music scene of the 1960s (as distinct from the rise of pub rock in the 1970s) was not fuelled by alcohol, as the majority of live music venues were unlicenced. 'Yeah, there was virtually no rock 'n' roll music in licenced venues,' confirms Phil Manning, who in the mid-1960s was playing guitar with Bay City Union, before joining blues behemoth Chain. 'The only licenced venues were these sort of late-night nightclubs that had, you know, Tony Pantano or someone, real cabaret sort of music. The rest of it was in these discotheques, which had DJs who'd play records in the breaks – they all had bands on – and the suburban dances. So there was just music everywhere. In '66, '67, there must have been twenty clubs in the CBD, all of which had music on, all unlicenced.'

'It is hard to believe,' Browning agrees, 'but I think during that period there was six o'clock closing in Melbourne, hardly any licenced venues around. So these venues weren't licenced, oddly enough, which didn't seem to matter; people still came and it was all about the music.'

Manning remembers seeing bands during the day as well as at night. 'You'd pay a couple of dollars to go in, bands every lunchtime at Tenth Avenue in Swanston Street, I think it was. It was pumping. And it was nothing in those days for bands that were popular to go out and maybe do a lunchtime show, then get in the van about six o'clock and go and do an early spot somewhere, drive around the corner to another dance to do a mid-evening spot, then finish off at an eleven o'clock spot somewhere else. That was quite common.'

Bertie's opened in a five-storey building on the corner of Spring and Flinders Streets ('My friend's eldest brother got the idea that he wanted to start one up, which really in a way cannibalised Sebastian's a bit, but nevertheless … that went off majorly,' says Browning with a smile.) The Catcher and The Chaser followed. Kids were thronging into these venues. The bands were filling stages.

And *Go-Set* was moving with it all.

* * *

In 1967, a little over a year into *Go-Set*'s reign, a development occurred that was to cement its popularity and influence. Tony Schauble, always on the lookout for ways to reduce debt and increase revenue, brokered a deal between the magazine and British Airways, then known as BOAC.

In return for 'a big, fat ad and editorial', the airline furnished *Go-Set* with two around-the-world tickets. These were given to writer Lily Brett, who by then had been contributing to *Go-Set* for around a year, and photographer Colin Beard, essentially a founding member of the magazine. Up until this point, avid Australian music fans could order in copies of UK magazines *Melody Maker* or *NME*, which would arrive months after their English publication dates, offering glimpses into what was happening in London and the United States, hotbeds of musical and cultural upheaval. Now, though, as Brett and Beard flew first to the United Kingdom and then to the United States, Australian music fans were about to get these insights first-hand, written by Australians for Australians. These two local music journalists were parachuting right into the beating heart of it all: it was one of the biggest things to happen in the fledgling music press to that point.

'The timing was phenomenal,' recalls Frazer. 'The fact they landed in California for Monterey Pop, *the* Monterey Pop, was luck more than anything else. So they got a terrific series of scoops. And it was tricky, with having no money to send over to them, but [Lily] figured out a way to sleep on somebody's floor, or whatever had to happen. And [she said] on the phone one day, "I've got a fashion special I'm sending you," and I said, "Do we care, do we need one?" She said, "Okay, the hippie fashions," and I said, "Okay, that's getting better." Then she said, "The models I've got are Cher and Michelle Phillips of the Mamas & the Papas." I said, "Send it on!"'

Brett recounts some of this trip in her novel *Lola Bensky* (2012) – not that it requires fictionalising. Brett, in her own words young and inexperienced, made the most of the opportunity not because she felt part of the rock scene, but because she was determined to produce quality journalism. As a result, the scoops came thick and fast.

'I think part of it was my sheer enthusiasm for doing a good and intelligent job,' Brett says. 'I mean, I just had an awful lot of very powerful people [assist me] … Barry Taylor at Apple helped me get into Monterey and sit with all the performers. Just having a lot of help from a lot of people with a lot of power in the rock world.'

Brett and Beard talked with the likes of Hendrix, Cher, the Mamas & the Papas, the Bee Gees. They covered Monterey Pop; they covered the scene it was inspired by; they covered the people and the places and the fashions and the culture that was heaving, undulating, a world away from home. And they recorded it all and sent it back to grace the pages of Australia's own pop music bible.

'I was so naïve, I arranged all the interviews, I did them, I organised the photography, and I look back at some of the people I spoke to on the phone, I was assuming they were the same age as I was … but they [surely weren't], and I felt terrible for calling them by their first names and being so catty,' Brett says. 'It turned out to be a trip that involved interviews with just about everybody who was important in the rock world in England and America. I think if you give people responsibility and not much direction, you can have a very good outcome. I just plotted where to go and what to do.' She laughs. 'And when I think about it, there were very few people my age travelling on their own from Australia … in New York and California. [And] at that age, an age difference of three or four years can make a big difference, and I think it was a great example of how not having a dogma to preach grew something that was thrilling in itself.'

Readers of *Go-Set* were finding out about what was happening from a source close to home almost as it *was* happening – anyone who had doubted the publication's validity or influence was now eating their words.

'It made Australia seem very connected to the rest of the world,' Brett says. 'And when I wrote, I wrote for readers, and I was one of them in many, many ways. In one of my articles, I couldn't believe it, I'm telling them that New York is really behind Australia in fashion, and my knowledge of fashion was laughable … [and I'm] shopping in Carnaby Street with Barry Gibb, and I'm making these big announcements and I'm telling kids to travel, they need to travel, it's a big education.

'I was speaking to them as though I was very experienced at everything, but I was so excited, and it was contagious in Australia, I think. Also, I think I was very, very lucky because I was completely ignorant about how unimportant Australia was to the English and American rock stars. I mean, we were a relatively insignificant newspaper … I didn't understand how insignificant we were, so I just thought, *Of course they'll give me an interview.* Not understanding that in America they didn't even know what language we spoke in Australia.'

It was not only her naivety but her natural tenacity and diligence that got Brett – someone truly interested in the music and the scene, not with selling papers or scoring points or wanting to be cool – these coveted interviews.

Beard cites the duo's relationship with UK journalist and the Beatles' press agent Derek Taylor as the golden key. 'When we got [to the US], we tried to make appointments in LA: The Byrds, Sonny & Cher, the Mamas & the Papas and so on, and people said, "Who the hell are you?" So we got onto Derek, a good friend. And then the next morning the phone rang hot with people saying we were the most recommended press people they've ever come across! And all these managers and press agents in London were sending telegrams to their counterparts in LA, which was terrific. And I think we did really, really well – which I think was largely due to Lily, you know, she was very charming and very good at getting in and explaining to people. But also, people remembered my photographs ... so between the two of us, we were probably quite unique press people.' Beard was several years older than Brett, and his reputation, in particular, had preceded them, with the UK's *NME* providing the pair with all their contacts in return for Beard furnishing them with 8x10 prints of all he ended up shooting – not a bad deal.

The fact that a small, newly launched publication was able to send two journalists on an overseas trip – for seven months – is astounding. Brett and Beard both recognise this, even if at the time there were annoyances to deal with. Brett mentions more than once that money was a concern. 'How to pay us was not really worked out very well, and it'd often take a long time to get money to us, and it was never a huge amount anyway.'

'We had *no* money,' Beard concurs with a laugh. 'We got stranded in LA at the Ambassador Hotel and couldn't find the money that Phillip and Tony had sent us to get out of there. I was plotting to go down the back stairs and through the carpark before we finally found the money.'

The degree of freedom given to the journalists more than compensated for these practical niggles. 'I think there was something about the freedom and the flexibility that created a lot of good things,' says Brett. Both *Go-Set* founders embraced Brett's ideas. 'There was an open-mindedness: both Phillip and Tony were very receptive to anything you pitched. They were significantly open-minded ... anything I asked if I could do, they said yes to.'

Beard is more direct: 'Basically, I was never given any brief by either of them,' he says. 'Because to be quite honest, they didn't know what was happening. Phillip knew about the printing and the issues, Tony did a bit of the negotiation in a business sense, Terry Cleary handled most of the advertising, so in a sense [what they got] is what they got.

I mean, obviously Tony might say, "Can you get photographs of so and so," that sort of thing, but basically a lot of the stuff we got, [we] got by being out there.'

It was the readers of *Go-Set* that benefited from this arrangement, and they came to support the publication in droves.

* * *

When the Monkees toured Australia and Japan in September and October 1968, *Go-Set* was nearing the peak of its powers. It'd been two and a half years since the first issue, and in that time as the Australian music scene had grown, so too had the magazine. *Go-Set* had branched out from its spiritual home in Melbourne and truly become a national publication, its readership outstripping that of its only real rival, the glossy *Everybody's*.

In Sydney, the pace with which *Go-Set*'s popularity grew necessitated a local office. David Elfick, these days a successful film producer and a co-founder of surf bible *Tracks* but then an Arts student at the University of New South Wales, was chosen for the job based almost solely on the fact he was active within the arts on one of the most 'creative campuses' in the country. He was running the drama club at the University of New South Wales when Frazer offered him a job on *Go-Set*. 'I thought I may as well do that, I dunno what else I'm going to do with an Arts degree.'

'I started off with a typewriter, which I couldn't type on, one telephone line, and the rather over-important title of Sydney editor of *Go-Set*,' continues Elfick. 'The first thing to do was become friendly with the DJs at 2UW, so those people got to know me as I took the mag around each week, and then they'd put me on air for a few minutes to talk about what was in the mag that week, and that helped raise the profile. And of course I went down to Melbourne to meet all the *Go-Set* people in Melbourne, and Melbourne was a really jumping scene, but I realised that EMI Records, Festival, RCA, CBS, all the big companies were based in Sydney. And of course you also had Albert's [music company] in Sydney, so while Melbourne thought they ran the pop scene, in fact it was really run out of Sydney. And that's where the money was, and that's where the power was.'

Elfick sought to use this to his advantage, quickly securing advertising from companies such as Fender, who was owned by CBS. 'Yeah, so Fender would put a quarter-page ad in and then EMI would put a half-page in,' he remembers. The Sydney operation gathered momentum, to the extent that Elfick began to need help. 'I said to Phillip, "I need an assistant," because every time I left the office, no one answered the phone,' he explains. 'So I said, "I've gotta have an assistant." So they gave me a paltry sum each week to employ one.' Cleo Calvo, today known as Clelia Adams, went on to forge a career in country music, but at the time she was an aspiring musician and a fan of the publication. 'So we had a little office with a good person virtually running the show.'

Phillip Frazer describes Elfick as 'an editorial guy, but also a business guy', praise Elfick counters with, 'I had no business training and not much business sense, but there was a bit of entrepreneur in me.' As the Sydney office grew, Elfick built a small yet incredibly effective team around him, complimenting what was happening at the Melbourne base.

'I said, "Look, I want someone to do promotions. So this guy came in … his name was Donny Sutherland,' remembers Elfick. 'Each week we had a lot of unsold copies left over, you know, a few hundred lying around the office. So I thought, I've gotta do something with Donny, to give him a job, because he's a very likeable guy. So I went to Polaroid and said, "Will you give me a Polaroid camera every month, and unlimited film stock, and we'll promote Polaroid cameras?" Those cameras were a revolution. So I gave Donny a Polaroid camera and last week's back copies of the paper, and he would stand outside schools at 3.00pm every afternoon and give out free copies of the paper and take people's photographs. Usually in groups. Then we'd publish one of the pics each week … and that person who had the photo published would get a free Polaroid camera and some stock. So needless to say, everybody who was given a copy of the paper or who had met Donny – and we're talking about hundreds of kids each week, 'cos he's doing this job Monday to Friday – bought the paper the next week because they wanted to see if they'd won the camera!'

Sutherland, who was given his own column, 'Donny's Place', also headed out every day to badger newsagent owners, making it his mission to get the magazine in prominent positions in as many outlets as he could. Elfick hired his own advertising manager, and *Go-Set*'s Sydney office was ticking.

'We were a very formidable office,' Elfick confirms, with no small amount of pride. 'And it wasn't long before sales in New South Wales were up to the sales of Melbourne. And of course the ad revenue we brought in was enormous. So I would immodestly say that the Sydney *Go-Set* team – and it was a team – really saved *Go-Set*'s bacon, because it was a magazine that expanded fast, and it was the leading magazine, but it needed both Sydney and Melbourne to be functioning on all cylinders to financially survive.'

Under Frazer's leadership, with Elfick in Sydney, where the industry had made its home, things were running strongly from an editorial standpoint by 1968. The publication wasn't making a great deal of profit, but the printers were happy enough to keep bankrolling what they saw as a business still finding its feet.[7]

For Elfick, the 1968 Monkees' tour was a no-brainer for *Go-Set*. He pitched to Frazer that the paper should send their Sydney photographer, Phillip Morris, as well as someone in Melbourne, to all the Monkees' Australian shows. The plan was, Frazer recalls, 'to cover the shit out of this Monkees tour'. 'We'd blanket it,' he says, 'put out a special, a Monkees Tour Special.'

Before they could get started, one thing had to be taken care of. Frazer had just hired a new designer, who until recently had worked for a graphic arts firm, essentially an advertising agency, as he recalls. 'She took me aside and said, "Look, my friend's girlfriend still works at this firm, and she said one of their customers is Shell petrol, and they're preparing to do a young people's magazine about rock 'n' roll." She said they had the idea to call it *Gas*. Cool, groovy, got it? So I called my dad, who was our lawyer, and said, "Can you find out if there's a registered trademark or any such thing for a magazine called *Gas*?" And he said okay. No, he found out, so I said, "Can we register one, right now, *Gas* publication?" And he said, okay, done.'

A major petroleum company outwitted with a shrewd business move, it was back to business, except now there were two titles in Frazer's stable – *Go-Set* and the yet-to-be-launched magazine *Gas*.

Gas's debut was hastened by a sudden turn of events. The Monkees special had been laid out and was ready to send to print when disaster struck. The Monkees' media machine reached out to Elfick: having heard about the impending 'special issue', they were threatening to sue for 'a million dollars'. '[They said,] "We own the name, we own everything about them. You try to put out a special Monkees anything without corporate backing from us … fuck you, we'll kill you."' Frazer laughs. 'So we didn't. We put out *Gas* issue 1 instead, killed two birds with the one issue.'

And they didn't get sued?

'No, because we didn't sell a [stand-alone] Monkees special, we sold *Gas*, where the first issue was all about the Monkees tour … we had to keep [producing the magazine] to defend ourselves against [any legal action].'

'That is how I recall it,' Elfick reflects. 'We did *Gas* magazine for the Monkees; I don't recall that their management was going to sue us, but I'm sure it's true. And I thought ... we could continue to do a magazine that was glossy, and just was a bit different to *Go-Set* but catered to the same audience, and it was probably even more, if it was possible, a bit more of a poppy fanzine than *Go-Set* was. I also realised if the mag worked, it would be another source of income, and we probably needed that, because we were a bit overhead-heavy, very much reliant on sales and advertising. The main competition was *Everybody's* ... and that was of course a glossier paper. So *Gas* could sort of compete with *Everybody's* as well.'

And so *Gas* became the pilot fish to *Go-Set*'s shark. It lasted for around ten months, edited at various points by Elfick, Molly Meldrum and Bob Weis (who also went on to pursue a successful career in film), and became a handy place to drop the more pop-oriented stories that were, by the late 1960s, deemed not a decent fit for *Go-Set*.

For *Go-Set* had evolved along with the scene it was covering and with its readers. 'It was like the culture itself, it changed,' says Frazer, 'repeatedly, constantly, permanent-revolution sort of thing.'

By the late 1960s, pop music had begun to splinter. According to Frazer, the bubble-gum music that had so captured the paper's readers in the mid-1960s was falling out of favour at a rapid rate. 'Pop continued its fragmentation into subgenres – heavy metal, acid rock, bluegrass, singer-songwriter ...' he says. 'Neither I nor the various *Go-Set* managements created this devolution of the "youth market". Rather, we tried to devolve our publications along with it. That left *Go-Set* with a young pop subset of the sixties and seventies generation, shrinking by the year.'

One thing Frazer prided himself on was an ability to read cultural shifts and moods, appreciating that there were dozens of cultures co-existing at any one moment. When we meet at his home in Coorabell, northern New South Wales, he tells me by way of example that what a thirteen-year-old girl would have gotten out of *Go-Set* would obviously have been very different to an eighteen-year-old boy with a blues record collection 'as long as this room'. He understood that, and he understood that a lot of his Monash friends who'd said they would not be seen dead reading the music paper would be reading it at home. And so he and Schauble made sure the magazine reflected these rapidly diversifying audiences. 'We were changing the magazine every week, introducing stuff that did talk seriously about music or about the politics of music, or sex, or drugs, or whatever.'

Other innovations in the content became iconic. One morning, Frazer arrived at the magazine's offices to find a note slipped under the door. It read, according to Frazer, 'I like your magazine, and you run this chart of the Top 40, and I get it, but it's a national chart, or is pretending to be, but it's not. It doesn't appear to be based in any statistical reality. And I myself have been interested in the subject, and I've called dozens of record shops and companies and have compiled my own chart, and here's a copy of one, you might be interested.'

'So I rang him up, as we used to do,' says Frazer, 'and I said I'm printing this one, and you'd better show up every week with another one, and he said okay.'

The compiler of this chart was a young architecture student named Ed Nimmervoll. Upon migrating with his family from Austria at ten years of age, Nimmervoll had become a rabid music fan, a true devotee of what was happening in Australia. And not just in terms of the music itself – he had an inordinate interest in the ins and outs of the scene: how it ticked, not just how it sounded.

'That changed things,' remembers Frazer, 'because not only did he do that, which was an industry-oriented type thing, which I kinda thought was cool – well, not cool really, but good, good for us – but he also, of course, had a musical sensibility that was definitely of the "I'm interested in the more grown-up stuff", the social context of the lyrics and so on … I knew plenty of people who had that mindset, but I didn't have one on staff until Ed.'

Journalist Jeff Jenkins recalls Nimmervoll's charts with no small amount of awe, having been glued to them as a young reader of *Go-Set*. '[One reason why] *Go-Set* was really significant was Ed creating that chart,' he acknowledges. 'Until that came along, with Ed creating it, there was no national chart at all. He *created* that. He had this formula for working out the charts … [it was] just mind-blowing that he did that. It gave *Go-Set* real authority, too. And people loved it … they loved the chart; you might love Zoot or the Valentines, you'd be watching them go up and down the charts, what's going on? And that was fantastic that Ed gave real prominence to that, created it all … he was a pioneer.'

* * *

By the late 1960s, *Go-Set* had a staff of around thirty, at least a dozen full-time. It was still not a money-spinner, but it was proudly independent, progressive and never pretended to be something it wasn't. *Go-Set* was just a pop-culture newspaper with a strong music focus, but it became *the* music magazine in Australia, the most trusted.

'I think today *Go-Set* could never happen,' marvels Brett. 'It would require the most immense capitalisation – you couldn't possibly owe the printer money and other people money and keep going until you sold enough newspapers. But it just was. I meet people today who tell me that they were glued to *Go-Set*, they read every word, which was more than I did. It really had a very, very powerful effect; it [had] a remarkable cohesive effect on the readers, you really felt part of the movement.'

The late 1960s was the birth of celebrity culture. While Brett and Beard were navigating their way through the heady American and UK rock scenes, the idea of the 'celebrity musician' was becoming part of the zeitgeist, as performers were idolised due to their status within certain circles or scenes. *Go-Set* was complicit in this, if unintentionally. In the late 1960s, the reporting of what was happening across the western world was eye-opening. Many rock and pop stars were at the forefront of this cultural change, promoting a new set of values and way of life. No one could have known at the time that the culture of celebrity would eventually turn sour.

'Today, celebrity culture is what sells all publications, it's shocking,' says Brett, who is remarkably happy to talk at length about her time with *Go-Set*, even so many years after the fact. 'And of course, today you wouldn't find out anything about any celebrity because you have to sign a contract before you go into the interview … I was just left alone with the people I was interviewing, I came into their homes. It was all so makeshift, you know? I interviewed Sonny and Cher in London, but I also went to their home in California. I interviewed the Mamas & the Papas at John and Michelle's house. It was all so much more normal, you know? John gave me a tour of the house, a tour of the garden, and it was the same as speaking to equals in many, many ways.

'That could never happen now. I mean, celebrities are so shielded … in Australia, we did it with a bang with *Go-Set* … I interviewed and talked to Jimi Hendrix several times in the UK and America, and you could actually just see him in the club and have a conversation, chat with him, no PR person, nobody around … and Monterey, which was an organised festival, there was massive freedom, Brian Jones was wandering around and no one had any security and the cops were wearing flowers like everyone else … it was remarkably egalitarian.

'Now, everyone that is recognised by more than 500 people isolates themselves. Surely they don't do anything normal at all … and you'll never ever know who they really are. And I watched Sonny and Cher bicker, I watched John and Michelle have an argument, nobody was at all bothered by the fact I was there. And if I said anything interesting, they responded. It seemed normal; I thought it was normal to chat with Janis Joplin about our mothers, both talking about our difficulties with our mothers and our love for our mothers, and I thought that was really normal,' she remembers.

Go-Set had a hold on the market, and with good reason. It had seen off its competitors by being agile, but it had also stayed true to its ethos – it was still being written by kids for kids, by Australians for Australians. With journalists of the calibre of Brett and Beard reporting from the cultural frontlines, the magazine had an imprimatur that lasted for many years.

Nothing lasts forever, though. And not everyone thought *Go-Set* was the business. As the 1960s morphed into the 1970s, new developments in the Australian music press were afoot. *Go-Set* would not have the market to itself for much longer.

5

LIFE ON ANOTHER PLANET

'It was just in a time when rock 'n' roll was the supreme entertainment form, really it was.'

Adrian Barker

In July 1970, Adrian Barker was sitting at his desk in a house on Drummond Street in Carlton, in Melbourne's leafy inner north. The desk was strewn with papers, the walls were covered in posters; music was blaring from a large stereo. Issues of *Go-Set* were scattered around the room, not least because the magazine, now at its peak after four years of solid growth, had offices in the building just next door.

Barker was running Drum, a booking and management agency whose roster included Company Caine, Tamam Shud and The Flying Circus, among a dozen or so other acts. Its main draw, though, was Melbourne-via-Adelaide mainstay The Masters Apprentices, a band Barker had roadied for since mid-1968, after clearing stages and packing trucks for Max Merritt & The Meteors and Ram Jam Big Band. Barker was astute and organised, so after the Apprentices ran into management troubles in late 1969, he offered to team up with them to open their own agency.

As Barker sat surveying his burgeoning empire, The Apprentices were in England. The year before, they'd come runner-up (for the second year in a row) in Hoadley's Battle of the Sounds, an annual Australian rock and pop competition established in 1966, and the comp had packed them onto a ship and sent them to the United Kingdom, a six-month sojourn offering the band a chance at cracking one of the oldest markets in the business. They and Barker would part ways prior to the band's eventual demise in 1972, but at this point, it was all systems go. And so Barker was on the job – a young bloke consumed with rock 'n' roll, making a go of it as an early-twenty-something smack-bang in the middle of one of the hottest scenes on the planet.

Yet his world was about to change, and it was because of another young, ambitious industry wannabe, a nineteen-year-old named Michael Gudinski.

Widely acknowledged today as the godfather of Australian rock 'n' roll, Gudinski, who passed away in March 2021, wasn't that far above Barker, had there been an established pecking order at that point, but his profile was rising. Over the phone, which was buried somewhere on Barker's cluttered desk, Gudinski pitched an idea: Barker would close down Drum and come and work with him and fellow agent Michael Browning (who had recently thrown in the towel as booker for city discotheques Sebastian's and Bertie's). The three of them would form a new agency.

Given Gudinski's evident passion and drive, it would have been an enticing proposition. Barker, though, was loyal to his stable of bands, The Apprentices in particular, who needed him at home '[running] the fucking business' while they made a go of it in Old Blighty, and so he decided to stay put. Another reason was location: Gudinski had leased a house slated for demolition across the river, on Punt Road in South Yarra, and Barker was willing to countenance his offer if the two Michaels used Drum's well-established and, quite frankly, nicer offices instead. But Gudinski was set with his Punt Road base.

In the music business, however, things have a habit of changing quickly. With the Apprentices not bringing in any money at home, given they were halfway around the world, Barker and Glen Wheatley (then playing bass with the band and an active role in their affairs) decided to dissolve Drum. And so, only a couple of months after Gudinski's offer, Barker, now a free agent, took a booking position at Consolidated Rock – the Michaels' new agency – and settled in at what would prove to be one of the biggest businesses in Australian music.

'When I was [booking] Sebastian's and Bertie's … Michael Gudinski and all his Jewish mates used to come round from Melbourne High at lunchtime – they ran dances at Caufield town hall – and they'd come round and hassle me for bands and whatever, and it just evolved from there,' Michael Browning says on the origins of Consolidated Rock. 'Michael was the smartest of them all. We talked and got together eventually, and started up Consolidated Rock … basically to create a monopoly. Which we managed to do. We basically represented just about every band in Australia who were playing and who were half-decent. And it kind of just got too big. We hired Michael Chugg and he opened our Sydney office, and it got quite massive.'

So for Barker, joining the Michaels was a solid career move as well as his only option. With Consolidated Rock, Barker became part of a group that was changing Australia's music scene. Their roster soon included the likes of Billy Thorpe & the Aztecs, Chain, Carson, Healing Force and Bulldog, bands peddling a heavier, harder, grittier sound, very blues-based, a far cry from the bubble-gum that'd come to define the mid-1960s and which *Go-Set* had covered with such fervour. The Michaels very quickly had Melbourne and Sydney sewn up. They carried huge influence with the bookers from myriad venues, they pushed their bands in and they developed a reputation for being the only game in town; as Browning told journalist Stuart Coupe in Coupe's book

Gudinski (2015), Consolidated Rock was 'a fully operating monopoly – if your band wasn't with us, they didn't work in Melbourne or Sydney'.

Barker revelled in this new sound. 'We changed the Melbourne music scene completely,' he says today. 'When I say we changed it, we were part of that change, you know – Billy Thorpe & the Aztecs, the La De Da's, Chain, Carson, and all these other fucking bands. And, you know, it was burning.'

Except in one quarter. *Go-Set*, well established and, as Barker readily concedes, 'incredibly influential', wasn't giving Consolidated Rock's artists the coverage the agency's heads deemed worthy. In fact, as far as Barker remembers, *Go-Set* was barely covering this newer, heavier scene at all. 'We were having a lot of trouble getting our bands in *Go-Set*, couldn't get stories in there,' he muses. 'We hassled constantly about getting editorial and they didn't think it was appropriate to cover any of those bands. They ended up suggesting that we write a column, which I think we did, and I think I wrote it – I can't quite remember, it was a long time ago now. Or at least we fed them the info for the column, which I would have collated.'

What happened next was to change the nature of Australia's rock 'n' roll media landscape, and exactly how it came about is a subject on which all who were there have an opinion. Michael Chugg, running Consolidated Rock's Sydney office, says it was the Sydney version of the company's successful Melbourne town hall concert series that broke the relationship with *Go-Set*. 'It was a fucking nightmare,' he remembers of the event, which he confesses went pear-shaped. 'The nazi guards were arseholes … as soon as Lobby Loyde finished, he fucked with the PA and it never worked properly again, so Thorpie ended up going on at ten to eleven … so Molly [Meldrum] wrote a front-page article in *Go-Set*, and he denies he ever wrote it, but it was titled "Rock Con at Sydney Town Hall". So Browning got the shits, and started *Daily Planet*.'

Barker agrees that this – *Go-Set* so ardently panning something of Consolidated Rock's that the agency saw as beyond their control – was, for Browning, the final straw. 'He said, "This is fucked, it's not good enough,"' says Barker. It was felt that *Go-Set* was meddling with their bands and their business. 'So he comes up with this crazy idea [that] we'll start our own paper. And of course, none of us know a damn thing about running a paper!' According to Stuart Coupe's account in *Gudinski*, Gudinski was toying with the idea of starting a record label at the time, but such was Browning's ire at *Go-Set*, and his confidence that a competing paper was the answer, all available funds were channelled into this new venture.

'We thought it was a revolution,' recalls Barker with a laugh. 'We were young guys on a mission. And we felt that everything to do with *Go-Set* was yesterday ... [*Go-Set*] was from a different era by then.' And so *Daily Planet* was born, mooted as a true competitor to *Go-Set* – another independent music paper designed to capture what was happening within the sticky-carpeted confines of the nation's live music scene.

(It's worth noting that, while these conversations were going on in Melbourne, in Sydney a very low-key and under-the-radar publication had appeared called *Sound Blast*. There is very little in the way of information on this title, which ran from early November 1970 through until the middle of 1973, but it was published by Times Parade Pty Ltd, and edited, at least early on, by David Frith. It seems a blueprint for a number of later publications, and certainly appeared to take rock 'n' roll and its concurrent culture very seriously. Notably, from its January 1973 issue, it incorporated long-running paper *Music Maker* into its pages, which it seemed was a death knell for both publications, as both wound up together only a few months later. The fact that neither Browning nor Frazer had rated *Sound Blast* as either an advertising opportunity or a competitor speaks, perhaps, to how low-key it truly was.)

According to Browning though, it wasn't so much that *Go-Set* weren't featuring his agency's bands. In fact, as far as he was concerned, *Go-Set* were part of business at that point within Melbourne. 'When we were running the clubs, they were paramount to our getting the word out as to who was playing. That was the only advertising we did,' Browning explains. 'We had a weekly ad in *Go-Set*. So everything just went hand in hand. Molly was always at the clubs, and Lily Brett, who was a really important contributor at that time, she was there. You know, it was just all one big family.'

The reason he recalls the agency starting *Daily Planet* stemmed from Consolidated Rock's monopoly: '*That's* kind of [why] we decided to open up … because *Go-Set* were having *editorials* about what a bad state of affairs it was that Consolidated Rock had this monopoly, every week … and *that* gave us the shits. So we thought, if you wanna be like that, we'll just start up another music paper, see how you like that. We should probably have just ignored it, but we were just young and stupid … that's how *Daily Planet* started. For all the wrong reasons, really.'

It was, as Barker says, a huge gamble. But something as trivial as not knowing what they were doing was hardly going to stop these three; nothing had so far. 'It was like everything at that time, you didn't need to know anything,' says Barker. 'You didn't have any mentors. Didn't have any yardstick to relate to, any background; any field we were undertaking, it was all new. Everything – running an agency was new, and we had to work out how to do the booking books and collate phone enquiries and how to market. It was all just common sense, in a way.'

Barker, the agency's go-to man for any new side venture, was tasked with getting the paper off the ground, and was listed on the magazine's masthead through its entire lifespan as editorial director.[8] The task of launching and running a successful publication was huge. 'There was a lot of trouble with the paper actually, a hell of a lot of trouble,' he recalls.

'Number one, it was a stupid idea because we didn't know what we were doing, big time. And it's an expensive thing to do and no one had deep pockets. And the money doesn't come in from the first issue, it takes weeks and weeks before you get any result. The only thing that was keeping us sort of afloat was venue advertising money, and that wasn't much. We got the money from pubs and clubs, venues. Because we were at the core, because we had the agency and were on the side of the bands that were earning the money, we were able to get quite a bit of venue advertising and stuff like amplifier companies' advertising and bits and pieces like that. But that really wasn't enough, and the bills started piling up. That's one problem the paper had, the finances.'

The second problem set a precedent that dogged *Daily Planet* for its entire existence. 'Somehow or other Gudinski, who managed Chain at the time, chose the roadie from Chain to be the editor,' Barker says. 'Now Jiva Lawler was an absolute, full-blown hippie, 100 per cent. Vegetarian hippie religious guy. And way ahead of his time in a sense, with his philosophy about the Earth and conservation and diet and, you know, looking after the rivers and plants and all that sort of thing. But when he got his bands on the paper, that's what he turned it into, from day one. Because that was his philosophy, and somehow or other, Gudinski thought he was an intellectual. I reckon that's what he thought. And he admired him, big time. And everybody kind of admired him, but we were trying to start a music paper.'

'I was still roadie-ing for Chain, but I was losing interest,' Lawler says of the time. 'Then out of the blue, to offer a roadie editorship of this new magazine was quite something.' He adds with a laugh, 'They must have seen that I had a bit of nous, you know? [So Gudinski] saw something in me, and I was grateful because it was a wonderful experience. They gave me a handful of cash, said go out and rent a house in South Yarra and set up a darkroom, set up art boards – because we did everything by paste-up then – and then go and find some artists to help you set up the paper each week. There was a band called Madder Lake back in those days, and three of them became the artists on *Daily Planet*. And they were just so much fun to work with.'

Despite Barker's misgivings about Lawler as editor, *Daily Planet* first appeared on 13 August 1971, Australia's first true alternative to *Go-Set*. 'Get a paper on the street,' Barker says on his initial brief from Gudinski. 'And [make] it a music paper.'

'But it wasn't, it wasn't that,' he says with no small amount of frustration at the memory. 'It was a bit of a communal thing, there were a lot of people having their say, you know? There wasn't any one person. Gudinski was hardly ever there, Browning was hardly ever there – they were running the agency and managing bands, backing CR and manipulating alternative arrangements with that, and that sort of stuff. And I'm in South Yarra trying to run this fucking paper, trying to get it on the street, under this hippie communal vibe. Oh my god, it wasn't my background, it wasn't my dream to have this thing!'

Lawler maintains Gudinski and Browning gave him no brief. 'They just said, "Go for it." They were busy themselves, they couldn't get much involved, they trusted me completely.'

At least initially, perhaps. 'It soon became very obvious to us that Jiva was probably not the best choice,' Browning says today. 'He was just so radical; it certainly wasn't our idea to be as underground and out there and radical as it was. We thought it was gonna be a hipper version of *Go-Set*, that was our plan. But between Lobby [Loyde] and Jiva, it just turned out to be an even more radical version of *Rolling Stone*. And it was great, everyone loved it, but we couldn't make it work because the advertisers, the powers that be in the advertising world, didn't embrace it, it was just too radical for them. Jiva would write editorials saying "don't buy CBS records because CBS provide component parts to the war in Vietnam"! So we're like, right, well, we'll strike them off our list of potential advertisers.' He laughs again.

Lawler's final issue with *Daily Planet* was number 14, dated 12 November 1971. 'Gudinski and Browning were pressuring me to take advertising from record companies [and] to run articles on their bands,' Lawler says. 'I just couldn't do it. I recognised they had to pay – we had very little advertising in the first few issues – but I just couldn't do it.'

Lawler, staying true to his ideals, decided he was done. And so in his final issue as editor, he penned a short note, letting his audience know why he was leaving:

> I began as editor of the *Daily Planet* with (x) amount of knowledge, equally proportionate to that of naivety. It was a total venture into the unknown, but ideals were fought for immediately. Sticking to these provided my only guiding light. The second and third Planets were crises – which happily passed. Each additional issue moved closer to my ideals, the only possible set under which I could edit the paper, for those alternatives being suggested to me were without valid principle …
>
> But this cannot be. Today new laws were handed down (or up), opposite to my ideas, and so I must resign. The *Planet* is to be guided by new motives, new ideas – not better than mine, not worse – simply opposite.
>
> *Daily Planet* may soon be very different. Buy it, read it with love. We who had to leave believe in you all and thank you for your continued hope and guidance. Keep writing, so that the new leaders may also benefit by the beauty of your communication. As for us, we'll have to find another way.
>
> Nevertheless, we'll see you on the 16th July 1978 – and probably not before. Remember that popstars died with gonorrhoea.[9]
>
> Jiva

After Lawler's departure, it was Barker who reluctantly stepped into the editor's chair to pull together the remaining half-dozen issues of *Daily Planet*. In an apparent effort to set the editorial direction back on track, in issue 17 (3 December 1971) an editorial appeared penned by contributor Margo Huxley:

> The original idea for the *Daily Planet* was a paper designed to help encourage the growth of a truly Australian rock scene. The changes that have occurred in the paper in the last two issues have been an attempt to recapture that original direction – a paper that takes' seriously' Australian music and musicians. Jiva saw a different role for the paper (valid and worthwhile which should be taken up again somewhere soon), but it was not the role originally intended.
>
> ...
>
> We don't want to kill good music by making hype of it – we want an honest appraisal of what is really happening. We still need your articles, drawings, comments, letters and poems. We don't have enough pages to print everything we'd like yet, but if you can share our faith in Australian music with us, there'll be lots more in the future.
>
> Margo

Lawler had never followed the ideals with which Gudinski and Barker were aligned, and he claims he was never informed of them. He took the paper his own way. After he left it seemed, at least for a while, that *Daily Planet*, guided by Barker in a more hands-on role, was firmly back representing the safe agenda favoured by the Michaels.

* * *

By the time *Daily Planet* first hit the streets in August 1971, *Go-Set* co-founder Phillip Frazer was winding up his tenure at the magazine and had on his hands a few other countercultural projects that would consume his time and efforts over the coming years. In Frazer's own words, he was transitioning out, and so any competition for *Go-Set* wasn't really on his radar. 'From my point of view, it was not a major concern,' he says on the appearance of *Daily Planet*. 'They made it perfectly clear that they were interested in [their] bands and whatever else they were doing, which wasn't going to give them a mass market if they didn't go beyond that.'

Molly Meldrum, who was still writing for *Go-Set* – and who today is very close with Michael Browning, as he was with Gudinski – recalls with a smile, 'Back then, I think our idea was, "Oh, fuck 'em." Yeah, we called 'em radicals and hippies.'

Regardless of what the *Go-Set* staff thought of their new competitor, *Daily Planet*, despite its difficulties, had hit the ground and the editorial team tried its hardest to make it run.

Barker, as was in his DNA, was still helming the venture with gusto. 'Okay, these first few issues are coming out all wrong,' he says, 'but we can push it in the right direction, get more music in there, which we did. And Jiva didn't last very long anyway, so we moved it around. I changed the format a bit.'

Named with a nod to Clark Kent's workplace (or perhaps the St Kilda brothel – no one really knows except for Lobby Loyde allegedly, and he died in 2007), *Daily Planet* presented a very different picture than that painted by *Go-Set*. A music paper, yes, but with greater concerns, *Daily Planet*, due to Lawler's editorial direction and the communal dynamic of the magazine that resulted, set itself up as a counterculture publication, looking to delve into the social and political issues – the much more adult issues – of the day.

'They took a lot more of an *OZ* magazine approach at that time, which Gudinski wasn't happy about,' remembers Jen Jewel Brown, who came to work for the paper as an eighteen-year-old. 'I mean, he wasn't really that interested in counterculture or politics.' There were articles on masturbation and the history of swear words; profiles on Allen Ginsburg and *OZ* editor Jim Anderson; a piece by 'TK' entitled 'What the Nuns Told Me', about his experiences in the Catholic education system. 'Articles like that were a lot more counterculture,' notes Brown.

Former roadie David Pepperell, who was by this time establishing himself as a rock writer and who'd come to write for *Daily Planet*, said they wanted to be more like *Rolling Stone*: 'We wanted to be a real underground paper.'

This was a significant point of difference between the two magazines. While *Go-Set* had evolved from its teenybopper beginnings, it had yet to fully embrace what was happening culturally outside of music in the early 1970s. The magazine's peak, according to Phillip Frazer, was 1969, and after that – indeed, after Frazer himself left – it struggled to keep up. This is where *Daily Planet* saw itself as superior.

'We were sort of aware that we had a lot more of a counterculture interest and we wanted to grow up, basically, compared to *Go-Set*'s background,' Brown explains. 'We had coverage of jazz, the London Scene, Glenn Wheatley had a column … We had more expertise, we had Broderick Smith writing about the old blues guys, he was extremely knowledgeable about it. So we had more of a broad scale of music and counterculture going on compared to *Go-Set*, which had much more focus on big-headlines pop stars … "this is the latest pop star that's arrived", that sort of thing.'

The writers at the paper felt they had a lot of freedom to pursue ideas and shape the publication's content. Concurrently, Barker was concerned with getting as much music into the magazine as he could, but found it hard to deal with the communal beast the magazine had become.

This essentially split the magazine into factions. 'I was in charge of the damn thing but [Gudinski] should have taken a stronger hand, and I complained to him, enormously, but as I said, it was very much a communal thing,' says Barker. 'Lobby Loyde had a lot to say and insisted on his own column – he used to write these rambling, hand-written, four full pages of stuff that could vary between stories about modern warfare to music, to amplifiers, to the music scene, all this stuff, and it would just go on and on, disjointed stuff. And I'd have to cut it up and find a way for it to go in the paper, because we couldn't print the whole thing.'

Loyde had begun his musical tenure playing with popular Brisbane band The Purple Hearts, who had a number 9 single with 'Early in the Morning'. The Hearts disbanded in 1967 and Loyde joined Wild Cherries (the Cherries ended up supplying a number of members to Chain), before going on to play with Billy Thorpe & the Aztecs and forging a notable music career. Along with fellow musicians Broderick Smith and Matt Taylor, he was a regular contributor to *Daily Planet*, as well as one of its most vocal critics. According to Barker, Loyde told him regularly that the magazine looked like shit and asked why he was being so conservative with the layout: *Why don't you have an article that starts at the top of one page and continues across the top of subsequent pages? Why do you use borders?* It is a small miracle Barker did not turn prematurely grey.

Detractors of the paper made much of it being little more than a publicity sheet for Consolidated Rock artists too (particularly in its second incarnation), a point that was also raised by some of the paper's writers. 'We wouldn't just write laudatory articles about any band [Gudinski] managed, which he also wanted us to do,' David Pepperell says. '[According to him], we were supposed to be a publicity arm of … Consolidated Rock.'

'When I'm pushing for more music content, they're saying, "It's more ideological than that, this is a paper about counterculture and alternative music, we're not gonna be involved if it's gonna be Gudinski's publicity sheet,"' Barker says. 'Well, fuck you guys, what we're trying to do here is actually promote music.' He laughs. 'We'd argue back.' This explains why the paper's content was so scattergun, a continual (and mostly non-acrimonious) negotiation between the rock 'n' roll bosses and their alternative staff members. 'The constant back-and-forth seemed, in a way, to be kind of acceptable,' Barker says now.

It was acceptable because those were the times. This was the beginning of the counterculture. Whether *Daily Planet* was ever a proper counterculture magazine might be debatable, but its contributors were undeniably individuals who were living it, who were part of it, and who realised as it was happening what a revolution it truly was. A different movement that sparked the advent of *Go-Set* in 1966, but a revolution in its own right.

'For us, this was the universe. I sometimes refer to it as the youthquake,' says Brown. 'It was the period leading into Whitlam's time, we were in Vietnam, people were getting drafted, the politics of the day were seriously affecting people right around us. And the media hadn't learnt to clamp down on its coverage of war, which it did after Desert Storm [in the Gulf War] … and we got those images of napalmed children and people being shot in the head and things like that which were so horrendous. Many of my friends were facing the draft and people were conscientious objectors, or they were hiding from the draft. So they were serious times, as well as exciting times. And the music scene was tremendously vibrant, and there were a huge number of venues, especially in Melbourne, which had been the centre of music, really … Sydney at times has really surged, but in terms of ongoing power and venues open, Melbourne has been a real pumping scene, and was right through those days.'

It was the musical aspect of this counterculture that Gudinski, Browning and Barker had been trying to cover all along. 'Gudinski was rather cross that we hadn't concentrated so much on bands,' remembers Brown. 'Not that he was against counterculture or all those things, but you know, he always envisaged it being primarily music.'

For the staff of the magazine, the writers and editors who were living the counterculture, music and this social change were one and the same – it made sense to them to be writing not only about the music that was the soundtrack to this culture shift but about the culture shift itself: the newfound freedoms, the liberation, the change.

'[They were] the same thing, for me,' Brown agrees. 'They were intricately interwoven. The free expression … When you see a band like Led Zeppelin that put together these elements of the old blues and the kind of sexual revolution – Robert Plant would always perform with a little vest on, basically naked, long flowing hair, and sing songs like "Whole Lotta Love" or "The Lemon Song", overtly sexual. And the old blues songs, a lot of them are overtly sexual too … rock 'n' roll is a very sexual kind of music and it was intricately interwoven with the sexual revolution, the coming of the pill, women's liberation, gay liberation.'

It was the birth of a new era, and it seemed like the magazine was just beginning. But what no one knew was that its days were numbered; it was only a matter of time before it all collapsed.

* * *

At the end of 1971, Adrian Barker departed *Daily Planet*. 'I just packed up and left,' he says. 'By now I'm getting frustrated [with the communal nature of the paper], so I told [Gudinski] I've had enough … I'm not an expert anyway in running a newspaper, I'm not a journalist as such, and it's not the direction I wanted to head in, so I'm out.'

As a result of Barker leaving, *Daily Planet* appeared on 24 December 1971 and then the paper lay fallow for a short while over the new year period, but 'they had a very loyal staff in David Pepperell and Jen Brown, and Peter Walsh and the art department … everybody wanted to keep it going. And I think they decided to revamp it.'

'I think everyone realised it was a cock-up, complete fucking cock-up. And it could be done better,' Barker reflects. 'I don't know exactly what happened, but what I do know is when I pulled out, it pulled the rug out from underneath the bloody thing.'

Barker's departure and the subsequent revamp led to a re-branding of the publication as *Planet*. The first issue appeared on 19 January 1972, in a new broadsheet format, similar to US *Rolling Stone*, which was likely a major influence. Barker was still listed as editorial director, and was to remain on the masthead for a couple more issues, but his involvement, both with the paper and with Consolidated Rock, was essentially over. He fled north to Brisbane because the paper 'was just chaotic' and the agency 'was not really where I wanted to be'.[10]

Meanwhile, neck-deep in the revolution, the remaining team, led by Brown and Pepperell in particular, continued on. *Go-Set* was faltering, failing to capture the zeitgeist as it had in the late 1960s, and its visionary co-founder Phillip Frazer had moved on. Despite being owned by part of the establishment they were railing against, rail *Planet*'s staff did, continuing to produce a paper that aimed to portray what was happening in and around the youth scene of the time. But events were conspiring against them.

Michael Gudinski and Michael Browning were considering parting ways. The magazine was Browning's idea in the first place, and as Gudinski's client list picked up steam, it was obvious the money was going to come from touring international artists, as opposed to running a local underground rag. His patience for the paper began to wane.

This was also fuelled by jibes from within the publication's pages itself.

'I wrote this article saying what a shocking [load of rubbish one of] Gudinski's town hall concerts was,' says Pepperell. 'What happened was, you were waiting half an hour between the acts, because all the acts had roadies with all this competition who wouldn't let each other use each other's equipment. So you're sitting there for half an hour while they pull one whole band off and put another one back on ... So I wrote an article about that which he really didn't like.'

Money was the most contentious issue, however. No one had pots of money to continue funding the paper, and despite the fact that its circulation figures were allegedly decent, *Planet* just wasn't achieving the reach it needed in order to cover its costs.

I suggest to Pepperell that perhaps, despite the times, Australia just wasn't ready for a paper like *Planet*.

'Maybe,' he says. 'I think more because people didn't see it. It didn't have the penetration of *Go-Set*. It was hard to get it in the shops, distribution didn't seem to be as good. *Go-Set* used private contractors, which I think worked better. A mate of mine was the Victorian distributor – what he used to do was get a carful of kids and he'd drive around and drop them off, pay them a dollar. That seemed to work better, they certainly seemed to get in the shops better than we did.'

After a pause, he muses, concurring with my theory, 'But, you know, we were a bit before our time. We were early seventies. If we'd been, say, mid-seventies, we would have gone like a bomb. Australia wasn't really ready for an underground paper, and it just couldn't gain traction.'

Being one of only two music papers in the entire country was by no means a guarantee of survival. As well, as the counterculture picked up steam, the revolution became mainstream and so readers peeled off, looking for something else, something edgier and newer. *Planet* wound up as a kind of cultural detritus, consigned to history, even if that history had been the present just a year or so before.

The final issue was dated 4 July 1972. While some maintain that the issue was seized by the Victorian Vice Squad and the repercussions of this were impossible to come back from financially, the truth is more mundane. Ultimately it just ceased to exist, Gudinski pulling the pin on what he saw as a money pit.

And so Michael Browning's battle cry of 'we'll crush *Go-Set*' remained unfulfilled, and Australia went back to having the one music paper.

Daily Planet produced twenty issues, *Planet* twenty-six – it was a flash in the pan, but its significance outweighed its longevity. While Michael Gudinski might not have been fully invested in the publication, while Adrian Barker might have torn his hair out in frustration over finances and vocal contributors, the writers and photographers and musicians and editors believed in it (and gave everything to make it happen), and so made it a true chronicle of its surroundings, all that was happening in those heady days when anything seemed possible and probably was. It was about music, because music fed the growing countercultural movement. But, despite what Consolidated Rock were after, it ended up being about more than that.

Meanwhile, Phillip Frazer had new ventures in mind. Frazer was 'always full of ideas', Brown recalls with a smile. 'He came in with his cape on ... In a way, he's like a hustler, but he's not a hustler in the way of conning anyone or pocketing the money, he's just a brilliant man, an absolutely first-rate editor. He always gave women a huge run in his publications, a feminist from an early time. And an intellectual, somebody very committed to political freedom, and not having the people confined to little, narrow spaces [built] by capitalism, basically.'

The Australian rock 'n' roll press, careening head-on into the counterculture and all it promised, was hardly done for yet.

6

HIGH TIMES AMID THE COUNTERCULTURE

'It's pretty clear now that what looked like it
might have been some kind of counterculture is,
in reality, just the plain old chaos of undifferentiated
weirdness.'

Jerry Garcia

The counterculture. A push back against prevailing social norms, a concerted effort, mainly by youth, to forge for themselves a set of ideals that not only eschewed what an older generation has impressed upon them but also represented what it was they were after. What they wanted. What they believed.

The term is relatively new, but the concept is not. The metaphorical yoke of oppression has been thrown off many times in history, with the consequence being the emergence of a new set of attitudes, pitted against the old and taking society in exciting directions informed by freedom, by sexuality, by lust and passion, race and religion. Countercultural movements have never been without tension, but then nothing worth having ever has been.

The countercultural shift of the early 1970s in Australia was not unique in that it stemmed from the movement already underway in America and the United Kingdom. Australians emulated what they saw, heard and read, as ripples spread, eventually making their way across the Pacific Ocean.

The youth market had not been short of publications of dissent. The Sydney-based *OZ* magazine, formed in 1963 by Richard Neville, Martin Sharp and Richard Walsh, had run through the 1960s, courted by controversy and fielding charges of obscenity. Its last Australian issue was published in 1969, after Neville and Sharp had relocated to London and started a successful UK offshoot. Yet unlike the rock press, *OZ* was designed to be satirical and focused on politics. *OZ* didn't cover much in the way of music, which was a huge part of what made the counterculture tick.

And so what can be termed the Australian countercultural rock press, heavily invested in the changing musical nature of the time, ran for a brief period through the early to mid-1970s, burning quick and bright before morphing, for good or ill, into what had by then become the mainstream.

The one driving it all was Phillip Frazer, the man responsible for *Go-Set* (along with Tony Schauble) and an advocate for dissident writing, having co-edited *Lot's Wife*. The Monash student newspaper – along with the University of New South Wales' *Tharunka* (and the far more underground *Thorunka*, or *Thor*) – had already made a name as a publication for young people. And so by the time the counterculture hit Australia, Frazer was well equipped to capture it.

Frazer had long since realised, as the 1960s came to a close, that *Go-Set*'s original readership were growing up and moving on, and their tastes in music were changing. No longer was it the Beatles and the bubble-gum popstars of the 1960s. Now, it was well and truly about rock 'n' roll, psychedelia, sex and drugs and all the rest of it.

In mid-December 1969, within the pages of *Go-Set* Frazer inserted a section entitled 'Core', which focused on the grittier, dirtier, grungier aspects of the constantly evolving youth culture.

Long-term *Go-Set* writers like Ed Nimmervoll and Rob Smythe featured heavily in 'Core', which was just four pages, not even a lift-out, but its clear aim was to capture an older reader. 'That was to give the eighteen-year-olds, or the more serious people who saw themselves as more serious than *Go-Set*, [something new]. They could buy *Go-Set* and trash it if they wanted to, and just walk around with 'Core'. That was kinda the idea.'

Frazer's musical tastes were changing too. Where once he'd been content to be a spectator to trends in Australian music, concerned mainly with tapping into what he and Tony Schauble saw as a lucrative youth market, the newer music coming out of the United Kingdom seemed to him more exciting, more adventurous, more indicative of the cultural change happening around them. 'I was having fun [as] the music changed,' Frazer says. 'There was some of that music I liked a lot. Not that [much] local, but the Americans and the Brits were turning out some amazing shit. Those were the golden years, so to speak, of rock 'n' roll. Plus it was a roller-coaster that wasn't stopping, so there was no way off. If we stopped, either one of us – well, Tony stopped – but if I stopped, I knew the whole thing would come apart and I'd probably be sued for a debt. So it was the *Macbeth* thing, blood so deep, the only way out is forward, right?'

For the vast majority of its lifespan, *Go-Set* had been in debt to its printers, Waverley Offset Press. As the paper had become more successful (in part due to the success of sister paper, *Gas*), the debt had plateaued, but the printers, with whom the editors had had a relationship since the *Lot's Wife* days in the early 1960s, were still owed money.

Frazer, an entrepreneur as well as a publisher, sought to expand on the concept of 'Core', which he saw as a money-maker in its own right. His aim was to offset some of the debt owed to Waverley Press. And so while still at *Go-Set*, Frazer took 'Core' and turned it into a stand-alone publication, the rather predicably titled *Revolution*, which first appeared in May 1970, a good year or so before Consolidated Rock's counterculture wannabe, *Daily Planet*.

'*Revolution* ... was also being paid for by the printer,' Frazer says with a laugh. 'I'd convinced them if we did this, we'd make more money, which to some extent was true – I mean, we were holding at that point, we weren't losing any more money. And the *Gas* sideshow had produced some degree of profitability.'

Revolution, which Frazer says was one-third to one-half music-related, ran monthly for eleven issues. Perhaps its most notable issue was 4, which contained as a four-page insert: the first issue of the Australian *Rolling Stone*. The Australian *Stone*, which at that point was essentially an abridged version of the US version, continued as an insert until *Revolution* was shut down, at which point it was rebirthed as a stand-alone magazine.[11]

Revolution was a mixed bag, covering a plethora of issues deemed pertinent to an audience who'd long since outgrown *Go-Set*. Articles such as 'Chicago: The Trial of "Youth Culture"', 'The Moratorium: An Exercise in Revolutionary Politics', 'Macrobiotics: A Stomach Revolution for Western Man', 'Out: A Black Manifesto by Dick Gregory' and '"There Are Two Sorts of Time": The Student Movement in Australia – A History' appeared alongside in-depth musical analysis and interviews on and with Jack Bruce, Wendy Saddington, Pink Floyd, Eric Clapton, as well as opinion pieces ('was "Let It Be" an obituary for the Beatles?'). It was brash and confident and knew its politics in a changing environment.

Its contributors included Rob Smythe and Ed Nimmervoll, who'd both written for Frazer in *Go-Set*'s 'Core' section, as well as cartoonist Michael Leunig, artists Martin Sharp and Ian McCausland, and writers Helen Garner, David Elfick, Jen Jewel Brown, Margo Huxley, Abbie Hoffman and Lillian Roxon. It was a small dynamo, which tried to capture in a serious fashion what was happening in the culture.

It was 'very exciting', Brown confides. 'Because you felt that there was a new frontier … this was the coming of a national consciousness of music and culture expressing itself, a much more liberating kind of expression.'

Change wasn't only happening culturally, though. And so when Waverley Press began to tire of this debt around the middle of 1971 and passed operations across to the accountants, it was a clear sign that *Go-Set*'s days, and *Revolution*'s, were numbered. 'The family who owned the printers had sensibly turned over their affairs to a bunch of accountants and lawyers, and you can imagine they weren't all that polite to us,' Frazer recalls. 'Especially when things happen, like I start doing *Rolling Stone*. They thought this was pretty blatant – confronting, as far as they were concerned.'

Revolution, as was bound to happen in these still-conservative times, had also begun to attract the attention of the authorities, who issued summons over certain articles printed in the magazine. Most notably was a piece in issue 9 (March 1971) on 'cop and court suppression of counterculture mags worldwide, which led to … a court hearing where we discussed the size of Mick Jagger's balls,' Frazer recalls. Yet it was, quite ironically, an excerpt of Abbie Hoffman's *Steal This Book*, which was printed in *Go-Set*, that was one of the final straws.

'Hoffman wrote this book … where he said each chapter was about ways to survive without having to go and get a job at a bank and wear a tie, which he'd never do, and also about subverting, you know, the mean and nasty people who run capitalism.' Frazer laughs. 'Including such gems as "go into a supermarket, buy a pizza, and then slot some LP records in the box with the pizza, and get away with that" … this was the level of this thing, it was amusing.

'So we published maybe five paragraphs of this in *Go-Set*. And the then attorney-general of Victoria went apeshit because his two thirteen- or fifteen-year-old daughters read *Go-Set*, and here was this preposterous invocation to break the law. So a cop came around and told me, somewhat embarrassedly, that his job was to summons me to a court hearing for inciting diverse persons unknown to commit larceny at supermarkets.'

It was around this time that Frazer left *Go-Set* for good. The printer's accountants and lawyers were pissed off by the court cases (another of which centred around Frazer distributing copies of the extremely controversial *Thor* in Melbourne), as it meant they were kept waiting longer for payment. Frazer was also getting itchy feet. For a while, he had been looking to sell *Go-Set* to fund future ventures, shopping it around to various potential buyers, including Rupert Murdoch.

'I had a meeting with Murdoch, person to person, and he was ready and willing to do it,' Frazer says. 'And he said he needed to know how long I was willing to commit as editor, and I said, "Do you mean working for you?" And he said, "Yeah." And I said, "Not at all." "Okay, well we don't have a deal, because it'll fall apart." So I said, "Fine, nice talking to you." So that was it.' He shrugs. 'I thought, okay, after this court case, that was the end of the relationship with Waverley. [The lawyers and accountants] sent me a letter saying our agreement is over … and I said, "Yes it is," and that was it.'

And so Phillip Frazer's association with *Go-Set*, the magazine he'd co-founded and overseen over the course of five years, guiding it through the musical and cultural minefield that was the 1960s, wound up.

The parting of ways served to kill off *Revolution* too, and for a brief moment in the early 1970s, Phillip Frazer was not involved with any publication – aside from the Australian *Rolling Stone*, which at that point was only eight issues old.

Of course, he wasn't done; parting ways with his long-term backer and moving on from *Go-Set* was hardly going to slow down a man for whom the counterculture and its associated movements (up, down, sideways), along with an appreciation of the music that soundtracked it all, ran deep within. With fellow counterculturalists Pat Woolley and Macy McFarland, Frazer essentially picked up where *Revolution* left off, starting *High Times* in August 1971 (the same month *Revolution* died). It was a similar countercultural paper with a strong music bent.

Issue 5 of *High Times* contained an interesting article, written by Frazer himself. Titled 'The Freap Magazines', it goes into reasonable depth analysing the most prominent counterculture magazines of the time: the US *Rolling Stone*; *The Berkley Barb*, one of America's first underground papers; the London version of *OZ*; *Friends* (or *Frendz* as it became from issue 29, which was released on 21 May 1971), a London underground paper; the Australian student newspapers *Lot's Wife* and *Tharunka*; *Revolution* and *High Times*; and *Daily Planet* (briefly). It's a fascinating insight by a 'freap' (freak press) magazine into itself and its contemporaries.

'In the London offices of *Rolling Stone* last month,' writes Frazer in the December 1971 article, 'there was a chance gathering of freaks who had all worked on different papers – one from *Rolling Stone*, one photographer who had worked on several American freaps, one from *Friends* and myself (*Lot's Wife*, *Go-Set*, *Revolution*, *High Times*)':

> We identified the stages of 'development' common to all these papers. The first phase was the initial enthusiastic launching that centred as

> much on the group of people involved as on the ideology or 'purpose' of the paper. The energy generated within those groups was such that the end product was inevitably as much an expression of the group, and more particularly of the attempt at establishing relationships among people within the group, as it was a document for public consumption.
>
> The second stage is the critical one, in that the looseness, the lack of concern for the harsh realities of delegated responsibilities, and ultimately the ability of the group to produce a workable means of handling the money, has to be reckoned with. The paper becomes an imperative imposing itself on the group and the dynamics of deadlines, debtors, creditors and the outside world generally. Instead of a group of people, each one proceeding to do whatever he or she does best, people are replaced by roles, and new people are chosen by their ability to fulfil those roles, rather than their compatibility within the social group.
>
> Some magazines never get through this stage, some resist it and survive by eventually forming around a different group, some go through it and become relatively efficient highly-structured businesses. There are probably thousands of magazines that suffer the first of these fates (Melbourne's *Source* was a recent example), there are a few that fit the second description – London *OZ* is one, *High Times* (née *Revolution*) and *Frendz* (née *Friends*) are others.

Rolling Stone and *Go-Set* come under the third category, Frazer writes. These papers, while they went through the enthusiastic stage, managed to survive the second stage, eventually organising themselves in such a way as to thrive. Sure, not a lot of money was flowing in (not in *Go-Set*'s case, anyway), but they were functioning businesses with purpose, the results speaking for themselves.

The first phase Frazer mentions, that of the 'initial enthusiastic launching' that is as much about the people as it is the paper, was certainly true of *High Times*. It was a collective, for want of a better word, each issue reflecting the interests of whichever group of contributors was ready, willing and able to make it happen. Frazer has said the magazine 'consciously avoided imposed systems of operations or of editorial control, attempting to allow a free-flowing involvement by anyone who [could] connect with what was in previous issues'.

The reason Frazer and fellow *High Times* financers Macy McFarland and Colin James decided to stick with this model was linked to the reasons why *Revolution* had met its demise. Frazer writes in the same article that *Revolution* was incompatible with its stablemate, *Go-Set*, in that the latter, as a mass-circulation pop-focused newspaper, had already been through phase two of development, effectively 'inhibiting *Revolution* from ever making it to stage one!'

Revolution, despite its importance (at least in hindsight), was doomed from the get-go – it was geared to go through the stages Frazer describes in his article, but because it never really got past stage one, it was never going to last. *High Times* suffered much the same fate – while it ran for a respectable six issues, appearing monthly and covering, like *Revolution*, a large amount of music-related material, it too 'ran out of distributors and therefor money', Frazer explains, putting paid to another publication deemed too risqué by the powers that be. But Frazer had learned from these experiences, and more was to come from him.

* * *

Phillip Frazer's final countercultural publication, and the one which was to last the longest and perhaps burn the brightest, was *The Digger*. Today regarded as *the* seminal Australian countercultural paper, *The Digger* provided a platform for 'at least ten radical new communities which coalesced between 1968 and 1975', Frazer notes. 'For saving environments, helping oppressed people rise up, working/playing/

living collectively, outing prejudices, demanding equality, that sort of thing. Most of these groups had local newsletters, but *The Digger* offered a national platform for all, so it sold more, got more ads and bred collaborations.' Frazer has called *The Digger* 'more serious' in nature than any of his previous publications, and there is little doubt it was.

Jen Jewel Brown, who'd had her first piece published in *Revolution* and who was a refugee from the very recent demise of *Planet*, was a foundation staffer for *The Digger*. She did film and music reviews, as well as features, interviewing public figures such as Bob Hawke (then at the ACTU) and Margaret Whitlam. 'It was this gigantic broadsheet that you could really stretch out in, it was intensely political,' Brown remembers of the paper. 'There was a lot of reporting about women's collectives, women's theatre groups, rallies and the Women's Electoral Lobby, news from America, the Black Panthers connection, black writers getting published, Roberta Sykes, so it was the start of all that kind of thing in Australia.

'It was quite feisty, it was a publication where there were cliques and bits and pieces, and it gave a lot of room to women,' she goes on. 'Some of Helen Garner's earliest pieces were published in *The Digger*, her stories about working for the Education department, teaching at Fitzroy High, where a kid came and asked her about four-letter words and she locked the door and started using the blackboard, which was a bad idea – she ended up getting fired, and that was the start of her career as a writer.'

Formed by Frazer, Gary Hutchinson and an American journalist and 'draft dodger' by the name of Bruce Hanford, *The Digger* was birthed in August 1972 (less than two months after the demise of *Planet*) and ran through until December 1975, appearing fortnightly (going monthly in the later part of 1973), producing a total of forty-eight issues.

The Digger didn't publish editorials – there was no first-issue screed proclaiming loudly what its ambitions were. But from the get-go, the paper's intentions were obvious, as Frazer himself explains in a 2018 article for arts publication *Daily Review*:

> Like with social media today, new technologies bred new cultures: the new tech of the '60s was electrified music, photography-based printing, transistors, TV, and the biggest culture changer of all, reliable contraception known as The Pill. But unlike social media, the counter-culture arose with a purpose: it demanded social changes – which I considered urgent and undeniable – and that was what all these papers were about. *The Digger* took on culture change as its mission: it brought together writers, thinkers, artists, and activists, all eager to take over the dying cultures we'd inherited and redefine them.

A closer look at the masthead reveals how the collective nature of the paper developed. In the initial issues, Bruce Hanford and Phillip Frazer are listed as co-editors. From issue 5, the pair are listed under 'Editorial', while issue 9 lists under 'Editorial' Hanford, Frazer 'and all the diggers'. From the following issue, Helen Garner joins the pair under the heading 'Editing', an arrangement that lasts until issue 16 (May 1973), in which under 'Editing' Garner, Colin Talbot and Virginia Fraser are listed. From issue 17, the heading is 'Editorial' again, and listed are all who have been involved in the issue, giving the impression the publication had stepped away from a model with firm roles (if, indeed, it had ever really embraced such a model officially) and towards a more communal way of working.

And it did work. Intensely political, as Brown says, the paper was dense – a lot of type, interspersed with pictorial and cartoons and illustrations. It gave space to the writers to really delve into their topics of choice. And these topics were many and varied. *The Digger* touched on subjects not being covered in-depth, or at all, by the mainstream media. *The Digger*, always on a financial knife-edge, threw itself into reportage on an incredibly diverse range of issues. Histories of abortion, drug-taking and growing, investigations into overseas affairs, Australia's part in the Vietnam War, profiles on political and social leaders, exposés into aspects of Australian culture not even thought about by those in the mainstream.

In a single edition, you could expect a lot. April 1974's issue 29, for example, contained: 'Collective Management in Melbourne's Pram Factory Theatre' by Helen Garner and Tim Piggot; 'World Bank Involvement in South Vietnam's Tiger Cage Prisons'; an interview with André Menras, a former political prisoner of South Vietnam; 'Patty Hearst – Did She Fall or Was She Pushed?'; and a piece on Leichhardt women's community health centre.

A few months later, August 1974, issue 35: Joni Mitchell interviewed about her records, loves and loneliness; an article about 'the land rights con on Australia's blacks'; a profile of Terry Darmody and Sydney jug band music; a review of a Lou Reed concert by Jenny Brown; a piece on 'the perils of having babies at home – one woman's amazing tale'; and articles on Bruce Cathie's grid theory of UFOs and N-bomb explosions, women's prison Fairlea and corruption in Victoria's Hospital Employees' Federation.

Human interest stories with timeliness or political implications played a part too – a firsthand account of a friend of one of the paper's writers who'd spent the past four months working as a male prostitute in Sydney ('What Can A Poor Boy Do, 'Cept Sell His Arse …'); a piece in which Bruce Hanford interviews female prostitutes working in the Cross ('Notes on the Nature of a Game'); stories from inside jail, with accounts by prisoners, jailers and critics ('Prison: How It Looks …').

The Digger was no lightweight, and it was viewed by its loyal reader base as *the* paper to be reading if one was in any way interested in what was really happening behind the headlines.

'I can't tell you anything about sales figures,' says Brown, 'but it was certainly revered among certain left-wing uni students, music fans, counterculture fans, theatre fans – we had a lot of coverage of theatre. We were Melbourne-based; we had an office in Sydney, but I guess there was coverage on local fertility clinics, corruption in the cops, some things that really stirred up some ants' nests.'

This was all done through a desire to cover the ever-changing counterculture, employing true journalistic instinct. *The Digger* was no conspiracy rag; nor was it merely trying to stir trouble. Its aim was to shine light on what it, and its audience, saw as social, political and cultural injustice. It was a true counterculture paper in every meaning of the phrase, down to being run by a collective, with no real 'boss', despite the fact it did exist for the most part under Phillip Frazer's publishing control.

Incorporated into all of this solid journalistic fare, of course, was a steady diet of music, which, even as the 1970s rolled onward and the music continued to change and polarise more than ever (even within countercultural ranks), still drove what the disaffected youth were after.

As well as a gig guide, in-depth album reviews were common, as was coverage of live tours like The Stones' 1973 run. 'What Happened to Joe Cocker in Australia' was debated in issue 6, with a long story on Cocker and band's deportation from Australia written by Colin Talbot, Martin Fabinyi and 'assorted mudsharks'. There were previews of New South Wales' Bungool Festival of Music and Victoria's Sunbury Rock Festival; long interviews with Frank Zappa, Jack Bruce and Joni Mitchell (the latter syndicated from Canadian magazine *Maclean's*); and a feature on women in rock 'n' roll, written by Margaret Macintyre, which ran on the cover of issue 39 (December, 1974). Jen Jewel Brown also wrote stories on the costs and business traps of rock groups, while Alistair Jones reported on the 'country music dream centre' that Outback town Tamworth had become.

These reviews and articles were on a completely different level of sophistication to those published in *Go-Set*, not only in its early years but as it ran concurrently (sans Frazer) alongside *The Digger* until 1974. The world had changed dramatically since the mid-1960s – things were serious now, and serious were the people who wrote about them. There's a real feeling within the pages of *The Digger* that it all matters, that nothing is trivial, that nothing is left unquestioned – whether it be politics or music. As Phillip Frazer wrote, *The Digger*, 'by scraping the rust and mold from our culture to reveal its true shape', hoped 'that might point to new solutions'.

Due to its focus on reportage and pushing boundaries, *The Digger* was not without controversy. Several of the articles on politics erred close to The Line, or in some cases crossed it completely.

'Yeah, we were seized,' Brown confirms, referring to involvement from the Vice Squad. 'We had an issue on pornography, a story written by Beatrice Faust, who's a known academic, but it was seized nevertheless. So we were being harangued. Apart from the Vice Squad, ASIO had a great interest in [fellow publication] *Nation Review* as well … [they] discovered at one stage that their accountant worked for ASIO.'[12] She laughs at the memory of the story.

Faust's pornography feature ran in issue 3 (23 September 23 – 7 October) of *The Digger*, a three-page story complete with various images that were said to contravene what the establishment deemed worthy of public consumption. 'I think ASIO had this insane idea that all these groups were going to somehow blow up Australia, really. There was no violence associated with any of our publications,' Brown says on the paper's ongoing battle with the Australian intelligence agency. 'It does seem ridiculous. But they were very suspicious, so there was always that kind of thing dragging along, and legal things were very expensive.'

The Faust case was eventually won by the prosecution, in April 1974, resulting in a fine of $1350. This amount effectively crippled the paper, contributing to its eventual demise.

* * *

The final issue of *The Digger* was in December 1975, 'the year the magazine ran out of money and lawyers', as Frazer puts it. It'd run its course, served its purpose perhaps. The counterculture was already ceasing to be so revolutionary, as the cultural values it had tried to institute as a counter gradually became the norm.

Phillip Frazer had drifted away from *The Digger* in its later months, looking for something else. In 1976, he pulled the pin on his decade-long involvement with the Australian 'freak press', moving to America, where he remained for almost three decades. But he looks back on those years and the work he did, the movements he was involved with, as incredibly important. 'We were, in fact, inventing a radically different culture from the one our parents tried to force upon us,' he says. 'And it didn't fail, it didn't collapse. Counterculture was not a fad here, a stupid thing to do, it was generally a success, and it's still going on. And I think that's what it did – it rode a wave that was part of a cultural shift of tremendously powerful stuff, and I just kept moving with it, so to speak, and beyond it. But it left a very different place behind, after its time had finished.

'And if I was to define a type of press versus another type of press, I'd say that's it – the culture is writing its own stuff, as opposed to the previous, which was corporates writing *to* the culture. That's the turning point.'

A year or so before Frazer left the country in fact, and even before *The Digger* had ceased to be, a new press was blooming. It was equally serious in its reportage, but was pulling the focus right back to the music itself, leaving the coverage of underground politics and social movements to others. This was the beginning of a new age of the Australian rock press, an age that was to become golden.

* * *

While it took a while to gather steam, the Australian edition of *Rolling Stone* was to become an integral part of the local rock press. Before Frazer relocated to the United States around 1976, he'd travelled there years earlier, while still running *Revolution*, ostensibly to obtain the license to bring this still fledgling, music-oriented counterculture title to Australia.

Prior to appearing as a four-page insert in *Revolution*, *Rolling Stone* had first made its presence known in Australia via the pages of *Go-Set*. Keeping his finger on the pulse of the underground, Frazer subscribed to all the freak press he could find around the world – all the freak press, he says, rolling his eyes, who 'had their shit together to get something … and mail it'.

Among those publications was the new American magazine *Rolling Stone*. Started by a young Jann Wenner and music critic Ralph J. Gleason in San Francisco in 1967, much like *Go-Set*, *Rolling Stone* quickly established itself as the record of choice among young people. It spawned a short-lived English edition (1969–72), followed by Frazer's Australian version. Since the early 1970s, there have been more than twenty international editions, in countries such as China, Colombia, India, Mexico and Indonesia.

In 1968 and 1969, Wenner ran a two-part feature interview with John Lennon. Frazer, always a visionary, negotiated an agreement to syndicate it in the pages of his Australian rock paper. 'I dealt with [Wenner] by telephone, possibly letters – I don't remember that part,' Frazer says. 'I made an agreement to buy the interviews and print 'em in *Go-Set*, which we did.' A lot of the freak papers swapped material; there was a 'global syndicate, loosely speaking', as Frazer describes it. And so *Rolling Stone* made its first foray into the land Down Under.

A year and a half later, July 1970, and Frazer was in Chile. He was there in the lead-up to the presidential election, eventually won by the left-wing Popular Unity head Salvador Allende. 'It was scary, guys with helmets and canons,' Frazer recalls. 'People had vanished, et cetera. [It was] just chaos. There were thousands of business types trying to get in – thousands of guys in tweed coats with leather arm pads who were trying to get in. Spanish-speaking countries had rolled over. I got out, somehow.'

He'd come in via San Francisco. Prior to flying into South America, he had dropped in on Wenner, and the two spent a day talking all things shop, before driving south to a Beach Boys gig and a Janis Joplin gig, where he met Joplin, taking photos from the side of the stage. He ended up at CBS Records a few days later, no doubt drumming up business for *Go-Set*, when the guy on the front desk told him to 'Go down there, third door on the right.'

'I went down there and the third door on the right had a red light on, so I stopped, waited,' Frazer says. 'Red light went off, I walked in, there's Janis and [the Full Tilt Boogie Band] recording. So I turned my tape on and got my camera ready and sat down. I could hardly see what was going on through the smoke.'

He pauses. 'But I come back from Chile, whenever it was, six weeks later or less. And she's dead.'

This brought home to Frazer that it was time for him to go home. He met with Wenner again and the pair agreed to syndicate excerpts of American *Rolling Stone* in Australia. Frazer would print them as a four-page insert in his then-fledgling *Revolution*, the more serious stablemate to *Go-Set*. And so, eighteen months after the Lennon two-part syndication, *Rolling Stone* made its debut in Australia, albeit in a small, quiet sort of way. A year previously, an English edition of *Rolling Stone* had appeared – a venture which was to last only a few years. But it was Australia where it stuck, initially in the pages of *Revolution*, the seeds for its longevity and influence sowed early by the man who had the vision to get it happening in the first place.

'*Rolling Stone* had similarities with *Revolution*,' Frazer says, 'in that it covered rock 'n' roll and politics, and it covered them from a national point of view – in their case, USA – and from an intelligent, young activist point of view and language, a worldview. And they had in common that they were run and owned by people of that generation.

'Jann wasn't doing what anybody told him to do … well, he was constrained by the creditors and, you know, his staff, and so was I,' Frazer continues. 'We were both interested in a social, political world, not obsessed by music per se. And in England … there would have been more competition for the English *Rolling Stone* … *Friends* [for example] was more of a hippy, alternative, counterculture paper, rather like *Revolution*. But I wasn't competing [against *Go-Set*] with *Revolution*, because I was it, both of them, so I just went from one to the next.'

When *Revolution* folded in August 1971, *Rolling Stone* became a stand-alone paper in Australia, still run by Frazer, along with *Go-Set*'s business manager, Geoff Watson. 'I could see that I could do a *Rolling Stone* Oz edition because I'd established that with Jann directly, and I knew what to do and how to do it,' Frazer explains. 'And I only needed one other guy to start with, and that was the business manager at

Go-Set, Geoff Watson, who was the only person over thirty.' He laughs. 'So Geoff and I started *Rolling Stone* while I was still at *Go-Set*.'

Australian *Rolling Stone* was up and running.

7

THE DEATH OF *GO-SET*

'It was a disease that was eating at it.'

Ed Nimmervoll

In 1966, as times changed and the culture began to shift in earnest, the appearance of *Go-Set* could almost have been considered the act of a benevolent god to young Australians. Here, seemingly out of nowhere, was a platform from which to shout. For a generation excited for growth, coming to the realisation that they could forge their own identities beyond the prescribed confines of their parents' lives, it was intoxicating.

It was almost too good to be true – their own paper, focused on their own beliefs and concerns, written for them and by them alone. It was revolutionary. It became, with time, a trusted chronicle of what was happening in music and pop culture. A lot was happening, and quickly – as its audience changed, so too did the magazine, Phillip Frazer and his cohorts doing their best to keep up with it all, cover it all, explore it all.

As the paper grew, it became not just a companion to the Australian music industry, which was expanding concurrently, but a guide and a constructive critic; sometimes encouraging, at other times harsh, but always watching and nurturing, a voice not just for the people but for the industry.

'It was the bible of Australian pop music, as they say,' says long-time contributor Michele Williams, who rose to some modicum of fame as 'Mitch from *Go-Set*' during her two tenures with the publication, in between stints living and working in London. 'You knew that if you wanted to know what's happening in Australian music, you had to read *Go-Set* to find out.'

It would have seemed then, in 1968 and 1969, when the paper was at the peak of its popularity, that *Go-Set* would be around forever. How could a magazine as important and influential as *Go-Set* not last? How could a publication as dedicated as it was to the almost constant cultural shifts that defined the times ever fade away?

The sheer turbulence of these times, however, ensured it did. Even a paper as edgy as *Go-Set* couldn't keep up. And in truth, in its final years – certainly from 1971 until it finally *did* die in August 1974 – it wasn't cutting-edge. It lost that immediacy as its original readership grew up and it found itself unable to keep pace with the fractious nature of cultural change as the 1960s morphed into the 1970s.

By 1974, the paper was a shadow of its former self, having changed hands and cities, its ethos and influence long since diluted. It's generally recognised within Australian publishing that Phillip Frazer leaving the magazine in early 1972 was when *Go-Set* dipped in power, in potency. Frazer's direction, his proven ability to read cultural shifts and his tireless coverage of same, was what had driven the publication, what had seen it change with the times in order to remain as relevant as possible. But, weary of the threat of lawsuits and the demands of debtors, with a waning interest in contemporary pop culture and a burgeoning interest in the brewing counterculture, Frazer jumped ship, and the decline kicked in for real. The charge for 'inciting diverse persons unknown to commit larceny at supermarkets', stemming from the publication of excerpts from Abbie Hoffman's *Steal This Book*, was the last straw for Frazer – he agreed to a deal with the printer, Waverley Press, and the magazine now rested in whole with the family company that had carried the debt from the magazine's inception.

'Yes, the demise began when it was taken over by the printer. It lost some of its heart then,' long-time contributor Ed Nimmervoll said in an interview with the ABC's Barry McKay on an episode of Radio National's *Hindsight* in 2001. '[Then] the printers realised they'd picked up a tiger by the tail, and so they sold it off very quickly and it came under the control of people who looked at *every* aspect of it – how much it was costing, what it was doing, all those sort of things. How efficient it was. Rationalising everything and kind of ripping its heart out.'

In 1973, Waverley Press, realising they couldn't run *Go-Set* in a way that would remain financially viable *without* Frazer, sold the title to Sydney-based Sungravure Press, a printing and distribution group owned by UK publishing giant IPC, which was already publishing its own teen magazine in Australia, *Dolly*. The paper seemed a smart addition to their emerging youth stable.

As such, *Go-Set*'s corporate headquarters were now Sydney-based, although the paper itself was still based out of Melbourne. It was edited by Nimmervoll, who had taken over editorial duties after Frazer's departure. As a cost-cutting measure, and perhaps in an attempt to broaden the appeal of a paper in decline, the new owners began syndicating articles from veteran UK music papers *New Musical Express* and *Melody Maker*, and so *Go-Set* lost, over time, one of its most important qualities, which had endeared it to readers from the outset – its uniquely Australian bent.

'It was an English company ... the implication was, you've got *NME* and *Melody Maker*, you can fill this whole magazine with these articles,' Nimmervoll remembers. 'So what do you need that [local stuff] for?

So the budget wasn't big for Australian artists.' The publication was soon no longer consistently written for Australian audiences by Australian writers who were as much a part of the scene as the bands they were writing about.

'Just all of those things, it just ground down. It was a disease that was eating at it,' Nimmervoll laments.

Frazer agrees that 'under the new owners, personality writing and editing was supplanted by syndicated stuff', and the paper 'lost its verve and nerve'. 'They also failed to engage savvy women writers, photographers and designers or editors,' he says.

He theorises, too, that as 'pop continued its fragmentation into subgenres', so 'the market continued the process of disintegration that really began in '68'. 'At that time we introduced the 'Core' section to appeal to the late teen/twenties age group, or more serious followers of music and lyrics. Then we launched *Revolution* to take that a step further, basically creating a teen paper and a post-teen paper. Neither I nor the various *Go-Set* managements created this devolution of "the youth market" – rather, we tried to devolve our publications along with it. That left *Go-Set* with a young pop subset of the sixties and seventies generation, shrinking by the year. This, combined with a management style that had no real connection with what the paper was or what it had been, contributed mightily to its eventual demise.'

When Sungravure decided to move the paper *itself* to Sydney in early 1974, it spelt the end. 'When they moved to HQ in Sydney, [they] traded the cheeky, hip Melbourne zeitgeist for the hip-pocket Sydney one,' Frazer says.

'Part of the process was to take it from Melbourne, where it'd always been, and bring it inhouse, inside the publishing world,' Nimmervoll told McKay in 2001. 'That was when I left ... I didn't want to leave Melbourne and I wasn't enjoying what I was doing anyway.'

In his final editorial, towards the end of 1973, Nimmervoll announced the news that the paper was moving to Sydney. Melbourne had both 'loved and hated *Go-Set*', he wrote, and the question now was, would Sydney 'care about it in the same way?'

It very quickly became apparent that it did not, as readership figures declined.

A few years before the end, now-veteran Australian music writer Christie Eliezer had begun contributing to *Go-Set* while still at school. 'I used to turn up to the offices in school uniform, that was a bit of fun,' he says with a laugh. 'And ... *Go-Set* was unbeatable in those days – they just had everything.' But by 1969, *Go-Set* had a problem. 'Even the name was a really daggy ... it was meant to be a send-up, it was aimed at the fourteen- to twenty-year-olds. Now, three or four years on, those kids are older.' According to Eliezer, Sungravure and the paper's last editor, Jenny Irvine, tried to rebrand the magazine once it had relocated to Sydney, but 'I don't think they gave it enough time – I think they gave it four or five months and then they killed it off.'

A few months prior to *Go-Set*'s final issue, Michele Williams returned from her second stint in the United Kingdom. 'I had left [for the UK again] before Phillip had left,' she explains, 'but I heard that when he left there was a lot of trouble with Waverley Press ... and it was ridiculous, because there was no *Go-Set* without Phillip, I felt that right there and then. But I started doing a column from London, the occasional feature. As such, I didn't really have a solid connection with *Go-Set* at that point, but I was sending in my column.'

Once she returned to Australia, Williams ended up settling in Sydney, where, along with editor Jenny Irvine, she was the only staff member in the office. 'To be honest, I can't remember what I used to write then. So it was Jenny and me, and Ian [Meldrum] still sending his stuff up and Phillip Morris doing photographs. So there was some familiarity there. But it was pretty dull.'

Williams held on for a few months, but not having a connection with the music of the time and yearning for a vibe now long gone, she pulled the pin, a move which as she understood indirectly acted as the trigger for the magazine's demise. 'No one seemed to know this was the policy of IPC … that they would shut down a magazine if they could not continue publishing without replacing departing staff,' she says. 'And I was just bored. I mean, it was absolutely awful. So I just decided I was heading back to England again … so basically it shut down just after I left, which I assumed was due to the IPC policy.[13] The last [issue] of *Go-Set* was August 25, and that would have been put to bed some days before that date.'

It seems a terrible injustice that a paper like *Go-Set*, with its rich (albeit brief) history, its proven track record of influence, its relatability and its uniqueness, could fizzle out with barely a sound. After eight years, to end like this seemed inconceivable.

'I know,' says Williams, smiling, 'but if you think about it, it ended after five years, because of Phillip leaving, so it was really five. It's insane what went on at *Go-Set* – it was anarchy and chaos all the time, people just had such a brilliant time, and [Phillip] was responsible for all of it. It's really after he left, that's it, it's the *end* of *Go-Set*, but we just pretended it went on for a few more years.'

I suggest that her two stints working for the magazine on staff would have been very different – 1968 compared to 1974. 'Extremely,' she says. 'They're not the same magazine at all, they're worlds apart. Worlds apart. I don't even know what to say about that … I just felt that after Phillip left, as far as I was concerned there was no *Go-Set*. I was still sending my column over from England, but it was just going out to this faded memory. It wasn't *Go-Set*.'

'Culture and politics are always fluid and evolving, and like all evolutions, they have no predetermined destination,' waxes Frazer, adding, 'they sally forth in the face of the benign indifference of the universe.' And so it was that *Go-Set*, and along with it the first distinct era of the Australian rock press, ceased to be.

PART TWO

THE GOLDEN ERA

THE ROCK PRESS THRIVES

(1975–1993)

8

RAM, BAM, THANK YOU, MA'AM

'Waiter, have this man removed from the magazine!'

Anthony O'Grady

It's early 1975, and for the first time in almost a decade, Australia has no dedicated rock press of which to speak. *Go-Set* has been dead for a good six months. Gone too are *Sound Blast*, *Music Maker* and *Planet*. The local edition of *Rolling Stone* is still little more than a carbon copy of its American parent. *The Digger* is hardly the place for up-to-the-minute information on music. And shy of reading imported magazines from the United Kingdom and the United States, Australian music fans have little way of finding out what's happening in these bustling musical centres, let alone in their own backyard.

Despite this, music is everywhere. The Australian scene is continuing to grow – pub rock is dominating and the bubble-gum 1960s are now but a distant memory, shunted further into history after flower power, the UK blues boom and the advent of pot smoke–shrouded psychedelic rock.

So where to from here?

In Sydney, someone had already made a tentative move. Anthony O'Grady, a sometime ad copywriter and avid rock fan, had started a glossy, *Ear for Music*, along with publisher Kim Ryrie, in September 1973. O'Grady was no fool, but the magazine only lasted three issues before folding in December of the same year.

David Pepperell, formerly of *Go-Set* and *Planet*, remembers *Ear for Music* being 'a big flop'. O'Grady 'came out of advertising, and he did this thing where he guaranteed a circulation to the advertisers'. 'The idea was to do a full glossy rock 'n' roll magazine,' Pepperell says. But 'they guaranteed the advertisers that if they didn't get the circulation, they wouldn't have to pay. That was stupid. And it was a big circulation and they never got there, so they folded after a short time.'

Ear for Music was where journalist Jen Brown met O'Grady. 'I thought he was quite an operator, a young entrepreneur having the ambition and confidence to try and set up a national rock paper,' she remembers.

O'Grady was not to be deterred by *Ear for Music*'s failure, however. The experiences he had with the short-lived publication would prove immensely valuable, not just to him but to the rock press more widely – for a little over a year afterwards, a time in which *Go-Set* finally succumbed and local coverage was thin on the ground, O'Grady teamed up with newly minted publisher Philip Mason to launch *Rock Australia Magazine*, or *RAM*, as it was known, in March 1975.

An Englishman, Philip Mason had relocated from the United Kingdom in 1970, where he'd been marketing manager for the IPC-published *Woman* magazine, to take up a post with Sungravure, then publishers of *Go-Set*. He'd subsequently left IPC to start his own publishing empire, Soundtracts.

'I recognised with the closing of *Go-Set*, and with the Australian rock scene becoming more affluent and more active, that there was probably a hole in the market for a good, gutsy rock 'n' roll magazine,'

Mason says on the origins of *RAM*. 'I then needed to find an editor, and I'd read *Ear for Music* and thought Anthony was a fabulous writer. I'd never met him at that stage, but I rang him one evening and laid on the line what I had in mind … and [asked] was he interested in being the editor? And we met, and he was, and that's how it started.'

In *RAM*, Australia had the rebirth of a rock press, a natural progression from *Go-Set*. While unknown to anyone at the time, it would mark the beginning of the press's golden era.

* * *

O'Grady, who is known to many as the godfather of Australian rock journalism, died in late 2018 from a long illness. His death brought into sharp focus just how much of an influence he'd had over his tenure as a writer and editor, firstly with *RAM*, and later with myriad other endeavours. His funeral was attended by a who's who of rock-press luminaries.

Two months after his death, on 4 February 2019, journalist Stuart Coupe, who had a long involvement with *RAM*, wrote in *The Sydney Morning Herald*:

> O'Grady was a passionate, insightful, pithy journalist, a tough but giving editor and with his publishers had a clear and forthright perspective on marketing, distribution and image, something that was no doubt partially fuelled by a background in the world of advertising.
>
> After that brief advertising stint O'Grady wrote articles for *Go Set* magazine and edited the short lived *Ear for Music* before starting *RAM*. Amongst his inspired moves was arranging licensing deals with many of the overseas magazines he admired, thereby meaning that *RAM* had access to some of the best global music journalism whilst he nurtured a generation of Australian equivalents.

It was actually Philip Mason who had arranged the syndication deals with UK magazines *NME* and *Melody Maker*, before *RAM* even existed. Coming from IPC, who published these English rock press behemoths, his contact list proved critical. 'Yes, I had good links back to London and I was able to negotiate a syndication deal with those two magazines,' he confirms. 'I thought without those rights, it was going to be very difficult … to produce a good music magazine, so I thought it was essential that we had links to the British music scene, which at that stage was really more important than the American scene, I think.'

O'Grady's initial vision for *RAM* was to demonstrate that 'the calibre of the writing coming out of Australia was as good as what was coming in *NME* and *Melody Maker* in those days', remembers Coupe. The bar was high: influential English rock writer Nick Kent features heavily in *RAM*'s early issues, among other respected UK journalists. 'And it was very good. That's why we're all very lucky to come around in that time … he was a real stickler for *real* music journalism, that was his main [thing].'

'Anthony liked to think *RAM* was credible and not a teen-type thing, so, you know, I think he would have been more inspired by *The Digger*, the quality of journalism, than *Go-Set*', is Coupe's belief. *RAM* was a serious enterprise, as serious as the music scene growing alongside it, and for O'Grady it was imperative that the writing matched this. It was this vision that saw, via the pages of *RAM*, rock journalism become a respected pursuit in Australia for the first time since its inception.

Not that this vision was purely altruistic. 'I think he just saw a market opportunity,' Coupe muses. 'You know, *NME* was huge in those days, an unbelievably successful publication, so the idea was [to emulate]. There were ad dollars around, so I don't think he thought about changing history in any way, probably no more than Jann Wenner did in those days. But, you know, he was a tough, old-school editor, which was great. And I think he deserves more credit than he probably realises for the fact that that era of music writer, you know, we could all write. Without being egotistical, not saying we're geniuses, but we could write really well because we had to write really well.'

'He was a very good editor,' agrees Mason. 'He attracted a lot of very good, talented writers of the time. And he improved them – he said to them, we've got all this good material coming from overseas and we don't want there to be any drop of standards with the local content. And I think it's fair to say there wasn't.'

O'Grady wasn't in general one to editorialise, but the paper's first issue (appearing on 8 March 1975, priced at 40 cents) contained a short blurb, outlining what he saw as *RAM*'s purpose:

> Hullo. Welcome to our pages. I suppose you're wondering what we're all about, so I'll give it to you straight.
>
> Rock Australian Magazine is a new rock paper that aims to be world class because Australia is now part of the international rock scene. So we'll be covering top international groups with the same familiarity as Australian groups.
>
> Overseas groups are no longer the awesome, remote figures they appeared to be just a few years ago. They're now frequent visitors to our shores because they recognise Australia as a big part of the musical world. It's time Australians recognised the same. Rock Australia also aims to be an accessible magazine. Nobody on the staff has a star complex. We go to the same concerts as you, listen to the same records, get worried about the same things. We speak the same language as you.
>
> We also know that *our* rock and roll generation is a lifestyle and its expression is more than music.

> That's why you'll find articles on things such as the places you're thinking of travelling to, the clothes you're wearing, and information other papers won't give you ... such as our story on The Dole on page 25.
>
> But basically, and mostly, we want to be a good time. Because music and the people who give it are the most exciting time we'll all ever have.
>
> If you just want to share it and read about it, that's OK with us.
>
> But I'd also welcome anyone who wants to get involved. And here's a few ways ... jump on us if we're ever wrong. Point it out if we ever get pretentious. And when we knock ourselves out giving you a great story, why not respond to that too?
>
> Above all help us take pride in the fact that Australia is now a world class rock power and Rock Australia is its new magazine.

This editorial is signed by O'Grady, listing him simply as 'Editor'. And, in a similar vein to Tony Schauble's maiden editorial for *Go-Set* in 1966, it not only sets forth an agenda but acts as a call to arms, making clear the publication's mission is to become a hub in which like-minded people (the 'rock and roll generation') can receive and engage with all the cultural developments pertinent to their lives. O'Grady waxes somewhat lyrical with phrases such as 'we also know that *our* rock and roll generation is a lifestyle' and 'music and the people who give it are the most exciting time we'll all ever have', offering an insight into how he is looking to present *RAM*'s music coverage and encourage his readers to think about music.

O'Grady is right about Australia being an integral part of the international rock scene in early 1975 – and this is prior to bands like Midnight Oil, AC/DC, Skyhooks, Cold Chisel and INXS becoming international names, and before the advent of genres like punk (just) and new wave. At the time of *RAM*'s inception, international audiences were exposed to bands and singers such as Billy Thorpe & the Aztecs, Spectrum, Daddy Cool, Stevie Wright, The La De Da's, Wendy Saddington, Chain, The Dingoes, Ayers Rock. And international acts were in regular attendance here – Led Zeppelin, Roy Orbison, Cilla Black, Roberta Flack and The Rolling Stones, among many others.

O'Grady wrote a lot in the early issues, unsurprisingly (the magazine was yet to assert its influence and so staff were in short supply), and he covered a lot of ground. He wrote lengthy features on Skyhooks, Ariel, Jim Keays, Captain Matchbox, AC/DC, Sherbet, Buffalo, Stevie Wright, Dragon and Johnny O'Keefe.

Straight up, the syndication deals with *NME* and *Melody Maker* paid off. In the first issue, Nick Kent previews Zeppelin's *Physical Graffiti* and interviews, in the first of a two-part feature, both Mick Taylor and Mick Jagger, just before and just after the former left the Stones. To have this sort of in-depth coverage in a brand-new Australian magazine was impressive. *RAM* proved straight away it wasn't a wannabe but the real thing.

From issue 2, a fortnight later, O'Grady introduced news sections – 'Australian Graffiti', 'British Graffiti' and 'American Graffiti' – with developments and tidbits from these respective musical hothouses. Testament to his support of Australian music, while the British and the American news was each confined to a page, the Australian section very quickly grew to two pages.

Advertising was relatively sparse within *RAM*'s pages, at least initially. It's immediately noticeable – it seems most unfeasible these days that a publication like *RAM* could have survived without pages and pages of ads. Those which did appear were, according to Clinton Walker, who also contributed to the paper for a number of years, of a piece with the magazine's aesthetic. 'You'd have a couple of half-pages somewhere, [ads from] some shitty record company.' He laughs. 'And record companies didn't have art departments, and so they'd say, "We'll buy an ad for this new Australian Crawl album," and Gary Fletcher, who was the art director at *RAM*, would do the ad. You know, gimme a bromide of the album cover and I'll just put a bit of font on it … and yeah, the ad might look like the mag.'

How they could survive with almost no advertising? The economics of producing a magazine are different to that of a newspaper, and *RAM* was also commissioning longform pieces.[14]

'You know where [the money] was coming from?' Walker says, eyebrow raised. 'It was coming from *Tracks*, the surfing magazine, which sold shitloads.[15] It sold *shitloads* … everyone was smoking weed all the time, everyone smoked dope all day long, that was one of the things too. I do remember that Philip Mason – who owned Mason Stewart, which published *RAM* (and *Tracks*), who actually looked a bit like Bryan Ferry – I think he used to despair: "Those clowns up in the *Tracks* office, they're out of their minds, but they're selling so many magazines I can't argue with 'em."

'And Anthony would have *RAM* on a vaguely tighter leash, but it was still the same. And I think *RAM*, within that empire, was the prestige. *Tracks*, they were ratbags … they were just surf rats, we were rock 'n' roll rats.' Walker laughs. 'Although I don't really know what the distinction is … [at least] we had some literary pretentions.'

Issue 6 of *RAM* (17 May 1975) was different in that it marked the first of a semi-regular occurrence: a guest editor, in this case Bryan Ferry. 'Ferry was [Anthony's] ultimate guy,' Stuart Coupe says. Ferry was enlisted to pen a number of pieces in the issue while on tour in Australia with Roxy Music, which he did with great humour and grace.

His intro to a page-long piece entitled 'Confessions of a Debonair Degenerate', essentially his guest editorial, read:

> Editorship of a magazine is not something to be undertaken lightly. The RAM project has proved that. It seems everytime one turned around there were demented people screaming 'Copy, copy!' … 'Deadlines! Deadlines!' Nevertheless, it's a well known fact I'd do anything for RAM, so here we are. RAM by the way is a good magazine – required airport reading for all rock groups and (I am assured) a mainstay of suburban street life. This issue was put together with the help of the regular staff, while the band played table tennis in the basement. Hope you enjoy it. And thank you Australia for some very kind reaction at the concerts we were able to fit in while putting this issue together.

Yarns followed on London and New York nightlife ('In Search of the Perfect Hangover'), 'a jaundiced guide to the pop world', and the Debonair and Suave Test, all worked up by Ferry himself. A short missive on the Letters page added humour: 'I've got this $10 bet with a lady I know about the Bee Gees (pretty boring subject … but when $10 is at stake …),' a reader wrote in. 'Who was Lulu married to – was it Maurice or Barry? I say Maurice, but she refuses to believe it. Thanks a lot – you've got a great magazine there.'

The letter, signed by a Corporal Matchstick, was replied to thusly:

> See Dirt pages for Maurice Gibb's latest plans for Lulu. Also send the usual 25% bet deciding commission – A.O'G.
>
> While we're talking about money, how much do you owe me for all that writing … ? – B.F.
>
> 'Waiter, have this man removed from the magazine!'

(Another notable guest editor was supposed to have been Elvis Costello, except that Elvis didn't actually agree to it and so the only inkling that it was on the cards was a photo of a cardboard cut-out of Costello, standing behind O'Grady's desk.)

All of this was in good fun, which was important. *RAM* had set itself up to be serious, taking both the music and the journalism as things that mattered – it was imperative, though, that humour played a part, given the focus on humour in the Australian music publications that preceded it. This humanised and levelled the publication, avoiding the risk of it seeming elitist, and endearing it to even the most hard-headed of music fans. 'Anthony and I discussed the tone of the magazine from the outset,' Mason says, 'and we agreed on the "character".'

There was also content for those who wanted something aside from music. Like *Go-Set*, *RAM* wasn't just about music, even though that was its key concern. In the first issue, Australian rock writer Annie Burton wrote a piece on the dole – the term 'dole bludger' was popularised by politicians Bert Kelly and Clyde Cameron in the early 1970s in an effort to shift the blame for high unemployment from the government to individual welfare recipients. It was only a page-long article, but it was veracious and pertinent, in the vein of pieces that would appear in *The Digger*. Burton became an integral part of *RAM*'s lineup, and this article is an early harbinger of what was to come from her and others in this new magazine:

> … the thirty-one dollars you get is intended to keep you alive, but not ecstatically so, whilst your social conscience whips you to find work. Once upon a time, thirty-one dollars each week was a sum. You could pay the rent, feed the budgies and, while the town was not constantly red from your revels, you could afford a pink tinge every now and then. It's bad manners to go into how far it stretches now. And for this fortune, you will probably encounter personal denigration from bureaucrats reeking of employment …

Burton alludes to having spoken to a number of people on the dole, but the article contains no direct quotes. It's essentially an informed op-ed as opposed to an investigative piece, but it gives a taste of what *RAM* was about – representing issues close to their readership of music fans.

* * *

O'Grady would no doubt have been delighted by a letter written by a reader of *RAM*'s first issue, which he printed on the magazine's new letters page in issue 2. 'Dear Sir,' it read. 'Congratulations on your new music magazine. I have just arrived here from England, and *RAM* is as good as the English Rock papers such as *NME* and *Melody Maker*.'

To have his vision for the magazine recognised after only one issue would have been a tremendous boost, validation for the hard work that had been put in to get the thing off the ground. Yes, a good portion of *RAM*'s first issue contained syndicated material from both of those English papers, but in among these stories were yarns about Australian musicians and Australian music written by Australian writers (or O'Grady under various pen names, at this early juncture), creating a uniquely Australian feel.

'Yes, the writing was very fresh,' Mason agrees. 'I don't think any other magazine in Australia was running the sort of pieces we were running. And Anthony unearthed some great talent, and he has to get all the credit for that.' O'Grady poached Stuart Coupe from fledgling Adelaide publication *Roadrunner* in 1978 in order to further his vision for what *RAM* could be. 'I remember Anthony calling me up and saying, "How would you like to come and work for a real music magazine, dear boy?", Coupe, who had been working in the industry for some time by this point, says with a laugh. Also on the staff at various times in the early years were Annie Burton, Andrew McMillan, Dennis Atkins, Jen Brown, Richard Guilliatt and Miranda Brown.

That salutary reader was not alone in his positive impression of *RAM*. It struck a chord with readers very quickly. *RAM*, like *Go-Set* before it, appeared at the right time. Australian rock 'n' roll was huge and people were eager to read about it – in a publication that was more than gloss and swoon, but offered deep investigative pieces into these bands, these figures, this music that was so important to them. Throw in a little travel, a little fashion, and *RAM* was the magazine to fill not a niche but a need.

The majority of letters printed in the first issues made a point of congratulating *RAM*. 'I am writing to congratulate you on your suave magazine and to offer what little encouragement I can give,' reads one. 'First of all, I'd like to congratulate your new rock paper on its first issue. It'd have to be the best Aussie rock paper ever!' enthuses another.

The interesting thing is that once this rhetoric is out of the way, most readers go on, often at length, to share their thoughts on the music topic uppermost in their minds. Yes, this is a great publication, but down to business, they seemed to say.

And this is what *RAM* was for – discussing the business of music, and its readers were veracious in their need and want for it.

Clinton Walker, who wrote for *RAM* (among many other titles) in the late 1970s and well into the 1980s, has his tongue firmly in cheek when describing music writers in the early 1970s as the 'lowest of the low', until *RAM* disproved this and rock journalism became a *thing*. *RAM*'s pieces sparked opinions and admiration. Australia had become a player in the rock world, and *RAM*'s people were the only ones writing about it and analysing it with the passion and zeal and journalistic integrity with which all other facets of life were written about daily in other publications.

'Anthony held a standard that we should be as readable as [UK and US] music writers, people we looked up to, Hunter S. Thompson included,' says Jen Brown, who came to work at *RAM* in 1978, after stints at *Revolution*, *Planet* and *The Digger*. As *RAM* grew, so did the writers' skill and eye for stories. 'It all happened pretty organically,' she says. 'I followed my nose. I was always attracted to Australian music, I had a real passion for it, trying to analyse it, listening to all the lyrics. The excitement of the bands … they played live for weeks on end without playing anywhere twice, and they were really tight. There wasn't heavy editing on the pieces very often, there wasn't a lot of interference on the writers. The writers – Andrew McMillan, myself, Mark Mordue, Greg Taylor, Annie Burton – they were very capable writers … [you'd] talk through the idea with Anthony first, figure out when the deadline was going to be, how many words you were aiming at, who's gonna take the photographs, then bang. You had to do it quick … you'd go to press conferences, you'd interview people, chase people around. Nobody had mobile phones, you had to go on foot to things, there was no internet – it was very different.'

Annie Burton went on to become regarded as one of the country's best independent press writers. 'She had this unusual style, a lightness and a touch of absurdity, a lot of curiosity,' Brown recalls of Burton, with whom she shared a flat in her early days as a contributor. 'She was very readable and interesting. Anthony thought really highly of Annie. I think she wandered in there with no credentials, said she wanted to write for *RAM*, and so Anthony let her try and it all worked out.'

Another writer of note was Brisbane expat Andrew McMillan, who came to write for the magazine in its early years, when he was fresh out of school. His writing was visceral, in the vein of one of his literary heroes, Hunter S. Thompson. His work was already attracting attention by the time he came to write for *RAM*: one of his earlier pieces on Brisbane punks The Saints had been published in UK music bible *Sounds*. 'I think Anthony somehow got the wrong impression that

Andrew was an impressionable boy who could be moulded,' Brown says with a laugh of her good friend McMillan, who died in 2012. 'And even though Anthony's suggestions were professional, nevertheless Andrew clearly ignored everything and kept submitting things that would have Anthony saying, "No, my dear boy, I've told you about this before!"'

'Oh yeah, definitely,' Clinton Walker says when asked whether McMillan's writing was important to the magazine's success. 'He [also] definitely wanted to be Hunter Thompson. And it worked for *RAM*, people loved it. He suited that stuff, he had the language that seemed to suit all those bands.'

In 2012, Jen Brown produced a documentary called *Paper Trail* for ABC's Radio National, detailing her time writing for various rock magazines. McMillan was quoted on the episode, explaining in his laconic way how he got into the game:

> As a teenager, I read *Go-Set* and *Sound Blast*, and *Nation Review* and things like that. And then when *RAM* came out, I bought the first issue because it had the Rolling Stones on the cover, and I was really impressed with the life of the magazine. They had one story in there called 'Jesus Just Pissed Me Off', about life on the dole.[16] I was quite impressed with the language, and felt a certain affinity with that paper.
>
> And so I wrote a letter to the editor of *RAM* ... and a couple of weeks later I got a letter on a *RAM* letterhead from the editor, Anthony O'Grady, saying, 'Well, thank you for your letter, I've tweaked it into a concert review and there'll be a cheque in the mail next week.' And suddenly I was a rock journalist.

A rock journalist with Australia's newest rock magazine, a publication which at that point essentially had the joint to itself. *RAM* had found a gap and very quickly began to fill it. Most importantly, it filled it well. Rock journalism in Australia was coming of age – those covering this scene were not the 'lowest of the low' but dedicated young men and women reporting seriously on serious business: rock 'n' roll and all that occurred in its grungy sphere. As the 1970s continued its march, *RAM* was destined to grow.

9

A TALE OF TWO RIVALS

'It was never a case of fuck, how do we cover this?
It was, fuck, there's so much happening.'

Christie Eliezer

As *RAM* started on its journey in Sydney, further south in 1975 things weren't as dynamic. Early the previous year, Melbourne had lost its only rock paper as *Go-Set* – distributed nationally, but spiritually Melbournian – had relocated to Sydney prior to its demise in August 1974; the Australian edition of *Rolling Stone* was published out of Sydney too. *RAM* was growing, but in its early days, before it truly became a national publication, it was very Sydney-centric. So when *Go-Set* left the southern capital, Melbourne was left bereft. The city's music fans would have been left frustrated by the lack of coverage, despite the strength of its live scene.

And it was an impressive live scene – a hothouse of bands and music, one of *the* rock 'n' roll cities of the world. Mainstream Australian rock was, arguably, beginning to stagnate, but Melbourne was fostering an underground scene, filled with diverse acts and experimental sounds.

'The Melbourne scene was the biggest in the world,' journalist David Pepperell states unequivocally. 'In the world. It really was. Even guys in New York would come over and say there aren't as many venues, there aren't as many people going out to rock 'n' roll. Melbourne itself, there were about fifty rock pubs in, like, a twenty-mile radius. Going up to Ferntree Gully, the Royal, places like that, they all had live bands on. So the scene was spectacular, lots to write about, lots going on. The fucking touring scene, about every month someone would come out, it was magic for touring. We saw every decent band, you know, certainly from England. I did all those tours ... the Stones did probably the biggest tour of Australia ever in '73.

'So the scene in Melbourne: the bands who came here couldn't believe it. The scene in Melbourne was ten times London ... Sydney, there was never any scene in Sydney.'

Pepperell goes on, nostalgically, about various venues around the city, recalling ending up in Brunswick at the Bombay Rock at 3.00 am on Friday nights. 'I used to go to five gigs on a Friday night,' he laughs.

Melbourne music fans, after an entire year without a dedicated music press to cover this fertile growth period, were champing at the bit for a new publication that catered to their interests. The man to see this and do something about it was Ed Nimmervoll. Three months after *RAM* appeared in Sydney, before it could find its feet nationally, Nimmervoll introduced *Juke*,[17] Melbourne's answer to *RAM*, and so the Australian rock press expanded.

'My big plan was to replace *Go-Set*,' Nimmervoll told freelance journalist Barry McKay in 2001 for a Radio National documentary, *Pop & Circumstance*. 'It took me a year and a half. One of the things I realised doing *Go-Set* is what it *wasn't* doing. Times had changed ... there was room for a magazine, but it had to be different. The original idea for *Juke* was more of a cultural magazine, still about rock 'n' roll, but ... there was a photo session for a major artist each time, so the cover shot was an actual studio session, like a *real* magazine. So there were a lot of thoughts about being classy, which *Go-Set* had stopped being; I just wanted to be really, really classy. Do it in a classy way, get a really strong group of journalists and all those [things]. And I did that.'

Nimmervoll, with this vision in mind, needed someone to publish his new paper and approached Thomas H. Williams, who ran a small but reputable publishing house, specialising in, as Pepperell recalls, adventure sport magazines. 'Surfing and motorbike magazines, that's where it really started,' he says.

It was a gamble – Nimmervoll had approached Williams with trepidation, but Williams was immediately receptive. Nimmervoll's gratitude can be seen in a small note that appeared in *Juke*'s first issue to 'Tom Williams, our boss, for saying "yes" to *Juke*. We hope we make you lots of money, Tom.'

The first issue of *Juke* appeared in Melbourne newsagents on 14 May 1975, retailing at 40 cents (the same price as *RAM*), with Skyhooks frontman Shirley Strachan gracing the cover. It contained articles on John Lennon, actor Reg Livermore, Ian Gorman joining Daddy Cool, the facts about songwriting, and a big piece on then relatively new television show *Countdown*: '*Countdown* has brought Australian rock 'n' roll into a new period – a revitalised new era.'

Despite the professional image this opening issue would have presented, things behind the scenes at *Juke* over its first few months were anything but smooth. As it turned out, Williams quickly got cold feet on the idea of the magazine, and so Nimmervoll was unable to instigate his vision, given the pressure coming from his publisher. He had to shoulder a lot of the load himself, unable to staff the operation as he'd wished.

'I had this dream, and at the time I didn't think I'd realised it, because I just had to spin too many plates all at once,' he explains. 'The woman that I picked as my deputy editor, who was supposed to be carrying some of the load, she was having a nervous breakdown; [and Tom] lost faith after three months and he thought we should stop there and then. And he said, "This paper is finished." And so those three months were really traumatic for me, because I was just trying to do too much.'

Pepperell concurs that launching the publication was an uphill battle. 'We didn't last too long with [Tom], and he was very good to us, but his reps didn't know how to sell us,' Pepperell says. 'Nice guy, but he did motorbikes and surf. He gave up after not long.'

Losing a publisher only a few months into its lifespan, *Juke* was in trouble. But Nimmervoll wasn't to be thwarted – he approached Fairfax newspapers, whose flagship publications were major metro dailies *The Age* (Melbourne) and *The Sydney Morning Herald*. 'Yes, *The Age* picked it up without losing an issue,' Nimmervoll remembers.

'Ed managed to get Fairfax interested, they took it over, and we went to the fifth floor of the Spencer Street Soviet, as we called it,' recalls Pepperell with a laugh. 'So that was great. We went there and we kicked on from there. It was a very successful paper, *Juke*. It had a big circulation, it was national. I loved it.'

Journalist Christie Eliezer tells a slightly different story. He remembers a 'big, screaming row about money' between Nimmervoll and Williams; but regardless of the circumstances, the situation ended with *Juke* settling in under Fairfax's magazine arm, Newspress, which at the very least ensured their financial future.[18]

'Ed took it off to *The Age* and in some ways it was a good move, and some ways it wasn't, because it gave *Juke* something of a corporate kind of look, which I don't think was justified,' Eliezer muses. 'But on the other hand, it was good because with *The Age / The Sydney Morning Herald* connection we had somebody writing for us in every capital city, which *RAM* didn't. None of the other magazines did.' This, before *RAM* caught up, was a serious feather in *Juke*'s cap, allowing them to report on music all over the country, for audiences who would not yet have heard it.

'I remember both David [McComb] from The Triffids and Grant [McLennan] from The Go-Betweens, by the time they first came down to Melbourne – this is before JJJ – people kind of knew their music,' Eliezer says. 'Same thing with Perth and Adelaide. So it was a real national thing.'

David Pepperell was at that time one of the most prolific rock writers in the country, having written for *Go-Set*, *Daily Planet* and *Planet*. 'I really churned out a lot of copy in those days. Seven or eight thousand words an issue,' he says with a laugh. He was an integral part of *Juke* from the get-go. At Nimmervoll's request he wrote a column that was to become central to the magazine's lineup.

'Ed rang me up, said he was going to do a new paper,' Pepperell remembers. 'He'd got this idea of me doing a column, like [Molly Meldrum's] in *Go-Set*, which I thought would be fun, I always liked that column. It was just based on listing as many names as you possibly could. So I said okay.

'So I was talking to a mate of mine, an old jazz fan, and he said, what about [calling it] Dr Pepper's Hot Sauce?' He laughs. '"Hot sauce" used to be a jazz term for the mail, the inside news. So … I called the first two that. Then I had this idea of writing it as a story of this person, who was the maddest guy in Melbourne, writing it in the third person. So I started doing that, and it was amazingly successful, the most successful thing I've ever done. I've been stuck with that name ever since; people still call me Doc. So I wrote in the third person, and it was just completely ridiculous, and it was really what I was doing, it was all true. It was just a mixture of things happening, wild ideas, incredible libels – I libelled everyone. The subs used to read it and say, "Twelve libels this week, mate!"'

Pepperell's column only lasted until the end of the year, mainly because the semi-fictional Dr Pepper almost killed his creator. 'It was just insane, and of course, the more successful it got, the more outrageous I got.' Pepperell laughs. 'By the end of the year, I said to Ed, "I can't continue writing this because it's just gonna kill me." I was drinking so much, I was going out every night of the week, I was doing every drug I could to keep going, I was truly nuts. I'd developed the dark side of my character to the nth degree, I'd almost become Dr Pepper. I'm not Dr Pepper at all!

'Finally, I just quit. I wrote a final column, which I was going to call "The Death of Dr Pepper", but I was too afraid to. I'd created a monster. So I called it "Dr Pepper Fades Out".'

Both *Juke*, which was weekly, and *RAM*, coming out fortnightly, evolved into serious music publications as they gained traction. This was a time when rock journalists practising the craft, aided by more-generous word lengths, began to really flex their pens, and the writing on the music of the day was deep and passionate. There was so much happening, in Melbourne and beyond – *Juke* was there, trying to capture as much of it as possible.

'When I look back at some of those early issues we did, fuck, we really covered everything,' Eliezer remembers fondly. 'Because we also had people in London, a regular column in London, we had a regular column from Los Angeles and New York. *Juke* was the first Australian magazine to write about the British punk rock explosion. I remember the London girl ringing me up at two or three in the morning, saying, "You've gotta listen to this – 'God Save the Queen' … fuck, you reckon these guys are gonna be big?" He laughs. 'And you know, we were the first to write about the whole Krautrock trend, the New Romantics trend, and I personally wrote the first ever hip-hop story for an Australian magazine, because I was in New York. I didn't think it was gonna be this bloody big, I just thought it was an interesting African American phenomenon. I thought it was a wonderful, wonderful thing.'

It wasn't all beer and skittles, though. One low point was the now-infamous *Juke* review of seminal Brisbane punk band The Saints' debut album, *Stranded*. Written by Jamie Dunn, it panned a record that is (and was at the time, by almost everywhere except *Juke*) universally lauded as one of the very first punk records. Detractors of *Juke* point to that review to this day as an example of how *Juke* was behind the times, how it struggled to keep pace with *RAM*, how it never really hit the heights it should have.

Journalist Clinton Walker is caustic in his views on *Juke*. It was one of only a handful of music publications Walker never contributed to. 'Both magazines started in '75. Given *Juke* was in Melbourne, it should have had first access [to Melbourne bands], but it didn't,' he says. 'You know who did have first access? Anthony [O'Grady]. *RAM* was way better, because Anthony was cool and he could get Skyhooks and all that sort of stuff.'

I venture that Ed Nimmervoll would also have been cool.

'Yeah,' concurs Walker, 'but nobody was cool like Anthony, it really is actually that linear. They were daggy guys, they weren't as cool. They were career journalists, and *Juke* was a bit corporate, it was owned by *The Age* or whatever. And Anthony was swishing around with his scarves and he knew Bryan Ferry, and he knew the Skyhooks, or AC/DC. And sure, *Juke* had something, but it didn't have that.

'And then punk came along, and *Juke* hated it, just totally spurned it. Anthony did the opposite – he recognised it straight away.'

This is, of course, contrary to Christie Eliezer's claim that *Juke* was the first Australian publication to laud punk, but Walker is adamant. 'If you talk to people in Melbourne, and I can mention two people who would tell you – Keith Glass and Bruce Milne – they both said,

"Fucking *Juke*. They were hopeless, we gave up trying." The problem child called *Juke*, or Joke as we used to call it. *Juke* made some bad choices … Anthony knew that if you wanted to sell magazines you had to put Ritchie Blackmore on the cover and Radio Birdman inside, and he was totally into that. And [so did] *Stone*, to its credit, even though Australian *Stone* was coming out of that west-coast vibe of American *Stone*, which I hated … And so what then happened? *RAM* was miles ahead [of *Juke*].'

Walker opines in his essay 'Lowest of the Low: A Personal History of the Literature of Australian Pop', which is published on his website, that *Juke*'s 'indisputable Melbourne-centricity, not to mention tardiness to embrace changes in music' meant it 'struggled for credibility on a national level'.

Of course, the rock journalism scene was small, and many journalists were fiercely loyal to the publications that supported them. Whichever publication you were writing for was genius; its rival was the 'enemy' and was less forward-thinking and progressive. A healthy competition was born, each paper and its staff (some of whom overlapped) striving to outdo the other – the winner, of course, being the Australian music scene.

'There always was [a rivalry],' acknowledges Eliezer. 'In fact, it got to the stage that if you went to a gig, if someone from *RAM* was there you wouldn't talk to them, you'd just ignore them. It was so silly, so dumb.'

Ed Nimmervoll had thrown himself into *Juke*. His vision for it, according to Eliezer, was 'a magazine that made you proud … that really supported Australian music. And the thing is, at that time, in the wake of *Countdown*, AC/DC, Skyhooks, Sherbet, all that, you could do it.' But being published by Fairfax presented problems for Nimmervoll. At heart, he was a writer, not an editor; at Fairfax, the two roles weren't considered compatible. '*The Age* had very strong ideas on what an editor does,' says Eliezer. 'The editor stays behind his desk. He's responsible for every word that comes along, and the editor is not the main writer. Unfortunately, Nimmervoll was a really good writer, you know, his sense of perception and predictions were spot-on. So what happened was, Ed would go home and write and leave the admin to other people, so there were a couple of dramas with *The Age* – ads that didn't go in, lots of typos and all sorts of shit, you know.'

At this time, Nimmervoll's second-in-charge was Julian Cummings, ably backed up by staff writer Frank Peters and reviews editor Al Webb. Cummings left, though, as tension over Nimmervoll's role grew, and Eliezer came onboard as features editor. 'I'd actually gone in and volunteered my services, because there were so many typos in that bloody magazine,' Eliezer says.

Six weeks later, in May 1976, a year after *Juke* had started, Newspress boss Leonard Shaw had had enough and asked Nimmervoll to work under an editor, something which did not sit well with the man who'd created the magazine in the first place. And so he left. *The Age* 'one by one wanted to put their staff in place of mine, and so one of the people who left in the course of that was me', Nimmervoll told Barry McKay in 2001. 'So after a year, although this is my magazine and I've named it and done everything, I left. And I kept an eye on the baby, I kept supplying its chart, I wrote for it under assumed names and then swallowed my pride and gave it my own name, [and] every time there was an anniversary of something, they'd come back to me and get me to do a story.'

With Nimmervoll leaving, Eliezer offered to leave as well. 'My plan was to move to New York to become a political journalist. I'd done Politics and Legal Studies at uni,' he says. 'Ed asked me to stay on. I told him, "Only for a year or two, New York is calling." I stayed at *Juke* for eighteen years, until the very end. New York is still calling.'

And so Eliezer became a kind of managing editor – not editor, that would come later – but the person looking at the big picture, ensuring

Juke carried on and became the heavy-hitting music magazine it aspired to be. 'One of the first things I did was to get the syndication rights for *Sounds* magazine in England,' recalls Eliezer. 'Because there was so much stuff there we could bring it in. We brought in a whole lot of those writers we were talking about.'

They also brought in a new editor in Tim Britten, who was, Eliezer says, 'basically an administrator, knew nothing about music and didn't care. But he basically pulled it together and the mag got to the printers on time … so he lasted for a while, about two years.'

Alan Webster ascended to the editor's chair next, in 1979, 'making *Juke* more musical than ever', according to Eliezer. He held the role as the decade turned, and *Juke* entered the 1980s.

'I think the biggest change for *Juke* came in '81 or '82 though, when Graham Simpson came in. I brought Graham in because he was a good editor in the sense that … sometimes, the problem with magazines is, if you get too close to the music industry, you start doing favours and you end up in each other's pockets. But Graham found another way: "Fuck you, this is the way it's gonna be" [he said].'

Under Simpson, the paper broadened its horizons even more. It also went through its biggest visual and editorial revamp to date ('He brought in colour, and I think the circulation really boosted up for that,' says Eliezer), which elicited advertisers from outside the music industry. Simpson also, via Fairfax management, secured syndication rights to their overseas sources, meaning *Juke* was able to publish music writing from the pages of *Los Angeles Times*, *The New York Times* and *The Washington Post*, 'which increased the quality of *Juke*'s editorial no end', Eliezer says.

By this stage, the early 1980s, both *RAM* and *Juke* were at the height of their powers. Both publications were national, revered by music fans, brought in writing from US and UK magazines and ensured that the standard of the local writing was on a par. It was a golden era indeed, for both the music and for the press that was covering it.

I venture to Eliezer that *Juke* aiming to be national so early, before it'd even established its reputation in its home city, might have diluted its power somewhat, but Eliezer disagrees wholeheartedly. 'Not if you're coming out every week, buddy, trust me,' he says matter-of-factly. 'It was never a case of, "Fuck, how do we cover this?" It was, "Fuck, there's so much happening." I remember, at the peak of the whole live thing in the late 1970s, on a Saturday there'd be eight or nine gigs you had to go and see, because everyone was talking about these bands. So you'd go to one gig, hang around there for about thirty minutes, then piss off to Bombay Rock or Martini's or whatever. You always felt you weren't covering everything, but so be it, that's what it was.'

This is how it was for many years, as the scene grew and evolved, as the industry surrounding it did the same, and as the press covered it all, expanding alongside the bands and the labels, the managers and publicists, the small and the big within a scene gorged on sounds, the money flowing as the 1980s marched on.

10

MEANWHILE, IN ADELAIDE ...

'It is important to place music within its context
– that should be the predominant function of the
rock 'n' roll press.'

Stuart Coupe

By 1978, *RAM* and *Juke* were veteran publications, as much helping to create the musical terra as they were challenging it. They'd been publishing for around three years, and along with *Rolling Stone*, were *the* recognised publications of the day.

It's no surprise they were well-regarded – these two magazines were capturing the healthy Melbourne and Sydney music scenes well and with gusto. The men and women writing for the publications in these early years were of a different breed to their mid-to-late 1960s counterparts – many had journalistic backgrounds or had honed their writing through working on earlier publications. It meant that these publications were able to wield some muscle, not just in an industry sense, but in a literary sense too. New Journalism was still new; apply it to 1970s music, and the potential was huge.

It seems odd, at least to the casual observer, that aside from *Rolling Stone*, the first real contender to *RAM* and *Juke* came not from another paper in one of the two big cities, and not even from sub-tropical Brisbane, the smaller yet geographically closer northern capital. It came from Adelaide, the sleepy South Australian capital to the west, in the form of a fanzine-esque publication called *Roadrunner*, a paper which was to prove more than just a throw-away rag.

Roadrunner had its origins in various scungy venues in London, set to a new score of visceral intensity – punk, a new form of rock 'n' roll, the complete antithesis of what was currently playing in the mainstream pubs, the bigger clubs, the arenas the length and breadth of England and Europe. It was at the point, in the mid- to late 1970s, that acts like Simon & Garfunkel were being labelled rock 'n' roll – the sound, the genre, the ethos behind the whole thing (down, dirty, wild and free) had lost its way. Hence punk. And this is what informed *Roadrunner*.

Donald Robertson, a native Adelaidean then in his early twenties, was living in the United Kingdom. He was there when this new music first sprung up in 1976, and it grabbed him like nothing ever had. Based in Bath, he worked in South Wales. Every Thursday morning, on his way to the train station, he'd stop at the newsstand and pick up *NME*, *Sounds* and *Melody Maker*, keen to devour all he could on this primal new sound.

When he returned home the following year, he lugged with him some twenty-five singles, collected evidence of what was happening back in the mother country, so far from backwater towns like Adelaide. 'I came back in 1977, late October, I came back with singles,' says Robertson. 'Pistols, Clash, Damned, Wreckless Eric, Elvis Costello, you know. And I ran into all my uni friends with all these singles – "You've got to listen to this music!"'

A mutual friend introduced Robertson to Stuart Coupe, who was then editing the Flinders University student newspaper *Empire Times*, and the pair hit it off, bonding over these vagabond sounds. *Roadrunner* had not been conceived yet, although Robertson couldn't have known that its seeds were already present.

Robertson, Coupe and a host of others, all turned on by this music from the other side of the world, hung out regularly at Modern Love Songs, a record store tucked away in a basement in the Adelaide CBD. It was run by a local musician called Bo Kostyszyn. 'There were a bunch of people hanging around the shop, most of whom went on to form the punk band The Accountants,' Robertson says. 'Bo himself was keyboard player in The Dagoes later. So that Adelaide punk scene, small as it was, was kind of congregating around this record shop.'

It was there that, inspired by the burgeoning fanzine scene that included the LA-based *Who Put the Bomp!* (which had been around since 1970), London's *Sniffin' Glue* (since 1976) and local versions like Clinton Walker and Bruce Milne's *Pulp* (1977, which came about from the merging of Milne's *Plastered Press* and Walker's *Suicide Alley*), a loose collective decided to do the same.

Fanzines had been born of punk, in large part because of the DIY ethic that punk promoted. The uncomplicated yet visceral sound, the small independent labels that pressed cheap records, the bands putting together their own haphazard tours, making their own shirts and badges and designing their own record covers – DIY was at the centre of all of it. And so fanzines proliferated, DIY projects themselves, inky paeans to the music they idolised. It stood to reason that this group of Adelaide punks should want to do the same.

Street Fever hit streets in December 1977 for the princely sum of 50 cents. It was 'the day after the election', Robertson recalls. 'I'd seen the Sex Pistols in South Wales, I'd seen the first Stiff tour with Costello, Ian Dury and Wreckless Eric, so I wrote pieces, reviews of those, and one of the guys from The Accountants wrote reviews of

Radio Birdman and Young Modern. There was an interview with a psychosurgeon. So everyone who hung around the record shop chipped in, wrote a bit, did a bit of layout. We got it printed at [the same place as] *Empire Times* because Stuart obviously knew the printer there. And we thought it was great fun, we kind of took it around to record shops to see if they wanted to sell it. I don't know how many people actually bought it.'

In exchange for a full-page ad for Modern Love Songs, Kostyszyn said he'd pay the print bill. Though, according to a laughing Robertson, 'I don't think [he] ever paid it.'

Street Fever only lasted the one issue, mainly because from a business perspective it was completely unsustainable. It seems odd, a couple of young punks thinking about financial sustainability, but Robertson and Coupe, while their love of this music was pure, quickly realised that bigger things were possible.

'Stuart and I really enjoyed the exercise,' Robertson says, 'so we thought maybe we could do something a bit more serious, like a magazine, a proper magazine.' *Roadrunner* was about to be born.

'We approached a guy called Chris Plumer,' Robertson explains, 'who was head of a booking agency in Adelaide. We said to him, "We'd like to do a music mag for Adelaide. Do you think you could get the bands, and the equipment-hire companies" – the music industry of Adelaide, small and cottage as it was – "to provide advertising support, and we'll cover the bands and the gigs and that sort of thing?" He thought that was a great idea, so Stuart and I and our group of friends put together the first issue of *Roadrunner*.' It hit stands in March 1978. It was early days of course, but *RAM* and *Juke* now had some competition, coming from the unexpected direction of Adelaide.

'Starting *Roadrunner* was, you know, it was youthful naivety,' Stuart Coupe remembers. 'We sort of perceived *RAM* to be the old guard; I mean, ours was very much a punk-rock attitude. And every time a *Roadrunner* came out, I'd send it to Anthony. A little "Fuck you, here we come."'

The Adelaide live scene in 1978 was fairly strong – perhaps surprisingly, given its remoteness from other Australian capitals. The bulk of it though, according to Robertson, was blues and boogie bands, with a fair sprinkling of jazz and rock. Precious little punk, save for a local ensemble called Riff Raff, who played regularly at the Seacliff Hotel on Adelaide's southern beaches and who 'were a bit like Flowers [later to become Icehouse], a punk jukebox, they were good musos'. 'So it was sort of the only way you could experience what you were reading about in the British magazines, and the American ones. So it was a bit like going to a Pistols gig, or a Clash gig, a bit. A bit,' Robertson says of Riff Raff. 'And The U-Bombs started up in Belair in the Adelaide Hills about the same time.'

'There was a big venue in the city, in Hindley Street, Countdown in the Old Mariner Hotel,' he continues. 'They would bring interstate bands over, say Jo Jo Zep and the Falcons would come over for three or four nights at Countdown, and make quite a killing because people would go out.' Countdown was Adelaide's biggest music venue until the late 1970s. 'There was another venue called the Arkaba in Eastwood [which] would bring over interstate bands. So there was a circuit in Adelaide – an interstate band could come over and play six gigs in a week and make money, and then go back east. And the local bands used to really resent that, because they were on subsistence wages and they saw these bands come in and then go out. But the interstate bands drew the crowds.'

With *Street Fever* behind them, and a scene that was growing, if not playing as much of the music they wanted, the time was ripe for Coupe and Robertson to launch a magazine like *Roadrunner*. Indeed, the time was ripe for a publication that could push the music they loved, hopefully fuelling the concurrent live scene.

'Our real motivation was to inform people about the music,' Robertson says enthusiastically. 'We were really evangelistic; we were really crusading for the music because we were so excited by it. They were incredibly exciting times, so we were looking to convert people. So the magazine was a vehicle for that message, but I guess it was a pragmatic way of building a vehicle that could carry that message.

'And look, we were pretty keen on the emerging Australian bands of that kind, so in that first year of *Roadrunner*, the bands we featured were pretty much all interstate bands, pretty much all Melbourne-based, like The Sports, High Rise Bombers, Stiletto – those were the bands we thought were in tune with what was happening with the new wave. They were the ones we wanted to focus on and give exposure to. And apart from Riff Raff and The U-Bombs and The Accountants, there wasn't really much, the bands in Adelaide weren't really playing the music that we really liked. That kinda came a bit later.'

While those creating *Roadrunner* were indeed evangelical about their musical tastes, there wasn't any firm editorial policy, at least not for the first few issues. Coupe maintains that the idea for *Roadrunner* was a serious music magazine that would give *RAM* and *Juke* a run for its money, 'but with what we thought was a street-wise/fanzine attitude to the writing and content'.

It was Coupe who, in the fourth issue of *Roadrunner*, penned an editorial that read:

> It has been suggested that rock 'n' roll press began in the mid-sixties with HIT PARADER which was a comic book like pulp magazine edited by Jim Delahunt. It was forgotten after 1967/8 when the era of ROLLING STONE hit. HIT PARADER used to print the lyrics to songs and articles on musicians and their influences and was very much a period piece chronicling early 60's American rock

'n' roll. 1966 saw CRAWDADDY begin. Its early format was that of a fanzine with mimeographed sheets stapled together.

From these early efforts developed hundreds of zines devoted to rock 'n' roll and its off shoots – some of them glossy, others run off by hand, and all being more or less dependent on the music business.

Australia's main publications are obviously RAM, JUKE and the back 4 or 5 pages of ROLLING STONE. The rest are regional fanzines like FAD, RAT, SPURT, COMPLETE CONTROL and PULP. Adelaide specifically had YOUNG MODERN between 1962-5, but nothing based here until ROADRUNNER.

In terms of mass circulation / audience magazines (thereby excluding fanzines), RAM, JUKE, ROLLING STONE serve a definite function. The major purpose, and I suggest, failing, of these newsy rock 'n' roll papers is that they serve to maintain the illusion that rock 'n' roll exists independently of the forces around it.

How many times have people written to the NEW MUSICAL EXPRESS after the occasional anti National Front article, saying, 'We just wanna read about music, not politics', or 'Keep yer politics for the SOCIALIST WORKER'??

Other magazines criticise concert promotions and the fans say they're just interested in the music and not the politics of the business. What this leads to is that ROADRUNNER seeks to be a Pop/Popular CULTURE magazine as opposed to a Pop MUSIC magazine. Future issues will focus on books, movies, rock 'n' roll theory, and the usual gunk you know and love: record reviews, interviews and info on new bands – 'ya pay yer money – yer take yer chances' someone once said!!!

It is important to place music within its context – that should be the predominant function of the rock 'n' roll press.

This is as good a manifesto as one would expect at this point, and it's a jab at the big boys – the punk-rock attitude still very much prevalent among *Roadrunner*'s staff. And it hit its mark: Robertson recalled that Coupe's editorial elicited a response from Anthony O'Grady himself. *Roadrunner* was on the map. He 'sort of [pushed] back', recalls Robertson, 'saying, "That's what *RAM*'s been doing from the start." But Coupe's journalistic nous had not gone unnoticed: he was poached by O'Grady not long after his manifesto editorial.

In fact, the original collective had been falling away with each issue. Bruce Milne and Clinton Walker had come over from Melbourne not long before, dossing at Coupe's share house in Torrensville and helping out with a couple of issues, bulking out the staff with their own brand of off-centre expertise. But they left Adelaide towards the end of the year, around the same time as Coupe. By the end of 1978, Donald Robertson was essentially on his own. It looked like *Roadrunner* was to fold after less than a year, despite showing so much promise.

However, *Roadrunner* had built enough of a reputation in only eight months to prove that what it had set out to do was viable, and important. And so new writers and photographers began to emerge just as Robertson feared things were done. Some of these writers were journalists who brought to the magazine a professionalism that had perhaps been lacking, the DIY ethos ironically being what had kept *Roadrunner* from truly reaching its potential.

And this is what it did through 1979. It was 'very amateur to start with, and I think the early issues reflect that', Robertson says. 'But towards the end of the year, that first year, I think you start to see a more professional design, layout, editing, you get journalists starting to write, rather than just fans. So it started to evolve into more like a proper magazine.

'I think as that first year came to an end, we wanted to be a competitor to *RAM* and *Juke*. *Juke* was published by *The Age*, so a huge backing there; *RAM* was published by Philip Mason's company, which was also doing *Tracks*, and he had a publishing background in the UK. So they were much more established businesses than *Roadrunner*, and when everyone else left, it was me. That first year we didn't have an office, it was all done out of my bedroom in a house in Norwood.' He laughs. 'But I did see them as competition. We were covering the same scene, we were trying to be a national paper out of Adelaide – so not just an Adelaide paper going national, but a national paper, produced in Adelaide.'

The February 1979 issue marked *Roadrunner*'s first as a national publication. It was an ambitious gamble on Robertson's behalf, but one that, at least on paper, looked like it might pay off. *Roadrunner* had correspondents all across the country – Stuart Matchett, a foundation presenter at 2JJ, wrote from Sydney; Scott Matheson, rhythm guitarist for The Numbers (who later changed their name to The Riptides), from Brisbane; Bruce Milne, from Melbourne. There was even a London editor in Keith Shadwick. 'We were getting stories from all over the country, and producing it in Adelaide,' says Robertson.

'It's been a long time coming, folks, but here it is – ROADRUNNER'S first national issue,' opened Robertson's editorial in the Feb '79 issue. 'For the first time, we're reaching music enthusiasts on a large scale outside of South Australia, confident that there is room in this country for an independent music magazine to cover the rising tide of original Australian rock and the changing patterns of rock music overseas, New Wave and otherwise.'

The gamble certainly worked with music fans. Roadrunner became highly regarded. Perhaps not on the same level as *RAM*, which was king across the late 1970s and into the 1980s, but as a magazine that curried respect among the people who read it, and who contributed to it, it was up there with the country's best. Clinton Walker lists it as one of the three Rs (along with *RAM* and *Rolling Stone*), the magazines that a writer of the time wanted to be in. Even Anthony O'Grady, upon seeing Peter Nelson's review of a Radio Birdman reunion show (the band split in 1978, though they did re-form in the second half of the 1990s), told Robertson he'd have been proud to run the piece in *RAM*.

'I remember Anthony telling me years later that that article made him think, *Shit, this paper really is a competitor*,' recalls Robertson. 'So we'd hit a quality threshold where he started to take us seriously in terms of the writing.'

Robertson engaged writer Ross Stapleton to write a number of industry-focused articles, which included an analysis of the country's touring circuit (based on interviews with a range of top bookers) and a deep dive into the business interests of Michael Gudinski, which played well with the industry. 'Because, you know, everyone loves reading about themselves,' he says with a smile. 'Australia had never really had an industry magazine like *Billboard*, or *Cashbox*, or *Record World* or whatever the British one is. So, you know, I guess there was a bit of a gap there.'

The magazine was humming along, having made it through those tough initial stages, and was blooming into something Robertson was very happy with. He cites this growth stage as the most exciting for him; the fact that this small magazine from a small city was beginning to make waves on a national scale was a source of great pride. As well, new writers were coming on board and producing high-quality content; the sky must have seemed the limit.

Yet as well regarded as *Roadrunner* was, and as happy as Robertson was with how it was running, ultimately it had a fairly short lifespan. Over time Robertson's thinking on the magazine's rivalry with *Juke* and *RAM* changed, and he hoped the publications could be companions as opposed to competitors. 'People in Sydney might buy *RAM*, but they might also buy *Roadrunner* just for a bit of a different view. People in Melbourne might buy *Juke* – mainly for the gig guide, I think – but, you know, they might buy *Roadrunner* as well. So I think we saw ourselves as complimentary to *RAM* and *Juke*.' But it was not to be.

For Robertson, the eventual decline of such a quality magazine was frustrating. 'It was quite depressing, actually,' he says. 'I guess it got to a point where people just weren't prepared to do it for nothing. And I could hardly afford to pay anyone for writing. I had to pay the printer obviously, I had to pay the layout people, the photographers – Eric Alber, the main photographer, I always paid him. I wasn't earning a salary or anything like that, I was making enough to pay my rent, put food on the table, but that was it, it was a subsistence existence. So production costs needed to be paid, but contributors, you know, it got to the point where I wasn't really about to … the revenue coming in got below a sustainable level. And so I thought it was all gonna fold. I applied for a job as program director at 5MMM [now Triple M Adelaide] because I thought *Roadrunner* was gonna fold, and I got the job.'

Robertson happened to be close with Michelle Higgins, National Promotions Manager at Michael Gudinski's Mushroom Records. Higgins was a huge supporter of the magazine, and upon hearing the end might be nigh, she spoke with guitarist Lobby Loyde in Sydney. Loyde called Robertson, saying he'd heard the magazine was in trouble, and told him he had space in his Sydney offices and a financial backer who he thought might be interested in investing in *Roadrunner*. Would Robertson be interested?

'Yes, please!' He laughs. 'So I moved up to Sydney, got a new production team in place, I organised a printer, typesetter, bromides. I got an ad manager, Andrew Savage – he used to work at *RAM*. So I thought, I'll take this opportunity to change format, because I could see the writing on the wall for what we used to call the inkies. *The Face* had started in the UK, *Smash Hits* too, and the music was changing as well towards that more visual style, which was incredibly important.'[19]

The magazine was essentially put on hiatus for five months while a Sydney team was assembled and the new issue laid out, but it seemed it'd be worth the wait.

And the new format did appear to hit a chord with readers. The January 1983 issue, which was printed around Christmas, sold a lot of copies. All was going well until late January rolled around. 'When Andrew went to try to get ads for the [next] issue, which we'd already laid out, there was just no interest at all,' Robertson muses. 'Like, none of the record companies. It's traditionally a quiet time of year, they put out all the big releases before Christmas to get the Christmas market, and then they go on holiday in January. And we needed ads to pay production costs, so the financial backer backed out and that was it.'

And just like that, Robertson, having put together what he thought was one of the best issues of *Roadrunner's* existence, watched the publication bite the dust. 'Oh no, no,' Robertson says when I venture that he wouldn't have known that would be the magazine's final issue. 'I thought it was the first issue of *Roadrunner* Mark II.'

Robertson was also, at the time, managing alternative cabaret act Quietly Confident, as well as co-hosting a show on 2MMM [Triple M Sydney], and so tried to work through his disappointment – a lot of effort had been put in, and now it was done. 'I kinda kept myself busy, I didn't sit in the corner and mope. But yeah, it was, you know – I guess it was sad. The next issue slated, the one that never came out, I still have the layout on what the stories were gonna be in my papers … there was a big Cold Chisel story, there was a Divinyls story, a Hunters & Collectors story. Probably one of them [would have been on the cover].'

While no doubt a solid issue, would this have been enough to save the magazine? If it could have held on for that one more issue, perhaps its fortunes would have changed, but of this we can never be sure.

* * *

For just shy of five years, *Roadrunner* mixed it with the big boys, proving a well-regarded alternative to what *Juke* and, particularly, *RAM* were producing.

It could be argued, given the higher profile of the latter two, their proven ability to attract the best writers and photographers, and their syndication deals with English and American magazines, that *Roadrunner* was never quite in the same league, not as slick and relevant and influential. But it was a clever publication put together by people who knew the music, who loved it and who wanted little more than to report on it, spreading the word to their readership.

Perhaps therein lies one reason why its lifespan wasn't close to those of its competitors – by keeping true, at least as much as it was able, to its street-zine ethos, it wasn't able to become sufficiently profitable. The love of the music was not enough of a foundation on which to build a financially sustainable enterprise. The economics of journalism were changing in the early 1980s, the times were changing, the music was changing – love wasn't enough. Both *RAM* and *Juke* had publishers with experience and money behind them, whereas *Roadrunner* never did. It was a good music paper, but Robertson was doing it alone. The remoteness of Adelaide might have played a factor as well, given the number of journalists and readers based in Melbourne and Sydney.

And yet, while it was around, it displayed a remarkable ability to tap into the zeitgeist, to cover and cover well what the average music fan wanted to read about. A compelling example of this is Stuart Coupe's lengthy interview with Bruce Springsteen, conducted in Paris, which appeared in the June 1981 issue. This was longform rock journalism at its finest, and the fact it featured in *Roadrunner*, as opposed to a better-resourced rival, is testament to the publication's value.

As well, the magazine showed it was willing and able to evolve, moving from a punk and new wave focus early on – featuring, on various covers, Elvis Costello, the Sex Pistols, Sid Vicious, The Clash and The Police – to showcasing a coterie of artists, several of them local: Redgum, Midnight Oil, Flowers (Icehouse), The Angels, Kim Wilde, The Laughing Clowns, Bruce Springsteen, Ross Wilson and, on the final issue's cover, Kevin Rowlands from Dexys Midnight Runners.

Contributors included Clinton Walker, Stuart Coupe, Toby Creswell, Ross Stapleton, Glenn A. Baker, Greg Taylor, Jillian Burt and Sue Wylie, as well as the odd name from overseas (such as legendary UK rock journalist Chris Salewicz), who all came together to give *Roadrunner* its voice. Articles were generally long, and even a casual glance at the contents of any issue shows a passion for and a love of the music – *Roadrunner* was the real deal.

* * *

Robertson's career as an editor didn't end with *Roadrunner*. Six months after the magazine folded, he was offered the editorship of *Countdown* magazine (the print version of the highly successful television show). It was floundering at the time, the ABC feeling it was not of a high-enough quality to co-exist with the Molly Meldrum–hosted music show.

'What happened was, a guy called Jerry Cooper ran a group called Fanclubs of Australia – he started the KISS Army [in Australia], actually,' Robertson explains. 'He approached the ABC to do a newsletter-magazine associated with *Countdown* ... And it was like an eight-page fold-out tabloid thing, kind of limited. So he'd done that for a little while and the ABC were getting a bit restive and felt it wasn't really up to the quality they'd hoped, so they gave him an ultimatum that he needed to get a full-time editor and it needed to be more a magazine rather than the thing he'd been doing. So I don't think I was the first to be offered the position, but I got a call in mid-'83, you know, would I be interested?'

He was, and after five years of running a successful stand-alone music magazine, he came with ideas about how things should run; changes needed to be made. 'I kind of inherited a production set-up. The layout was being done by a company who'd been doing some work on *Dolly* – I thought it was very '70s, I thought it was very dated. So the key new hire for me was the art director, a guy called Ed Gillen, who was English, and he'd come out of the same school as Neville Brody, who designed *The Face*, so he brought that English look to the magazine. And so once we got that, it looked great. I drew on much the same writing pool that had been writing for *Roadrunner* and *RAM*, so Greg Taylor wrote some pieces, Clinton Walker wrote some pieces, all the usual others, and we got some international correspondents. So very quickly, I think within a year, we were selling 100,000 a month.'

This was largely due to a very simple marketing strategy, one that money could not buy. 'The monthly endorsement by Molly,' he reveals with a laugh. '[It was] all based around that ad every month, with Molly saying on television, "Here's the mag." He smiles. 'And once it kinda got up to quality, *Countdown* really liked it, and they would do a little promo on the show.'

So successful did the magazine become under Robertson's tenure that it was bought by Fairfax, who already owned the then-struggling *Smash Hits*. They had cornered a market, and *Countdown* magazine continued to flourish. As for Robertson, when the magazine's London editor, David Rolly, left to join a band, he moved over to London and contributed from afar, a glorious stint which lasted nine months.

Robertson returned home expecting, on the basis of a verbal deal, to retain the magazine's editorship. 'When I came back, it wasn't as easy as that, so that didn't happen,' he says ruefully. And so his association with the magazine ended, as did, essentially, his involvement in the Australian music media. It was a short and sharp career, but one of which he is immensely proud, and justifiably so.

11

THE COVER OF *ROLLING STONE*

'We were, if you like, the Steven Bradbury of publishing; everyone else fell over.'

Phillip Keir

Like many music-obsessives-turned-writers of the day, Ed St John got his start in the rock press while still at school. It was the mid-1970s, and while the counterculture movement was winding down following the Vietnam War, the music was no less innovative. St John was getting turned on by what was booming from speakers via the newly launched Double J, a game-changer as far as music in Australia went.

The radio station, an initiative of the Gough Whitlam government, was aimed at the youth market. It had launched on 19 January 1975. 'The *world* changed when Double J came along,' St John enthuses. 'Prior to that you had AM radio, which was just Top 40, and then suddenly you had someone playing Led Zeppelin and reggae and African music and a whole cornucopia of amazing stuff. It opened my head up to a whole lot of things I didn't even know about before.'

One of Double J's early DJs was George 'Groover' Wayne, who hosted the show *Cooking with George.* Wayne had schoolkids drop in to spin some of their favourite records, and St John was one. It was to shape the course of his life. 'He asked me, "What do you want to do when you grow up?"' St John recalls. 'I said I had no idea, and he said I'd make a good music journalist. "Would you like me to introduce you to my friends at *Rolling Stone* magazine?" "Yeah, sure."'

Not really having any idea what *Rolling Stone* was about, the sixteen-year-old St John found himself 'standing in my school uniform at the *Rolling Stone* offices, presenting myself as a suitable candidate to be a music journalist'.

Not only did St John have little idea of what *Rolling Stone* was; he didn't have any idea what music journalism was, either. 'There really wasn't a great deal of it at that point in Australia, unless you knew where to look,' he says. 'Certainly [music] was never written about in the mainstream media. I think most people regarded it as not worthy of anyone's attention, much less serious attention.'

As St John stood before the *Stone* editors, clad in his school uniform, *Go-Set* was barely a year out of the picture, counterculture go-to *The Digger* was winding up and *RAM* and *Juke* had only just begun. There was indeed music journalism in Australia at that point, but it was at the beginning of taking the spotlight in the way it would come to do.

The Australian edition of *Rolling Stone* was at the time being published by Paul Gardiner and Jane Matheson, who, along with ad-man Paul Comrie-Thomson, had taken over the magazine from Phillip Frazer when he had left for the United States. It was being run out of an 'apartment-sized office' in Milsons Point in Sydney. According to St John, neither Gardiner nor Matheson were 'music people per se', but ex-journos who'd worked for *Australian Financial Review*, among other papers.

'Paul [Gardiner] was sort of the publisher and Jane was sort of the editor,' he recalls. 'There was also this very interesting, eccentric character called Paul Comrie-Thomson who was the advertising manager – he'd been in an ad agency somewhere. And it was kind of a bizarre enterprise because they weren't passionate music fans. I don't really know how they all found themselves there.'

'What we were attracted to was the profile of *Rolling Stone* in the United States,' Jane Matheson recalls. The US publication, still under the control of founder Jann Wenner, had asserted itself as a true chronicle of the ever-changing times, covering not just music but also issues pertinent to the social and cultural shifts that were happening across the Pacific, and by proxy, the world. 'We didn't look at it as a small insert – it was this wonderful magazine from the United States, and back then, the culture was so different. The generation that's now known as the baby boomers ... was very young and there was an air of change and excitement, new ways of thinking and new ways of approaching things.'

Matheson, Gardiner and Comrie-Thomson had seen the potential the magazine offered, and so banded together to form the company Silvertongues, sourcing money from various avenues in order to purchase the licence from the US parent and from Phillip Frazer, who by late 1975 was looking to extricate himself from both *Stone* and *The Digger*.

'We were impressed by not so much the music as by the journalism in general,' Matheson says. 'The music obviously was an important part of it, but *Rolling Stone* in the US also ran a lot of political comment, Hunter S. Thompson covering presidential elections, all that sort of stuff. So it was the total package.'

The deal was brokered with the help of Richard Hall, who had been an adviser to both the Whitlam (federal) and Wran (NSW state) governments, along with being a founding member of the Literature Board of the Australia Council, and who was 'great at lunching'. 'He'd have long lunches and by the end of the long lunch, he'd have signed up two or three more people to put some money into Silvertongues. He was our left-wing and political connection.' They raised the money and set about introducing this American magazine to an Australian audience properly.

A criticism of the Australian edition of the magazine in its formative years was that it contained barely a skerrick of coverage of Australian bands by Australian writers – indeed, under Frazer, the magazine was little more than a smaller copy of the American original (not too surprising given the annual licensing fee paid by the Australian owners to the US parent allowed them to syndicate as much material as they wanted – certainly cheaper than paying local writers, and more efficient, too). Matheson, Gardiner and Comrie-Thompson, however, set about changing this – an endeavour that took time.

'The Australian edition in those days basically just slotted a handful of Australian stories into the copy,' recalls St John. 'They sort of carved out little bits where they'd pull out a page of American coverage and drop in a page of Australian coverage. It was fairly minimal. If you go back and look at those issues, you'd not find a lot of [local] stuff.'

Says Matheson, 'We took a while to build up some good writers. Ed was terrific, Toby Creswell when he started sending stuff in stood out too, and a few other people. Clinton Walker was one. We had to build up a stable of good writers.'

It was these writers who allowed the Australian *Stone* to begin delving into the Australian scene. Around 1976 and 1977 a strain of uniquely Australian music also rose to popularity, acts that were to turn international audiences on to a whole new sound and scene: Cold Chisel, Midnight Oil, Rose Tattoo, Dragon, AC/DC. The sound was brutish and raw. It was a distinct shift from early 1970s rock 'n' roll.

'It exploded,' St John enthuses. 'There were milestone records like Richard Clapton's *Goodbye Tiger* (1977) or Cold Chisel's *East* (1980), Midnight Oil came along, and suddenly you had bands popping up doing really interesting stuff, and that actually created a roll for people like *Rolling Stone*, because suddenly there was this need to talk about it and write about it intelligently, interrogate it, in a way perhaps that people hadn't felt the need to do with Sherbet or the Ted Mulry Gang. So I think it was right place and right time, because suddenly [there was this] idea that *Rolling Stone* could lend legitimacy to what was emerging.'

Part of this legitimacy involved being pitched to regularly by the record companies. 'It was a different era,' says St John, who went on to become one of Australia's leading record company executives, running marketing for Columbia Records and BMG, then becoming managing director and president/CEO of Warner Music. 'There was a guy … who was head of PR at EMI, and his idea of promoting music to me was that I'd go in there once a week or once a fortnight, and I'd sit in his office down the street and he'd roll a huge joint. Then he'd play two or three albums to me to the point where I could barely remember what I was listening to or what time it was, and then he'd give me an armload of vinyl and I'd walk back out into the street. That was PR, circa 1979.' He laughs at the memory.

Having local acts on the cover of the magazine (with the cover story written by an Australian writer) was another thing altogether. The first Australian band to grace the cover of the local *Rolling Stone* was Skyhooks (9 September 1976). This preceded a seven-year wait for the next Australian cover – Men at Work (June 1983), although this was a direct syndication from the United States, with the cover story written by an American writer – closely followed that same year by Toby Creswell's profile of Michael Hutchence and INXS.[20]

'The idea of having an [Australian act] on the cover, that took a bit longer,' St John concurs. 'I remember that being a real milestone moment. There was always this question, did we consider ourselves to be as good as what was happening overseas, did we have a legitimate place in the pantheon of all these American artists? And it wasn't just

America that we were looking towards but also the UK, and what happened in '76, '77? Punk. The Americans kind of missed that boat, at least the initial part. So my friends and I were much more interested in what was happening in the UK.'

It's fair to say that Australian *Rolling Stone*, while it *was* beginning to awaken and show potential as an organ of Australian music and culture in the late 1970s, wasn't yet there. *RAM* and *Juke* were on the ground much more directly, and possessed a style well suited to the trenches of rock 'n' roll, of punk. Their writers were regular figures on the scene, and more attuned and better suited to cover what was happening.

Rolling Stone was never a direct competitor to *RAM* and *Juke*, but more a companion, offering something different. As St John makes clear, *RAM* and *Juke* were about live shows, *Rolling Stone* was about records. Matheson largely agrees: 'I think we felt we had an innate advantage in that we had that really great stuff coming over to us every fortnight from America. There was a rivalry (between *Stone* and *RAM* and *Juke*), but it was a friendly sort of rivalry.'

The magazine got in on the ground floor of punk (ahead of *Juke*, if majority opinion is to be believed). An unlikely friendship developed between seminal Brisbane group The Saints and the *Stone*'s ad man, Paul Comrie-Thomson. 'Before the cognoscenti cottoned on to The Saints, Paul and Jane and particularly Paul Comrie-Thompson, who was not a music guy in any shape or form, suddenly cottoned on to the brilliance of The Saints.' St John laughs. 'Bizarrely, and Chris Bailey and Ed Kuepper can back this up, they came and stayed at Paul's apartment and Paul cooked them spaghetti, and there was this weird [domestic] scene.' St John laughs again at the odd memory of it. 'If you ever met Paul Comrie-Thomson, he was the least likely person to befriend The Saints. So we became early champions of [the band] before anyone else figured it out.'

'So it was an interesting time, because suddenly there was so much great music,' he continues, 'and we just happened to be there at a time when it was just really fascinating.'

It was around 1981 that St John (who at that point had been writing reviews and had a couple of features under his belt, Air Supply being his first, Richard Clapton his second), scored his first big assignment, heading out on the road with Cold Chisel. 'That was a *serious* feature, a proper two- or three-page feature,' he recalls. 'A feature on Cold Chisel, that's when I was allowed to go on the road with them, hang out with them for more than a 45-minute interview.'

This was *Rolling Stone*'s trademark – features written by a journalist who had spent a week or so with the band, on the road with them; pieces able to reflect on the deeper thoughts and the lifestyles of the band members. 'That was something I was keen to do,' says St John, 'because that was the dream of rock journalism at that point. And around then [*Rolling Stone* in Australia] started to do that.'

St John talks of other *Rolling Stone* writers from that period – Toby Creswell, Stuart Coupe (who was still heavily aligned with *RAM*) and Clinton Walker, the magazine's go-to guy for punk and new wave. They were all part of this new guard of rock writers who helped turn the medium into one that commanded respect, at least in certain circles. *Rolling Stone*, as it grew into the 1980s, helped foster this, as Anthony O'Grady had done in the early years of *RAM*. Rock journalism was serious journalism, not to be taken lightly. 'What was great about that era, and what is always great about music journalism, is that you have to pull apart and understand, describe what it is you're hearing, in order to help other people do the same thing,' St John says. 'Someone plays you a record and says, "What do you think of this?" You've gotta put this into words, and you go away and describe that, and over time that actually becomes the way people see it.

'I can't think of a better example of that than all of us suddenly understanding that Don Walker was writing this really profound narrative about what it meant to be young and disenfranchised in Australia at that time. You know, tapping into themes like Vietnam veterans, unemployment, being in prison … all these amazing issues that no one had ever written about in a song before. And what a privilege, looking back, what a privilege to be the person helping to unpack that, and go, "Wow, this is really special."'

* * *

As the 1980s rolled on, *Rolling Stone* continued to be a beacon of high-quality rock journalism. Street press came to be in the early 1980s, but it was still largely underground, with the articles written mainly by novice journalists and music enthusiasts, and so offered little competition. *Juke* and *RAM* were continuing strongly, but there was room for all three publications in a hungry Australian market.

Toby Creswell, an active freelancer for the Australian *Rolling Stone*, impressed Gardiner and Matheson to the extent that he was hired as the publication's music editor in 1985. 'There wasn't anybody else,' Creswell says on his hiring. He had no prior editing experience, but 'I'd been writing for them since … 1979. Or earlier. It was like this small sphere, there weren't that many people involved. The industry wasn't that big.'

Meanwhile, St John, who'd been a very regular contributor, was winding up his tenure, but accomplished journos like Clinton Walker and Bruce Elder (who went on to contribute to *The Sydney Morning Herald* for many years) were writing for the magazine with alacrity. The proportion of Australian content was still reasonably low, but the magazine had found its readership and was here to stay.

Around this time, there seemed to be a dearth of women covering the scene, certainly less than there had been during the 1970s. Perhaps this was due to the more 'blokey' type of pub rock coming to the fore, which tended to reflect masculine ideas and concerns. Jane Matheson, presiding over one of the larger publications in *Rolling Stone*, agrees, saying, 'There were very few women. Andrea Jones, Lyn McCarthy (film reviews), photographer Violet Hamilton were a few. I remember Jenny Brown and Miranda Brown contributing to Stone in the seventies, and probably Annie Burton … [and I think] to some extent this reflected the overwhelmingly male gender of the musicians.' It could also have been editorial oversight at some publications.

Towards the end of the 1980s, the magazine had been running in Australia for almost two decades. Recession loomed, and the economic downturn brought about another upheaval within its ranks. Publisher Paul Gardiner and editor Jane Matheson were bound to the magazine's parent via an annual licensing fee, which was contracted to be paid in US dollars. As the Australian dollar fell against its US counterpart, then, the cost of the fee grew. Eventually, it reached an untenable point. Gardiner and Matheson looked to sell.

'The licensing fee *was* written in American dollars,' Mathieson says, 'and when we wrote it, the Australian dollar was riding high – I think it was worth something like $US1.50, very high. We were on the good side of the equation. But through the years we published, the Australian dollar dropped and dropped and dropped, and I think by the mid-1980s it was down to about 60 cents. And despite our pleas to re-write the contract, they weren't at all interested, and it just became very, very difficult. That was what led us to decide that we just couldn't continue, because we had to cut staff and cut staff … it was a real struggle.'

Toby Creswell, still music editor, was in the best position to carry the franchise on. After discussions with fellow writers Ed St John and Bruce Elder about a joint bid to buy the licence proved unsuccessful, he spoke with an old school friend he'd recently come back into contact with: Phillip Keir. Keir, who'd been involved in theatre up to that point, and who had freelanced as a music writer, had a solid business brain. And so the two teamed up – Creswell to helm the editorial side of things, Keir the numbers side.

As so often happens with such partnerships, memories morph over time and each party comes to see things quite differently. So while Creswell maintains that Keir was a 'tough businessman' in his dealings with Gardiner and Matheson (a move which he believes sullied their new relationship, and from which it never really recovered), Keir recollects that while he did have to make tough decisions, the deal came together a lot more intricately.

'Toby could see that the license was running out,' he remembers. 'The Australian dollar had dropped and [Paul and Jane] had a set contract fee in US dollars. I became aware of that, and around that time my father passed away … and ultimately I ended up with a [small inheritance]. So in late 1986, we started talking.'

Keir's then domestic partner, Lesa-Belle Furhagen, who came from a film and arts background, became the third player in this team. 'Yes, we hatched a plan, worked through the plan on my father's dining-room table, and went from there,' Furhagen says. 'We all worked in the arts … we all had a commitment to culture. So there was a continuity in terms of us getting involved with Toby in acquiring the licence to publish.'

It seemed, at the time, a good match. 'It became more of a reality Paul was going to cease publishing. Toby thought it was a great opportunity,' Keir says.

In February 1987, he set off for New York in order to begin negotiating a new deal for the Australian license – no easy task. 'I wasn't meeting with Jann, I didn't even know what the protocol was. I was told to meet with their business affairs lady,' Keir recalls, adding he'd put together a 'sales kit' with the help of some advertising friends, the content of which was largely uncertain, given his lack of background in publishing. 'She was dealing with the process of licensing, and at that stage there were no other licenses. So I pitched to her, went home and rang up to [see where it was at], but found out she'd been sacked. So I'd spent all that time and effort speaking to the wrong person.'

Keir was told to speak to the newly appointed general manager, Kent Brownridge ('Kent Brownridge the *Third*,' he says, raising his eyebrows in mock deference), in order to move the deal forward. It was in Brownridge that he found an ally, albeit indirectly.

'He'd come from radio, the Clear Network, a completely different type of person [to Wenner], not editorial, who thankfully ended up dividing their office into editorial and business. He basically said they were still talking, and it turned out they were talking to a few other people, particularly Fairfax (who at that stage published *Smash Hits* and *Countdown Magazine*), and that [would have been] a natural fit. And the other bidder at the time was the owner of [radio station] 2MMM. So they were waiting to see if there were *other* bidders.'

Keir and Creswell were deemed small fish – all they had in their favour was the fact that Creswell was a known music writer and had been music editor at the magazine since 1985. They had no experience in licencing, little money compared to their competitors, and none of the backing that comes with any big media organisation. It seemed their bid was dead in the water before it'd even begun to swim.

'Then a surprising thing happened,' Keir says with a smile. 'Warwick Fairfax, one of the sons, decided to take Fairfax private, and he attempted to borrow an awful lot of money … so what happened was Fairfax had to stop bidding for any corporate activity, so they pulled out. It turned out Kent Brownridge the Third was very distrustful of radio people; he thought a radio station would only use [the magazine] as a cross-promotional device. It turned out he'd just been unceremoniously sacked by a radio network. So I like to say we got lucky, because we were, if you like, the Steven Bradbury of publishing; everyone else fell over.' (Steven Bradbury was the Australian speed skater who won the 1000-metre event at the 2002 Winter Olympics after all his opponents crashed in a pile-up.) 'We were behind, we had no solid money behind us, solid business experience behind us, but we were there.'

'My opinion of it is that it kind of appealed to Jann [Wenner] that this young trio full of energy and motivation were going to grab it by the horns and take on the world, which is what *he* did when he started the magazine,' muses Furhagen. 'It was pretty exciting. They were great days.'

By this stage, Paul Gardiner and the US parent didn't, according to Keir, have a good relationship because the Australian publishers were behind on their fees. 'I don't know how far behind they were,' Keir says, 'but it was some way behind, to the point where [the parent] had cut them off, they'd stopped sending material.'

Matheson elaborates: 'Jann Wenner and most of the Americans had very little interest in what was happening in Australia. I think they were just concerned that we keep paying our royalty payments, and that was it. I think like many Americans, they were so obsessed with what was happening inside their own borders, and anything happening outside of that wasn't that important.'

Straight Arrow, the company publishing American *Rolling Stone*, asked Keir and his team for six months of licensing fees upfront. They managed to raise it among friends, family and industry contacts, in order to keep the magazine going in Australia.

A deal was worked out with Gardiner and Matheson for the subscriber database and other essentials – this is where Creswell asserts Keir was a tough businessman, although Matheson says the reason for any acrimony was because Keir negotiated with the US parent in the States without her and Gardiner's knowledge. The new owners worked out a shareholding deal whereby Creswell, Keir and Furhagen held shares, along with a few other investors to round it off. *Rolling Stone* was off newsstands for around four months, relaunching again in September 1987.

From there, it was time to bring about change.

'We saw that the music industry was changing in Australia, there were so many big acts around … and so right from the start, we thought that if we were to take it on, we'd have to increase the Australian content,' says Keir.

The deal with the US parent remained that the Australian franchisee's annual fee gave them access to all the content of the US version of the magazine. No matter how little you chose to use, the fee was the same. This is why, in each issue over the course of Australian *Rolling Stone*'s print life, there were long articles by any number of American journalists.

According to Keir, as the Australian dollar fell, Paul Gardiner had cut local content, opting sensibly for more US-produced material in order to reduce costs. Creswell and Keir's first move was to *up* local content, with the aim of portraying the local edition of *Rolling Stone* as more of an Australian publication – an arm of the main body in the United States as opposed to (what they saw as) an almost carbon copy.

'We better targeted the editorial, we were a lot more proactive about that,' says Creswell. 'We increased the coverage of Australian music substantially. [We] got better photography. I think part of my contribution was the fact that I was pretty obsessed with Australian music and Australian popular culture, so we became a bit more plugged-in, I think. And also the 1980s was … a boom time for that sort of thing. I mean, once things like INXS happened and all that international success, it really made a big difference. So it was a combination of all of those things. We just made the magazine better.'

'Well, nobody got paid very much,' Furhagen remembers with a laugh when asked how they managed to pay for this increase in local content.

'We were working on next to no money. We worked out of a warehouse in Surrey Hills that barely had running water. We used to carry buckets of water into the darkroom to do the processing.'

'We did have the support of some significant advertisers for the first time, though, and marketing presence,' she adds. 'And [we were] promoting the magazine in a certain way, and also [made] some smart cover choices. If you got a cover right, you could double the circulation of one particular issue.'

Furhagen's role in the venture was associate publisher, but perhaps more importantly she oversaw the marketing and advertising. It was how the magazine was being pitched to advertisers that began to make a difference on the financial front. 'There was this perception that people who read *Rolling Stone* were a bunch of hippies with no disposable income running around in a Kombi van,' she explains, 'when the reality actually was at that time the boomers had all grown up and were in big jobs and were driving Mercedes and had lots of money to spend. So the perception of who the reader was and the reality were quite different. And so *that* pitch is what I took to the ad agencies. And the readership numbers stacked up with that, and the demographics.'

Due to Furhagen's savvy work in the marketing and advertising sphere, along with Creswell's intimate knowledge of all things music and culture and Keir's guiding business hand, the magazine slowly came back to financial life. It survived the recession and came into the 1990s stable, if not making bucketloads of profit. From 1987 through until Creswell's departure from the magazine in 1992, the circulation tripled. While *Rolling Stone* was arguably no longer the counter-cultural title it was when founded, it still carried weight in music and cultural circles, still included articles on important social issues. It also began to cover burgeoning videogame culture and film, extending its readership.

It was actually the non-music covers that proved the most successful. Both Creswell and Keir noted the May 1988 cover of actress Lisa Bonet, who appeared partially nude on front, wearing just an artfully draped white shirt. 'I thought it was a really stupid idea,' Creswell, says, smiling, 'and I was completely wrong. Those sort of moments really pumped up the circulation quite a bit.' As the old saying goes, sex sells.

Keir remembers dealing with local writers, in particular Brisbane-based journalist John Birmingham, an unapologetic Hunter S. Thompson fan who'd barge into the office brimming with off-the-wall story ideas. 'I really remember the characters, John in particular,' Keir recalls fondly. 'He came down in the first year we were running [the magazine], just at the end of that period, where Queensland had suffered through a difficult period. He *loved* Hunter S. Thompson, told everyone he was going to be the Australian HST. He came down and had nowhere to stay, slept on the couch in our office, probably had no money. He thought it was great we were doing this, he really wanted to do stories, had a whole lot of ideas.

'He was interested in the music area, but by and large he was interested in the gonzo journalism. So we had quite a few colourful experiences with John, who sometimes attracted a bit of excitement on the defamation side. One particular story he wrote on Australian Nazis, very colourful, I don't know *where* the material came from. I seem to remember he got hold of a whole lot of shots of Australian Nazis and we got into trouble for publishing them ... people saying, "I'm not a Nazi," and we have no way of proving it one way or another.'

Around this time, another young writer arrived on the scene in John O'Donnell, a music tragic who'd been trying his hand writing reviews for Sydney street press magazine *On the Street* and had been persuaded by a friend to touch base with Toby Creswell. O'Donnell went on to become managing director of EMI Music Australia, but then he was a font of musical knowledge who wanted little else but to write about it. He could more than string a sentence together, and so *Stone* was a natural fit.

'I approached Toby through a mutual friend,' confirms O'Donnell. 'It was my passion. I wasn't any good at making music, and so that led me into writing about it.'

O'Donnell became, in essence, a trusted lieutenant of Creswell's, rising to the rank of associate editor as the 1980s passed into the 1990s and as *Rolling Stone* continued to focus on Australian music. It was becoming, as the original had in America, a trusted source, relevant to its location. 'Yeah, it became that,' O'Donnell says. 'Toby was out there to kick all the opposition and put out the best magazine he could. He worked on all aspects of the copy, photography, all of those things, and the money was being ploughed back into it to improve it. And he and Phillip weren't rushing to do [that], but there was an impatience to it that was really healthy. And then they started putting Australians on the cover, which was an important change which happened in the period that I was there. And so they were putting out the best rock magazine, if you like, but still very conscious of *Rolling Stone*'s history with the counterculture and producing non-music stories that were worthy.'

Shaun Carney came on board as the magazine's political reporter, a smart move and a throwback to the parent magazine's glory days of heavy, yet pertinent political coverage. The editors also commissioned big non-music stories, including Mark Mordue's in-depth piece on AIDS sufferers and the discrimination and ignorance they faced, which won him the 1992 Human Rights Media Award.

It was a story that, incidentally, almost never came to be. 'We pursued Mark all over the country to get him to file his copy. He'd been working on this story for many, many months, and he started avoiding our phone calls, doing that classic thing that only writers can do,' O'Donnell recalls, laughing. 'Because he'd done so much research that he was kind of lost in the woods of writing the story and didn't want to sit down and confront the writing of the story. And Toby found him at home one day – he was clearing his phone messages, as you used to have to, from his answering machine and the phone rang, and he couldn't let it go to the keeper because he was clearing the messages. So he took the call and it was Toby, saying "Where the fuck are you?" And we convinced him to come into the office and he wrote the story from Friday night through to Sunday night and delivered a really great piece, and I went into the office on Sunday night and edited it and it then flew off overseas to be published that Monday morning. He thought we were taking the piss on how tight things were, but we'd already missed one month and moved the story to the following month, and we were hours way from missing it again. Anyway, he won a Human Rights Award.'

'Oh yeah, Toby and John locked me in the office over the weekend to write it,' Mordue confirms. 'And they sent me in pizzas. I couldn't get out. That's totally true.'

* * *

By the early 1990s, the Australian edition of *Rolling Stone*, the only international edition of the magazine still in production, was firmly ensconced in Australian culture. It had taken a while, the magazine's focus on Australian music slow in coming, but under Gardiner and Matheson, then Creswell, Keir and Furhagen, with O'Donnell and a stable of trusted freelance reporters backing them up, the Australian music industry had embraced what had finally become an Australian version of the iconic original.

'Completely,' enthuses O'Donnell. 'It was a magazine that was moving forward, not just stuck in the great days of '67 … we kept it relevant.'

12

THE ROCK PRESS GROWS (UP)

'I offered them four, and they took it.'

Phil Stafford

A typical day in late 1981 might have found Anthony O'Grady sitting at his desk, perhaps enjoying a smoke, contemplating the future. Outside his door in the small, bustling office his creation was growing, a real and raw rock 'n' roll magazine producing content on par with anything coming out of America or England: just as he'd wanted it, just as he'd foreseen it, just as he'd moulded it. But his mind would have been on what next. Having largely achieved what he'd set out to do, he might have been restless, perhaps a little frustrated, ready for change.

O'Grady left the helm of *RAM* around this time. In the grand scheme his wasn't a long tenure – but in that half-decade, culture and music continued to fracture and change, growing all the while, and *RAM* covered this to the best of O'Grady's ability.

The magazine was across punk when it exploded in the mid-1970s; it championed pub rock; it explored the new wave; and it was almost the sole chronicler of the 'inner-city sound' that burst, ragged and raw, from Sydney's dark and dingy inner west in the early 1980s.

It was, five years in, still Australian rock 'n' roll's record of choice, its contributors talented journalists covering Australian popular culture from a range of perspectives.

'You got the flow of the city, of what's really going on, not just empty reviews: see this, do that,' says Mark Mordue of *RAM* at this time, a publication he came to write for prolifically in the mid-1980s. 'With the good writers, you got a sense of the political, and cultural, and fashion … the whole ethos of what was going down. Everything.'

'We thought we were serious and *Juke* was a bit throw-away, lightweight,' Stuart Coupe adds.

O'Grady's leaving marked the end of the first of three distinct eras of the magazine, each defined by its editor. According to Greg Taylor, O'Grady's deputy who took over from him, the magazine's founding editor left because he saw no future for himself at *RAM*. O'Grady had 'five per cent of [publisher] Soundtracts – obviously Philip and Barry had the majority share, and they won't let him do anything. Our way or the highway,' Taylor explains. O'Grady 'didn't have the capital, whereas Philip and Barry had come out of advertising and had some money … so it was a long-running, rancorous thing between them. He left because he wasn't happy. And he was never going to make any money out of it; he was being paid a salary, he didn't have a stake worth selling.'

As O'Grady told writer and music industry professional Dave Laing in an interview published on Laing's site *I Like Your Old Stuff* in 2016:

> I'd started slip sliding away long time before cutting the cord with RAM at the end of 1981. Regrets – I have a few. I'll always wonder 'what if' the publishing company had reinvested RAM's profits into 'growing' the magazine into investigative journalism and in depth profiling instead of starting up new, invariably unsuccessful publications. It was particularly frustrating that I was a minor

shareholder in the publishing company and continually outvoted on future directions.

Publisher Philip Mason has a different take. 'There was certainly no animosity between us – I think Anthony had just had enough. He felt [five years] was long enough to be editing the paper.'

Despite the fact O'Grady had co-founded the magazine, and despite the legacy he had created due to his passionate belief that Australian rock writing could be on par with anything being produced overseas, the time was right for him to move on.

Taylor had come on board a few years before, answering an ad for a feature writer, despite the fact he was a professional musician who'd had 'absolutely no experience writing'. 'I was playing in a band with Jeff St John, I'd been playing with him for a couple of years,' Taylor recalls. 'We were coming back from Newcastle and stopped off at Charmhaven, the big truck stop where everyone stopped, and there was a copy of *RAM* lying there, so I flicked through it at two o'clock in the morning and there was an ad for a feature writer – "Must be experienced." I'd never written anything before … so I raced off two or three record reviews, sent them in, didn't hear back for a month or two.'

Taylor needed a job and was idly contemplating something in computing, but his heart wasn't in it. And so he rang up O'Grady, who told him to come in for a chat. 'So I met up with Anthony, had a chat and got the gig.' Taylor smiles. The inexperienced Taylor did have a strong musical background, and perhaps the other candidates were similarly lacking in journalistic credentials. Whatever the case, he was in.

I ask what his vision for the magazine was upon taking it over, and before I can even finish the question he jumps in: 'Less Angels, less Cold Chisel,' he deadpans. 'Lots of new bands that Anthony had never been particularly interested in – Sunnyboys, Hoodoo Gurus, that sort of stuff. There were lots and lots of bands. And in Darlinghurst, we were right in the thick of all that.'

Another difference between the two editors was their emphasis on industry connections. 'I was never much into the industry side of things,' Taylor says. According to him, Anthony was an industry guy – 'people would drop by and have a joint or chat with him. I was the only one of that crew who'd been a working musician … so we tended to be a bit more focused on rock band Little Feat and [later] Elvis Costello, things like that, which had never interested Anthony much. In a snarky way, we liked people who could actually play.'

Taylor's thinly veiled dig at punk highlights differences between the focuses each brought to running the magazine – and it suited *RAM* well. While Taylor might not have regarded punk highly, O'Grady did, at a time when it was part of the culture and warranted coverage. O'Grady might not have given much truck to bands like Sunnyboys, but that was perhaps before they became an important part of the sound that defined the time. Each was the right editor for the moment. The result was that *RAM* continued as a popular, trusted source of musical information.

However, change was afoot – and significant change, at that. A year after O'Grady left, Soundtracts, in a move that stunned Taylor and the staff at *RAM*, sold the title to David Syme & Co., the company that published Melbourne metro daily *The Age*, and whose majority shareholder at the time was Fairfax. The following year, in September 1983, Fairfax would assume complete control of *The Age* and all its subsidiaries.

'I think they approached me,' Mason muses, struggling to recall details of a deal that occurred more than forty years ago and changed *RAM* forever. 'We were doing maybe ten magazines at that point, and it seemed to be a sensible commercial decision at the time.'

For the staff, the deal came with one great irony: *RAM* was now being published by the same group who were publishing their main rival, *Juke*. Clinton Walker, who contributed heavily to *RAM* during the 1980s, talks of how, prior to the sale, he and other staff looked down upon *Juke* because it was published by Fairfax. 'We had a bit of an idea it was a bit corporate [because] it was owned by *The Age*,' he says.

'I think we *were* a much better magazine than *Juke*,' Mason says with a smile, 'and certainly the editorial team at that stage would have regarded it as a much better magazine, so I could understand their feelings.'

And now here was *RAM* about to be published by the same mob, essentially under the same corporate umbrella. It was a turn of events then *Juke* features editor Christie Eliezer remembers with unrestrained glee, given the rivalry that existed between the two magazines at the time. 'Then came the fateful day when the people who owned *Juke* bought out *RAM*,' Eliezer says, smiling at the recollection. 'And we were supposed to keep our mouths shut. I said, "Oh no, you can't do this to me, I need to tell a photographer." They said, "You're not telling anybody until we tell the staff." I said, "No, I need to tell a photographer, I want them to go into the *RAM* office and I want them to take a photo the minute you tell them that you've been bought out. I want you to take a photo of the editor."' Because that would have been the ultimate humiliation for those idiots. It really would have been.'[21]

While Eliezer never got his images, *RAM* did end up being published by Fairfax, their offices in Darlinghurst abandoned for smarter digs in the city. 'They moved us into an office in Margaret Street, on the twentieth floor or the eighteenth floor,' remembers Taylor. 'And they appointed a manager who was a complete idiot – he knew nothing about publishing, nothing about rock 'n' roll, he just sat there all day doing his nails. He made Philip Mason look like a publishing genius.'

As significant a change as this was for a magazine whose spiritual home was the scungy inner west around Darlinghurst, as far as the day-to-day went, things essentially remained the same. 'There were people in the building who were from Syme who we nominally reported to, but they knew little and cared less.'

For the next eighteen months, until Taylor departed as editor, *RAM* stayed under the Fairfax umbrella, continuing to provide the Australian rock 'n' roll community with the quality of reporting they'd come to expect in the nearly ten years the magazine had been publishing. As this time passed though, there appeared other changes, not just in music and culture, but in the media that was covering it.

Rolling Stone, so long little more than an extension of its US parent when it came to music coverage, was beginning to shift its focus towards Australian music on a greater scale than it previously had. The staff of *RAM* had not worried themselves overly with what *Juke* was up to, the majority sentiment being that *RAM* was a national music magazine, whereas *Juke* was far too Melbourne-centric to be a true competitor (despite how national *Juke* truly was), but the fact was it continued in popularity. As far as Taylor was concerned, changes at these publications weren't going to rattle them.

In addition, the free press began to appear: *On the Street* in Sydney, followed not long afterwards by *Time Off* in Brisbane and *X-Press* in Perth. This was something entirely new in the Australian rock journalism landscape. However, Taylor was unconcerned. 'We thought it was rubbish' is what he has to say on the subject. Stuart Coupe and Clinton Walker are both on record as regarding street press, in its infancy, as drivel as well. Given how untested street press publications were as a publishing model – the idea of a free newspaper, written largely by unpaid amateurs, focusing on niche topics did not, on the face of it, seem especially viable – it's easy to see why those already in the business saw themselves as a cut above. 'We never saw it as competition,' Taylor says, adding with a laugh, 'we were up ourselves – we were *writers*.'

Regardless of how they viewed the competition – or lack of – *RAM* still needed to evolve in order to survive, to keep up with what was happening on the scene and, even if it wasn't the main priority, to keep ahead of other publications.

'We had these writers and they all had their enthusiasms,' Taylor says on how *RAM* changed to reflect cultural shifts. 'Frank Brunetti, for example, would come and say, "This is a fucking fantastic band, we've gotta do something on them." So why not? [I'd say] "Call Bob King, see if he'll go down and take some snaps." And I'd think no more about it, and then the snaps would arrive, then the article, and away it went. I didn't have any grand plans – people came with ideas, and if what they wrote was good, then why not?'

Taylor, influenced as so many writers of the time were by the New Journalism movement of the 1960s and early 1970s, was interested in experimentation of the form. He also wanted to mix up the content. An example was the *RAM* version of British author Stephen Potter's parody books on gamesmanship from the 1950s. 'Gamesmanship was how to win at games without actually cheating,' says Taylor. 'So we had Rockmanship and ripped off the whole idea, with cartoon illustrations. So we were just having fun writing things, which is probably pretty self-involved, but the magazine kept on selling.'

This continued for much of early 1980s. 'We didn't see on the wall though, what was going to happen,' Taylor says, turning serious, as he discussed the changing conditions around *RAM*, which saw the eventual demise of the magazine. *Juke*, down south, was continuing to grow in popularity. *RAM* was not. 'We never got real sales figures, but we could tell it wasn't going well.'

In addition, the advertising revenue on which *RAM* was sustained began to dry up. While street press was not (yet) a true competitor in terms of readership, it was a threat when it came to securing the limited advertising dollars of music-industry sponsors. The introduction of video pokies into bars and pubs in the major capital cities was also beginning to present a problem, not just to the music press but to the live music scene in general. 'First the street press ate our lunch as far as advertising went, because we were sustained entirely by record company advertising,' Taylor says. 'And then the pokies, because then you lost your pub advertising.'

'Did someone say perfect storm?' he adds with a laugh.

It was an eventual inkling of what was to come that saw Taylor hang up his editor hat and move on to other things. 'I think I began to see the writing on the wall,' he says of his departure from the magazine in early 1984. 'I'd just been doing it for a while, and at that stage I was thirty-three. It was time for me to become … anything else. It *was* [sad to leave], but it was … we had a big piss-up, and then the next day I thought, *okay, that was good, now what am I gonna do?* I wasn't pining.'

* * *

The third and final era of *RAM* began in early 1984, a time when punk and new wave were fading, but pub rock, as well as an underground and more alternative strain of rock 'n' roll, was thriving. Australian music was strong and the industry, at least parts of it, was beginning to bulge fat with profit.

In 1982, leading into this third era, *RAM* was still the rock press go-to, despite the fact its founding editor Anthony O'Grady had left the previous year and it was being published by Fairfax, who were also publishing main rival *Juke*. Greg Taylor was firmly ensconced and under his steady hand *RAM* was still relevant, evolving to cover the concurrently changing music of the time.

Early that year, a young Brisbane music fan and journalist named Phillip Stafford came on staff, looking to get back into the writing game after a couple of years spent as roadie for his brother's band, gigging regularly around Sydney. Stafford had written a review of a benefit concert on spec, which Taylor had run, so he was known to the magazine when he applied for an associate editor position. 'I applied for the gig a couple of weeks [after writing the review], and Taylor said, "You're the guy who wrote that review, come on in for an interview,"' Stafford explains. 'And he pretty much gave me the gig on the spot.'

For Stafford, these were good years. He was where he wanted to be: writing about music, for a paper he admired, a paper with cred, with influence.

However, towards the end of 1983, the reality of being published by a media corporation started to become apparent. *RAM* wasn't making much money – it never really had – and so its parent company started talking about shutting it down and incorporating it into *Juke.* Instead of two competing titles, the idea was to merge them to create a single, national music magazine – essentially a home-grown equivalent to *Rolling Stone*, which by this point was starting to shift its focus away from west-coast America and onto the vibrant Australian scene.

To most of the staff, this was anathema. *RAM* could not possibly be shuttered, much less merged with its long-time rival, *Juke.* Stafford in particular, who'd been reading the magazine religiously since its inception, well before he'd come on board as an editor, was very keen to not see this happen. So he and his then wife made Fairfax an offer. 'I foolishly said, "I'll buy it off you." I asked what they wanted for it, thinking I'd not be able to afford it, and they just said, "What have you got?" … We had about four or five grand to spend, so I offered them four and they took it.'

Taylor had previously been approached about buying the magazine and had passed, deciding instead to step away from the editor role.

And so in early 1984 Phillip Stafford, for the modest sum of $4000, became *RAM*'s third owner, publisher and editor, and the paper was back where it belonged, far from corporate ownership. 'You've gotta laugh,' he says today. 'It was a bit like Trump winning the election: what do I do now?'

Stafford reached into his own pocket to buy *RAM* simply to 'ensure its ongoing survival'. 'It would have been called *Juke*, and the name would be gone forever, lost forever. I couldn't let that happen. I was an absolute fan of the mag, right up to the point I came on staff; to me, it was quite overawing when I got the job.'

The first order of business was to move out of the swish Fairfax offices in the city, taking the magazine back to its spiritual home in Darlinghurst. 'I found an office, very scungy, an old clothing factory, perfect,' Stafford confirms. 'We got some co-tenants in to help us afford it … [the typesetter] came in and helped with the rent, and then we got a team of artists in who did graphic art for all sorts, and they ended up doing the art for *RAM* as well. So it worked out well, it was like a little commune under one roof.'

Taylor occasionally dropped by to visit Stafford. 'It was a loft in Darlinghurst,' says Taylor, 'and it had this lift and every time you got in it, you thought, *I wonder if I'll get out of this?* It was all pretty tenuous, a lot funkier even than the [original] Crown Street layout, pretty basic.' Stafford was, as Stuart Coupe has written, 'fighting valiantly' to keep the magazine running. 'It wasn't going forward; it seemed like it was marking time,' is how Taylor characterises it. 'I'm glad I wasn't there, on the other side of the desk with Phil, trying to run it.'

By that point, early 1984, *RAM* had been publishing for almost a decade. It wasn't iconic, but it was very well regarded, a magazine people trusted, written by people who knew about the music and the culture that surrounded it. But it needed to change. 'There was fragmentation all around, with MTV, the rise of FM radio, and we knew we had to move with those times as well, so we started to cover music video, TV, theatre,' Stafford says on the new era of the magazine. 'We diversified as well, but there was a danger – we were aware of the danger of diversifying too much, getting too far from the original charter. So we tried to steer a course down the middle where [it was] still basically about rock 'n' roll, but with these other elements to it, which hadn't been covered before.'

RAM's direction had been set by O'Grady: to capture 'the rock 'n' roll generation, a lifestyle', as he had termed it in the magazine's maiden editorial. And it was to this vision that Stafford wanted to adhere, championing the indie music that was fuelling the scene at the time. 'Like the *NME*, we didn't want to be afraid of putting independent bands on the cover, if we thought they were any good. We put people like The Go-Betweens, The Wreckery on the cover … no one wanted to touch The Wreckery at the time,' he says, laughing.

He tells of a lunch with O'Grady, who at that point was working 'as a publicist for one of the promoters'. O'Grady was managing a tour for English rock band The Stranglers, and as part of the media–promo dance, took Stafford out for a meal, thinking, according to Stafford, that this would secure a Stranglers cover. 'But in the end, I decided that The Wreckery was the stronger story,' says Stafford. 'They were touring from Melbourne, they were in Sydney at the time, going on to Queensland, whereas The Stranglers were only playing two shows, one in Melbourne, one in Sydney … And he let me have it, he was so pissed off! He said there was an unwritten rule, he'd taken me to lunch! I asked him if he'd have tolerated being treated as an extension of the promoter's publicity department? And he said, "Okay, you got me there." Anyway, we were never quite on the same terms again after that.'

RAM carried on though, continuing to track Australia's ever-growing rock 'n' roll scene, covering anything they deemed worthy.

'Stuart Coupe brought me his Dylan exclusive – he was the only Australian journalist who was allowed to speak to His Bobness,' Stafford recalls. 'Jodie Adams was on staff for a long time. She was the editorial assistant when I started there and went on to become a long-term contributor, one of the very few women who wrote about punk and heavy metal. We also had this great American contributor, Cary Darling – he was in Orange County back then and was an Australiophile when it came to music.' Stafford laughs. 'He loved a lot of Australian pop music, plus Split Enz. He was a lovely guy. We had a London correspondent as well, even though we were syndicating the two English mags.'

Others associated with the masthead included Clinton Walker, Frank Brunetti, Mark Mordue, Jon Casimir, Wanda Jamrozik, Bernard Zuel, Jack Marx, Paul Toohey and Mara Smarelli. The magazine had a 'new lease on life', and it showed in the writing. *RAM* was still, after all these years, *the* magazine in regard to Australian rock 'n' roll.

And yet it didn't last.

As the 1980s drew to a close, *RAM* saw more and more competition, diversified across multiple forms of media. In 1987, Phillip Keir and Toby Creswell had teamed up to buy Australian *Rolling Stone*, very quickly shifting their focus to Australian music. Street press had been around since the very early 1980s and was now becoming something of a force, particularly the Sydney-based *On the Street*. *Smash Hits* began to cover some rock 'n' roll as well as pop, while the metropolitan dailies were about to enter the 'golden age of supplements', affording more space for regular music columns and album reviews. Add to this the proliferation of FM radio and the continued rise of MTV, and Stafford was beginning to realise that the writing was on the wall for *RAM*.

'Probably a year before I jumped ship, about 1986,' he reflects on when it dawned on him. 'By that time, *On the Street* were hurting us advertising-wise – because they were a free paper, they could afford to undercut. They'd sell ads for dirt – we just couldn't compete with that – and they'd sign people to contracts, have them for the whole year. So it got harder and harder to get ads, and the fewer ads you've got, the more other content you've got to come up with, and your expenses start to go north while your revenues go south. So '86, it was starting to hurt, and by '87 I just knew that there was no future. As sad as it was.'

RAM's second editor, Greg Taylor, was 'amazed' the publication lasted as long as it did 'because by that stage it was pretty clear that times were hard for a paid-for rock press'. Its protracted survival was a tribute to the work of Stafford and his team.

Stafford relinquished his share for a single dollar in early 1988. His by-then ex-wife, Jackie, was still invested in the paper ('probably more so than I was', muses Stafford) and she kept it going. Stephen Cadbury, who had been working closely with the Staffords, came on as editor, soon after followed by long-time contributor Paul Toohey, who was in the chair in July 1989, for *RAM*'s final issue, a touch over fourteen years after Anthony O'Grady and Philip Mason's very first edition.

'All along, people had been telling me that what I needed was a couple more titles: "You need a publishing company,"' Stafford says, before adding, 'Great idea, but where do I get 'em from? How do I buy them? In retrospect it wasn't a bad idea, and if you think about it, most successful publishers have never done it from one title, it's two or three or a stable.'

'But yeah, it broke my heart to walk away,' he continued. 'Yet it [had the potential] to go down in a screaming heap of shit if I'd stayed on board, and sure enough, that's pretty much what happened.'

Contributors weren't paid for the final few issues, which, in relative terms, wasn't too bad given the paper's financial situation. As Stafford says, 'they understood, circumstances being what they were. By then, it was out of my hands.'

And so *RAM* took its final breath. It was another magazine consigned to the dustbin of history, if still alive in the hearts and minds of music obsessives all over the country. Its legacy, and indeed that of Anthony O'Grady, still lives to this day, as *RAM* finally moved from well-respected to iconic.

* * *

Juke's growth period – through the late 1970s, after they'd established themselves, and into the 1980s, as MTV arrived and the effects of globalisation rippled through Australian music – was slow but steady. It was never as slick as *RAM*, according to Christie Eliezer, who seemed to regard the slickness that *RAM* exhibited (as a result of having a fortnight to put together an issue, as opposed to a week) as not being in the spirit of the rock press. But Eliezer and his team knew *Juke* was steady, and as it was nationally distributed, with any number of regionally based Fairfax writers available to be called upon to contribute, they regarded the magazine as untouchable.

'There was so much money around,' Eliezer remembers, recalling the time he went to interview Renée Geyer, as *Juke* was hitting its straps. 'I rang up her manager and said, "I want to interview Renée, can you sort it out?" Half a day later, the manager rings back and says, "Yeah, look, we can get you on the four o'clock flight."

'"What are you talking about?"

'"Oh, she's on Great Keppel Island, we'll fly you up."

'Fuck, all expenses paid! You go for four days, the interview is thirty minutes, and that's it. You watch a show, you come back. And a lot of people were flown overseas too, [because] advertising was strong, especially in the early days when record companies advertised because they knew it was important to keep music magazines alive. Then the accountants took over and it became harder.'

The bean counters, as Eliezer refers to record-company money men, didn't assume control until later in the decade, when the free press began to be seen as an alternative forum for advertising, and so having an effect on the viability of magazines like *Juke* and *RAM*. Leading up to that point, *Juke* continued unabated. Before the advent of Triple J and the youth station's ability to give national exposure to new talent, it was *Juke* doing this. 'I'd suggest *Juke* had a more national coverage than *RAM*,' Eliezer argues. 'Certainly when [bands] came to the east coast from Perth, or headed down south from Brisbane, Adelaide, they were surprised that audiences in Sydney and Melbourne knew their songs intimately. It was because the magazines had written about them beforehand.'

There was, as Eliezer says, a major cultural difference between *Juke* and *RAM*, which served to endear them, or not, to the readers and the industry. *RAM* was very much based on the *NME / Melody Maker* model, with 'star' writers. 'They certainly had those with Jen Brown, Annie Burton, Stuart Coupe, Andrew McMillan and Richard Guilliatt,' Eliezer says. *Juke*, on the other hand, was part of *The Age* and so a more conventional newspaper mentality permeated the whole enterprise. '*The Age/The Sydney Morning Herald* management was against the concept of "star" writers – the feature story was the "star",' Eliezer says. 'This applied to the newspapers and their magazines. We were also constantly reminded that writers and photographers might have personal spotlights, but without the blue-collar workers in production, the magazines would never come out.'

Juke staff had to attend legal workshops every six months to keep abreast of libel laws. This might have given *Juke* a reputation in some quarters as being 'toned down', 'but so be it', Eliezer shrugs, before recalling with a smile, 'I remember to my horror Bon Scott saying in *RAM* that to get on *Countdown* "you had to bare your arse at Molly". Outrageous! If Molly or the ABC had sued at the claim that this was how acts were booked for the show, they'd have won! No way would that have got a run in *Juke*.'

Eliezer, easily the longest-serving staff member of *Juke*, became editor right at the tail end of the 1980s. '1988 or 1989,' he recalls. 'By then the street papers were starting to have an impact and I had to broaden editorial to include lifestyle and tech elements. The features editor under me was Byron Smith, who later started his own ad agency, and then Dino Scatena, who went on to be features editor at *Rolling Stone* and is now a full-time author, and then Andrew Mast, who became editor-in-chief of *The Music* stable.'

There were successes, and also near-misses. 'One of *Juke*'s best covers-that-never-happened involved John Farnham, Shane Warne and Andrew Gaze wearing each other's uniforms, with Warne dressed as a singer, Farnham as a basketballer, et cetera.' He laughs. 'They were all *Juke* fans and into it. It took [marketing manager] Greg Phillips four months to coordinate and pull it together, but on the week of the shoot, "You're the Voice" went Top 10 in Germany, so [Farnham] had to get over there pronto. By the time he returned, the careers of the other two took them abroad, and we had to let it go.'

Juke evolved alongside *RAM* as the 1980s progressed, changing in order to stay relevant. Such is the lot of any magazine covering culture, regardless of where the centre of that culture is thought to be located. 'Rightly or wrongly,' Eliezer says, '*Juke* was regarded in some quarters of the music industry as the Melbourne paper and *RAM* the Sydney one, but that's a simplistic way to look at them. You have to put it in perspective – the gap between the two cities musically and socially and culturally fuelled the rivalry. Sydney bands like The Angels and The Radiators were huge in their city, but initially made relatively little impact in Melbourne. On the other hand, Skyhooks were *massive* in Melbourne, but not so much in Sydney. Greg Macainsh admits he wrote "Somewhere in Sydney" to curry favour with Sydneysiders. As a flow-on, there was a friendly rivalry between the magazines, but more from *RAM*'s side. That we had weekly deadlines and they didn't was an issue because we regularly broke stories before they did.'

Juke survived into the 1990s in a solid fashion then. They were nationally distributed; they had access to a plethora of contributors, both in Melbourne and around the country (not to mention the world); their staff were knowledgeable and passionate; they covered music and culture in a professional manner. Backed by Big News, they didn't have the editorial turmoil that *RAM* did, as during its three distinct eras its fortunes waxed and waned as it shifted between the indie and corporate worlds. *Juke* survived, and this was all it needed to do.

* * *

For the Australian *Rolling Stone*, the year 1992 brought turmoil. Five years after their successful bid for the licence, and with five years of consistent growth behind them, tensions between publisher Phillip Keir and editor Toby Creswell came to boiling point.

'I don't remember what the actual tinder was,' Creswell says, 'but I got fired.' Creswell is, by his own admission, a shy man, not one to delve deeply into details of a past he's long since made peace with. And so he offers little more than this, aside from, in what seems an uncharacteristic outburst, calling Keir a choice word or two.

Keir concurs there was a 'difference of opinion' about the magazine's future. After a couple of years of barely keeping their heads above water in the late 1980s, things began to improve, he says, and so the logical step for him was to start looking forward. 'We had to ask ourselves, as owners, what do we do now?' he says. 'Is a one-title house sufficient? Where do we go from here? So that, in essence, is where the difference of opinion arose,' he explains. 'Because we were all quite unified getting *Rolling Stone* to work – we all had a shareholding in it, we had a great commitment to it. So that's what the break-up was about.'

Co-publisher Lesa-Belle Furhagen laughs, almost incredulously, when I relay this quote to her. The laugh is followed by a rather long silence before she says, 'That's really not how I remember it. It was a long time ago. I think there were a lot of reasons,' is all she says on the subject, before adding on the Creswell–Keir dynamic: 'It wasn't new; they had a kind of challenging relationship right from the beginning. Some of it worked to the magazine's advantage … but often it was debilitating. For both of them, probably.'

Regardless of the true nature of the split, Keir had a larger shareholding than Creswell or Furhagen. In addition, his marriage to Furhagen was falling apart, so the company was 'clearly splitting different ways', Keir says. Essentially, Creswell and Furhagen 'were keen on doing something one way, I was intent on another way. So we divorced and I bought my wife's shareholding out. [Creswell] didn't want to sell his shareholding, but he wanted to keep doing these outside projects with her … that's when it got messy.'

How was this stand-off resolved? 'He was fired,' Keir confirms. 'And then I bought his shareholding.'

John O'Donnell, Creswell's deputy editor, recalls being ignorant of the growing tension. 'I was kind of the innocent bystander in the middle of two partners who fell out spectacularly. They were all friends [Creswell, Keir and Furhagen] and the friendship just got divided in a way that can never be fixed,' he says. 'It started breaking down … over a couple of years, where at one stage they weren't talking. And I reckon the blame does really lie on both sides – Phillip was a tough negotiator and a firm kinda guy around the money. Toby was working on other projects besides *Rolling Stone*; he'd flirt with film scripts, he'd flirt with ideas. He did the Barnes book, *Too Much Ain't Enough*; he did that during that time.[22] And in that period, I was blissfully ignorant that this was going on, but it became very obvious that I was the person Phillip was talking to [in order] to talk to Toby, ultimately.'

It came to a head soon afterwards. Furhagen sided with Creswell, and the pair began working together on various one-off projects, culminating in what O'Donnell describes as unhealthy behaviour. 'There was a particular day that Phillip saw some stuff on the fax machine that was fairly disparaging about him, faxed to somebody else,' O'Donnell explains. 'And, you know, that sort of stuff … whether it was left out to be found? I would say it was sloppily left out, but you know, that sort of stuff was happening. Something's gonna give. And Phillip was the kind of person who would probably put that to the side, build it up into a little pile where he could take it to his lawyer and go, "I want this guy out," and I think that's where it kinda got to, I think.'

The firing played out in a dramatic fashion. Toby was removed from the premises, O'Donnell tells me. 'Yep, a security person came in and escorted him off. It's lost in the sands of time, but I think [Phillip did not speak to him first], or he may have come up with the security guy and said a few words and then exited, and then Toby had to leave and was not welcome back in the building.'

Creswell was no longer involved with *Rolling Stone* in any way, ending a seven-year period that had seen him in an editing role of some kind. He and Furhagen left at the same time and formed Terraplane Press. Within a few months, no doubt spurred on by a mutual dislike of Keir, they had launched a direct competitor to *Stone* in *Juice*.

John O'Donnell, as well as a large portion of *Stone*'s staff, freelancers included, followed Creswell to the new publication. As far as Keir is concerned, however, from the outside there was very little change to the magazine; in consumer land, no one would have noticed. 'I edited one issue, maybe two issues, to get it out,' he says. 'I put Sonic Youth on the cover of one of them. It wasn't one of the bestsellers.' He laughs.

The firing of Toby Creswell was to usher in a new era for the Australian edition of *Rolling Stone*. One cannot help but admire the job Creswell did while helming the iconic title – indeed, it was he who turned it into a true Australian magazine, his laser focus on and passion for Australian music leading it to become more than an offshoot of the American original. But it was his leaving that was to pave the way for *Stone* to, essentially, re-create its glory days; that is, return to its roots as a magazine that wasn't just a vehicle for Australian music but a record of the times themselves, as it had set out to be under Jann Wenner in the United States in the late 1960s.

The new editor, installed from the March 1993 issue, was Kathy Bail, a journalist formerly of News Corp and publications like *The Independent Monthly*. Bail was a serious journalist and had been honing her craft from a young age, with a background editing Australian film industry magazine *Cinema Papers* and before that *Farrago*, the University of Melbourne student newspaper. It was these bona fides that Keir was looking for when it came to taking his publication forward.

'I suppose the thing that really appealed to me about *Rolling Stone* was that from its inception in the late sixties, it had covered music and the sort of social and political environment in which all of that happened,' Bail says. 'And so it was an opportunity to cover music and politics and the full range of things in contemporary culture.'

Bail says that for her the quality of the journalism always came first, no matter the genre. US *Rolling Stone* writers and editors such as David

Fricke, William Greider and Holly George-Warren always found original angles for stories. Hunter S. Thompson had his own distinctive style and approach. The magazine had 'a reputation for publishing investigative stories that were relevant to a younger readership, and I thought I had strong credentials in that area', she says. 'And I didn't believe that the editor of a magazine like that had to be a music fan or a musician. I thought that having strong editorial skills was the main thing.'

Bail's first move was to hire a new music editor in freelance journalist Dino Scatena (who went on to write for *The Daily Telegraph* and produce a number of books on high-profile Australian musicians). Her second was to form a coterie of contributors, given a number had defected to new game in town *Juice*. 'I was really well connected to some of the top journalists in the country,' she explains. 'And I knew that many of them were interested in contributing to *Rolling Stone*. Some of them worked on newspapers and other magazines, but would've been in a position to do this as an extra gig. So I suppose I felt confident that I could bring in a new group of writers.' There were, of course, a number of writers who contributed to both titles – writers, like any professionals, follow the money, at least to an extent.

Bail was building around her a solid foundation. It was this that was to serve her well over her entire tenure at *Stone*, which started with a bang. Her first cover, the March 1993 issue, wasn't a rock star, local or otherwise. It wasn't a film star or an entertainment personality at all. The cover story for that issue, his face adorning the cover with a half-smile, eyes partially hidden by a pair of black sunglasses, was none other than serving prime minister Paul Keating. This was an announcement – the magazine was now heading in a more political direction once again.

'That was March '93, just ahead of the election, which he won. That issue sold well,' says Bail, smiling. 'And it also got an enormous amount of attention in other media ... because it was a different kind of interview for Paul Keating; there was interest in what he was saying to younger Australians. A different demographic. So it was a signal, I think, in that first issue, that we were going to cover politics seriously. We were going to report on politics in a way that engaged the readership of *Rolling Stone* and younger readers. And also in a way that older readers of the sort of baby boomer generation would recognise. Because they'd seen that *Rolling Stone* had been doing this ever since the late sixties.

'So I think we probably got a bit of a crossover readership,' she continued. 'And that cover was reproduced everywhere. I talked about it on ABC television, on the *7:30 Report* [with] Kerry O'Brien ... I think I did something with [him], I think it was in *The Sydney Morning Herald* and Fairfax papers ... it went viral, in today's language.'

I ask what effect this degree of media coverage had for Bail, as incoming editor. 'It was a signal that we were going to cover kind of everything, between music and politics and social issues. And that was very different to *Juice*, which was sort of aimed at ... well, it wasn't aimed at that sort of older reader who might've been reading *Rolling Stone* for some time. It was aimed at the younger demographic. And I don't think they invested the same resources as *Rolling Stone* in those political and social stories.'

Bail's first year as editor yielded two more covers with Australians in Midnight Oil (May 1993) and INXS (August 1993), along with international stars, chosen to reflect what was happening locally – for instance, Madonna graced the October issue, given she was touring that month. Although it's not one of Bail's favourite covers. 'I think it's a weak cover,' she says, commenting on the shot, a close-up still from one of the singer's music videos. 'We were doing something on her as a video artist – I was trying to convey that we were writing much more about music video and the role of music video to promote music. And we're kind of right in the heart of MTV. So I thought that was a way of sort of signalling that kind of music video culture. But looking at it now, it wasn't a strong cover image.'

The final cover of the year featured Janet Jackson – the now iconic photo of the singer topless with her husband's hands covering her breasts. 'That's sort of classic *Rolling Stone*,' Bail says of another cover image she wasn't particularly proud of. 'There were often women on the cover but … *Rolling Stone* was beginning to compete with the lads' magazines, you know, other kinds of men's magazines. So, not my favourite cover.'

As 1993 ticked over into 1994, Bail felt she had found her feet as editor of the publication. 'I was hitting my stride,' she says. 'I had a much, much better feel for the readership. There were more obvious subcultures … more of a sense of the alternative [back then] … And I suppose my role as an editor was to be aware of what was happening across all of these subcultures and, even though I wasn't part of them, to have good sources or people within those groups to say to me, "This is what's going on, we should be reporting on it."'

This was at the height of grunge. Rap and hip-hop were entering the mainstream. In the near future, electronic dance music would become a powerhouse in its own right. *Rolling Stone* was able to cover a lot of this, thanks in large part to how Bail was running the show. During this period, too, she was able to keep up a close relationship with her American counterparts, spending a good deal of time in the New York office, so she 'wasn't just on the end of the phone or email'. 'Both Phil [Keir] and I made a big effort to stay really close to Jann Wenner, the editor of *Rolling Stone*, and to the team there,' she remembers. 'So I went over regularly to the office in New York and worked out of the office and got to know the people on the magazine, and so I think it was a close relationship.'

As the Australian edition's 500th issue rolled around (September 1994), Bail asked Jann Wenner to write a note to help commemorate the milestone:

> Issue 500 and we're still rolling in Australia ... This edition of *Rolling Stone* is now the only overseas edition of the magazine in the world. I've seen French, Spanish, Japanese and British editions come and go since I started *Rolling Stone* in San Francisco in 1967.
>
> Mick Jagger, interviewed by David Fricke in this issue, had a stake in the British edition when it started in 1969.
>
> We've always had a close relationship with the three groups who have published the magazine in Australia since the early Seventies. This edition has succeeded because of the determination of the people working on it to maintain the distinctive design and feel of *Rolling Stone*. Also, both cultures obviously share many similarities: In music, film and television, as well as lifestyle, social values and political ethics.
>
> Our stories and those originated in Australia share the same spirit: A Smashing Pumpkins interview next to a story on new faces in Australian music; P.J. O'Rourke's view on Haiti next to a photo-essay on the Philippines; an Anthony Kiedis interview next to one with Nick Cave. But, of course, the success of *Rolling Stone* in Australia ultimately lies in its local perspective. It's not simply an import; it has developed its own larrikin style and idiosyncrasies.
>
> From the New York office, expect more dispatches from Hunter S. Thompson and groundbreaking stories from our unique team of writers, editors, photographers and artists. I'm sure we'll be matched word for word by the Australian contributors. Here's to another 500 issues in Australia!

Maintaining close ties to the American headquarters was important. For the Australian office, it meant less friction and more freedom – the ability to rely on the support while doing their own thing. And Wenner realised that the Australian offshoot was its own being, the 'larrikin style' having been a part of Australian *Rolling Stone* since Paul Gardiner and Jane Matheson had run it from the mid-seventies.

Bail, the magazine's fourth editor, was aware of the importance of the publication she was helming. By this stage, the mid-1990s, the Australian edition had been running for a little over twenty years, the American version almost twenty-five. The magazine's influence, its synonymousness with music and culture, could not be underestimated.

'Absolutely.' Bail smiles. 'I always had a sense that it was much bigger than any individuals working on the magazine. It was very closely associated with the founding editor, Jann Wenner. So he was always there pulling the strings. And I think you had a sense that if Jann didn't like it, it wasn't going to happen.

'I was travelling in Indonesia, a remote part of Indonesia,' she adds with a laugh, 'and I had a *Rolling Stone* cap on and people were saying, y'know, "*Rolling Stone!*" Yeah, everybody knew about *Rolling Stone*.'

One of Bail's Letters from the Editor, in the November 1994 issue, elaborated on what the magazine was looking to do with the fledgling internet. At the time, it would have read as refreshingly future-focused, but today it seems laughably old-fashioned:

> *Rolling Stone* now has its own ramp onto the information superhighway. From our offices in Redfern, NSW – a three-story power station built late last century – we can leap into cyberspace.
>
> Next Online is being launched on the Internet by Phillip Keir, the publisher of the Australian edition of *Rolling Stone*. While it is a separate venture to *Rolling Stone*, it will offer many benefits to our readers.
>
> There's a lot of hype about the digital revolution and electronic publishing but as an editor caught in the middle of it, I think there

are good reasons for the buzz. Imagine reading an album review, then listening to sound bytes from the recording so you can make up your own mind if it's worth buying. This is just one of many possibilities with new, interactive media.

This is what you can look forward to from Next Online – all you need is a PC or Mac, a modem and a sense of adventure.

We have a new e-mail address for 'Correspondence, Love Letters & Advice': rsletter@next.com.au So more mail please. If you hate a cover, tell us, not just your mates; if a feature story has made an impact on you, tell us why. You're not necessarily going to get an instant e-mail response, but it's very likely your letter will be published in *Rolling Stone.* E-mail is as fast as a phone call and easy to use. And more advice from you will help us produce an even better magazine.

…

Next will also be organising electronic forums, on the kind of people and issues we're covering in *Rolling Stone.* The discussions will be moderated – so you won't be able to hurl abuse all the time – and may be followed up in the magazine. Special 'live' online events are planned. So if an artist has a new album out or is about to tour, you can chat with them about it on the 'Net.

…

In future issues, we'll keep you informed about Next Online, particularly the development of its music services. There'll be regular guides on how to join us in cyberspace so, if you're not wired yet, keep reading!

'Reading it now, it's just full of this tech optimism,' Bail says with a laugh. 'It's just so optimistic about what the internet is going to deliver. And then, we've got an email address so people can email to get a response. This just seems bizarre now. "Email is as fast as a phone call and easy to use" – it's like an ad!'

'This gives you sort of some idea,' she continues. 'I mean, now we take all of this for granted, but this gives you some idea of how kind of new this was [at the time]. And I think you've got to kind of understand that sort of context. So that's November 1994. So I think in that sort of time, we introduced in the magazine the possibility of reading a print magazine but also beginning to have this life online.'

Bail's time as *Stone* editor yielded its share of highs and lows. Highs included the Keating cover; meeting Hunter S. Thompson in New York ('He was in the office. He was smoking a pipe, and he offered it to me. He was gruff. He was just hanging out.'); and the cover featuring *X-Files* stars Gillian Anderson and David Duchovny in bed together, which was shot by an Australian, being syndicated to the United States. Lows included seeing Courtney Love perform at Selina's in Coogee ('The performance was a mess … she was trashed. I just thought, I hope she's gonna survive.') But it was an experience she would not change.

Working with Keir had its moments: Keir had a reputation for being a tough businessman. ('He was demanding. He was incredibly demanding. And if one of the magazines in the group was not working financially or struggling, he let it go. I don't think he was sentimental.') But credit where credit is due: Phillip is 'someone who's very good at spotting young talent and giving people opportunities', Bail says. 'There were opportunities to experiment. So when I went to *Rolling Stone*, we all had Macs, and that was the early days of computers. [Mac] was one of the first companies to get email and so Phil embraced new technology and digital technology. So he gave staff these tools, these new tools, and then said "Okay, see what you can do with it." I think he was an innovative employer in that sense.'

Bail's tenure as editor lasted around four and a half years, finishing in May 1997. When she was offered the editorship of the Australian Consolidated Press–published *HQ*, a bimonthly culture magazine 'that ran lengthy features and profiles, like *Vanity Fair* with an Australian perspective', Bail found it too good an opportunity to pass up. 'It was time to hand over to somebody who was closer to the *Rolling Stone* readers,' she says. 'I'd had a really good run. And it was also, after being in a small magazine publishing company that didn't have huge resources, an opportunity to go and work for the biggest magazine company in Australia. So it was good timing.'

Under Bail's editorship, *Rolling Stone* became again a cultural record – with a strong music focus, of course, but with an eye on the environment in which this music was happening. It was a reliable beacon in a time of change. And change was indeed happening. Publisher Phillip Keir, while running *Stone*, had expanded his stable of titles, including to some focused on tech – computer games and the multifarious beast that was the internet.

Bail's leaving heralded a procession of editors and publishers over the next twenty or so years, as the magazine's fortunes waxed and waned. In 2008, NextMedia, the company Keir had founded to publish *Stone*, essentially gave the magazine (as part of a larger merger) to ACP Magazines, which became Bauer Media in 2012. *Rolling Stone* then returned to its indie roots via Paper Riot in 2013, owned and published by Matt Coyte, who'd been editing the magazine since it left NextMedia.

Bail's editorship remains a high point in the magazine's storied history. 'She was the best editor [Australian] *Rolling Stone* ever had,' says long-running street press editor Andrew Mast, who freelanced for Bail in the mid-1990s. She gave 'really good guidance, good editing and subbing. Everything they did as a team there was so good.' *Stone* was reinvigorated, cementing itself once again as the record of choice for the serious music afficionado. It seemed it'd keep publishing forever. And in the late 1990s, who would have argued?

13

JUICE AND THE SPECIALISTS (VOL. 1)

'It was completely insane. It was an insane thing to do.'

Toby Creswell

By the early 1990s, *Juke*'s run as part of the 'golden era' of rock journalism in Australia was coming to an end.

Of all the mitigating factors that combined to kill off *Juke*, street press was by far the most effective. First appearing in Brisbane and Melbourne as early as 1979, these magazines were free, localised and weekly. They made money by persuading advertisers that they had more eyeballs than anyone else, on a regular basis. It was this shift in advertiser focus that eventually hobbled the magazine as the 1990s dawned.

It wouldn't have seemed like that at first, though. As Eliezer tells it, when he was at *Juke* in the early 1980s, street press was seen as laughable. 'You gotta be joking, did you see that awful magazine?' he says, remembering when he and his colleagues first saw a street press paper. 'You've got to realise,' he continues, 'that at that time the street papers were, editorially, not challenging at all. They were all about making money, it was all about getting ads; it was a smart idea, whoever came up with it. The stories were basically press releases re-written. They didn't have much money, they looked awful, they printed badly. We really didn't think that they were going to be much of a problem because they didn't look good.'

But several factors coalesced to make street press a viable advertising alternative. First, the music industry was changing as it expanded. 'In the late seventies, the people that made decisions about ads, they were music people. So basically, they said, "Look, let's put an ad or two into *RAM*, let's put an ad or two into *Juke*, because it's good to have those magazines around." Once the bean counters took over though, it was like, "No, why would I put an ad in *Juke* for $500, when I can do it in some street magazine for $100, $150?" That was the way they were thinking.'

Second, street press could meet readers where they were. 'Kids were not going to newsagents as much as they used to, so the magazines went to where they went.'

Which was, unfortunately for *Juke*, away from it.

* * *

Throughout 1991 and 1992, Eliezer tried his damnedest to keep the paper alive in the face of competition – music television, radio, the national youth radio network Triple J, *Rolling Stone* and of course the street press. 'By that stage, the street papers were a real fucking problem,' Eliezer says, rolling his eyes. 'I mean, we were just gasping for ads, really. We tried all sorts of things.'

One of these things was a partnership with music retailer Brashes. It was close to a last-ditch effort for *Juke*. Brashes at that time, according to Eliezer, was selling CDs for around $28. The plan was to turn *Juke* into a monthly magazine, make it physically smaller and re-price it at $2, from '$3.50 or $3.80, as my memory takes me', he says. 'When people handed over $30 for a CD, the person behind the counter would say, "Instead of your change, would you like to buy a *Juke*?"

'At that time, Brashes had worked out that, throughout its stores, 650,000 people came through per month,' says Eliezer. 'Eighty per cent had no idea what they wanted to buy, they just wanted to go in there ... so we thought, *fuck, even if we get a quarter of these people, phew!*'

Alas, it didn't come to be.

'Unfortunately, we didn't realise at the time, the top people at Brashes were really interested in the *Juke* thing,' Eliezer explains. '[But] middle management hadn't been consulted, so they were hostile. And there seemed to be some sort of communication flaw between the top people and the drones working on the counters. What they should have said was, "This is a good opportunity ... we have basically our own magazine, this is our magazine as much as it is theirs." And I think, from anecdotal evidence, some of the girls who worked on the counter, and guys too, they resented that they had to share their counter space with this fucking magazine. Okay, I understand, it's a retailer thing ... so occasionally, instead of *Juke* being up there on the counter prominently, some of the shops were just putting it [anywhere] ... if people asked for it, they'd sell it. But if [consumers] didn't know it was there, they wouldn't ask for it.'

This partnership lasted five months before Fairfax pulled the pin, and for Eliezer too, it was the final straw. Before the Brashes deal, *The Age* 'was thinking that maybe they could do it as a lift-out in *EG* [the Friday entertainment supplement], or whatever it was called in those days ... urgh,' Eliezer recalls. 'There was all this territorial stuff, *Juke* staff and *EG* staff. Fuck that idea, let's go to Brashes.' After the Brashes deal fell through, Eliezer and senior *Juke* staff had a meeting with *The Age* 'and to their credit – they'd gone through a lot of management changes – they kinda said, "Look, what else can we do? Do we change the format and go back to newsagents?" Sometimes you know the party is over, so I said, "Look, I've got other things to do. I'd been wanting to go and live in New York for ages, so I'm gonna fuck off."'

Juke has the distinction of running for longer than its northern rival, due largely to the fact it was being published by Fairfax and so had more resources behind it to prolong the inevitable. But by mutual agreement, it eventually folded in December 1993, almost four years after *RAM*. Eliezer was still editing the paper, aided by features editor Andrew Mast, who went on to become the long-running Group Managing Editor at Street Press Australia.

Mast had been brought in two years earlier, in 1991, to cover dance culture. 'I was brought in for that particular reason – I was the only journo covering dance music,' Mast recalls. 'Not only was I covering it, I was covering it right from the underground up to the overground. And even though my interest lay in the underground, no one else wanted to cover the commercial stuff, so that just landed in my lap. So I was the guy going to the Vanilla Ice concerts and all that sort of thing. So I saw some really great hip-hop, but I also saw every bad pop act. It was absolutely fascinating ... Before dance, I came from punk, so they knew I had the balance. That was the intention – *RAM* is gone, we've got a chance to get our stake in the market back, but we also need to branch out.'

When he started *Juke* in 1975, Ed Nimmervoll had an ethos in mind – a magazine that really supported Australian music. By the early 1990s, it may have seemed to fans that this ethos was no longer driving the publication, not because Eliezer and his team didn't care about the music, but because so much of their focus was on money and survival. 'I always thought that we cover this, cover that, we'll be fine, but I didn't realise that the audience was changing; it wasn't obsessed with Oz music as it once had been,' Eliezer laments.

However, Mast is of the opinion that upper management, not to mention Eliezer, just didn't know where to look. 'I'd [already] been working in street press and the kind of bands I was reviewing there I wasn't seeing reflected in *Juke*; I was going to see unsigned bands at the local hotel. So I just went, "Fuck it," and, un-commissioned, sent them a review ... and I got contacted and they said they wanted to publish it, and it wasn't until later I realised they were *looking* for someone to go and see these bands. So I did get a sense that they were looking to support unsigned bands, and once I was there, even as the pagination was going down, I'd be allowed to do a double-page spread on a local band. I remember I was able to give Tim Rogers and the lead singer from Tumbleweed a double-page spread. And then there'd be a big international band with a half-page story after it. And not only that, they sent a photographer along with me! So they were budgeting for that local coverage.' Yet the covers remained big, international acts.

The corporate backing was also a double-edged sword, and Mast believes it contributed to *Juke*'s downfall. Budgets were generous, photographers were in good supply, international stringers could easily be found. 'I think that was one of the problems – instead of cutting the budget and trying to fix up the magazine from a budgetary angle, they just kind of gave up hope as the sales were dropping,' he says. The deal with Brashes 'was one attempt at rationalising the finances, but I think it was too little, too late, and they couldn't quite decide what the angle was. I honestly thought we'd saved it, but no, then it was gone.'

And to really drive the point home, street press, as it'd been threatening to do for a number of years, since before Mast joined the editorial team, finally toppled them.

'Street press always felt like a threat, absolutely,' agrees Mast. 'I'd already been involved with *Beat*, and I think I was also writing for *Inpress* at the time and had to write under a pseudonym because Fairfax didn't want me writing elsewhere. So even though the threat was from street press, I was already entrenched in street press.' He laughs. 'But yeah, it was always there, hanging over our heads, that all our advertising had gone to street press and as a national paper, you couldn't tap into that local, grassroots pool that street press had, and we knew they were doing a great job. And even though you could pull bigger names and stuff like that, you'd be jealous of the coverage they could get done at that grassroots level.'

Eliezer moved overseas and Mast eventually ended up at *Inpress*, moving through the ranks as a national network was established. It was a short ride at *Juke* for Mast, but a good one. 'You've gotta realise, this young kid with no journalism training ... *Juke* was the greatest learning experience of my life,' he says fondly. 'I must have driven Christie insane with my questions. The bands I got to work with, brilliant. Going out on stories with a photographer is still one of my favourite things, they were all really good. These were great experiences and very few people get to have them now because of how journalism has changed. It was truly exciting.'

'One of the saddest things that happened when we left, there was this photo file like you've never seen,' he remembers, a grin spreading across his face. 'Like, from that wall to that wall, three drawers in each cabinet ... Can you imagine? Those cabinets were filled with not just press photos, but ... I remember one day opening a drawer and picking out this folder randomly, and there were all these rare, never-before-published photos of ABBA's show at the Myer Music Bowl. When *Juke* closed they were going to be put in the Fairfax archive, but I heard there was trouble with the archive ... I'm hoping it's all been digitised, it was mind-blowing. I got teary leaving there, not because I lost my job but because of those photos. I *wish* I'd stolen stuff,' he jokes.

Street press won out over *Juke*. In the late 1980s and early 1990s, the free press wasn't even at its peak; that was still to come. But not all music publications were flailing; some were having a reinvention.

* * *

'I think I was a bit insane at the time.'

Toby Creswell sits at a small table in a busy café in inner-city Sydney, sipping a coffee as he says this. He is remembering times gone by – times hectic and nerve-wracking, but exciting, the possibilities thrown up by what he was doing fuelling a desire to keep doing it.

It was 1992. He'd just been fired as editor of *Rolling Stone*, after differences with publisher Phillip Keir had come to a head. He'd sold his shareholding in the magazine and, understandably, wasn't happy with how it'd all turned out. Creswell had been involved with Australian *Rolling Stone* since the early 1980s, more than a decade of this as music editor, then as editor and co-owner. He'd had a huge part in helping to make this Australian arm of the American original a record of note within the local music industry.

He'd helped turn *Rolling Stone* into a titan, with little to show for it other than the admiration of those who saw this and the money he'd received for his share. And so the time was ripe for revenge, so to speak – to throw a big, dirty rock into the pond that *Stone* occupied. *RAM* was gone and *Juke* not far off, almost flayed to death by the lack of advertising revenue. Now was the time for a new player to enter the market.

I remark to Creswell that that's a pretty strong middle finger – leave, start a direct competitor.

'Yeah. It was, um, crazy,' he says quietly, in his typical soft-spoken voice. 'And it was kind of, um … yeah. It was insane.' There was, he admits, 'a bit of desire for revenge'.

This direct competitor was *Juice*, the first major title out of Creswell and Lesa-Belle Furhagen's Terraplane Press. It was preceded only by a couple of poster books. 'I think the first thing we did was a Johnny

Diesel poster book,' Creswell recalls. 'The most successful thing we ever did was a poster book called *Get In the Ring Motherfucker,* which was about Guns N' Roses, just before their tour. And we printed every picture back to front. But the whole thing sold out. So we did that and then we launched *Juice* in '93 and went from there.'

'I didn't see it as revengeful. We didn't have any work!' says Furhagen on the beginnings of Terraplane and *Juice*. 'We were suddenly without jobs. So I didn't sit down and think, *how can I be vengeful?* I wasn't sure what I was going to do. I'd left my job to go and work for *Rolling Stone* and had worked my arse off – and, you know, women in the music industry back then were given very little acknowledgement for the hard work they did. And I've not said this in the past, but I felt that was the case with me. So the motivation was a) we needed a job and b) there seemed to be a gap in the market.'

Rolling Stone's readership had started to age, and with the rise of Gen X culture, there was a space that *Juice* could occupy. 'A bit like *Spin* magazine in America, more your eighteen-to-thirty-year-olds, slightly edgier, a bit grungier. There'd been the emergence of grunge culture, and that was the niche we wanted to fill,' she says.

Juice, to everyone's surprise, achieved a certain level of success, running for around a decade before finally imploding in fairly spectacular style. In hindsight, it's not terribly surprising that it made good – here was a competitor to *Rolling Stone*, essentially covering the same ground, the same scene, in a similar way, but with the core difference that it had majority Australian content and an Australian tone. *Stone* was an offshoot of an American magazine, and as much of a local flavour as it had developed over the preceding decade (thanks in large part to Creswell), it always felt American to some degree.

'It's kind of weird,' Creswell muses. 'What would I say about it? The model that I sort of liked at the time was this magazine called

Details. It had a particularly good editor whose name I can't remember right now.[23] But *Details* was great, it had this kind of real attitude to it. And there was also that grunge / Generation X moment. And so we were trying to position what we were doing as a sort of grunge / Generation X alternative.'

The first issue had a few teething problems. The cover 'was just a million percent wrong', Creswell says with a laugh. 'The cover line was something like "Jimmy Barnes Goes Grunge", which he was doing but didn't work for him at all. Like, he made that really kind of angry record that just died.' It also came with free condoms, a giveaway from an advertiser, which meant some newsagents wouldn't stock it. 'It was at the height of the AIDS crisis, so we thought it was a good idea, but when ringing around newsagents, some didn't put the magazine out because they were Catholic!

'Everything went wrong with the first issue.' Creswell laughs again. 'But I think what we did quite well was that people did buy that whole Generation X thing. That helped.'

Creswell was burnt out from his years at *Rolling Stone*. For the small staff producing the magazine 'month in and month out', it was all-consuming. 'None of us did anything except produce the magazine and go to gigs. It was wild.' I venture that surely it wouldn't have been much different at *Juice*, particularly given they were starting from scratch. 'It was.' He laughs. 'It was crazier. But actually we did employ more people. We had less money to play with, [but] we employed more people.' This is probably why the publication did not make much money, he concedes. It's at this point he grudgingly calls Phillip Keir a good businessman.

But Creswell was quickly reinvigorated by producing *Juice*. He was now free to experiment with form and style, with layout, how the magazine looked and felt. 'I think I was bored with the formula, with the *Rolling Stone* kind of formula,' he says. '*Rolling Stone*'s got a very rigid style. And we were looking for different ways to kind of break that down. [We] were kind of mucking around with the way that information was conveyed. So we would do things like the history of jazz in graphs and pie charts, and also I got to open up the writing a bit more. So that's kind of what was really exciting about it. We really tried to get a lot of artists doing interviews with other artists. The first one, we had Grant McLennan interviewing Nick Cave, which is just fucking genius.'

Essentially, *Juice* was to Australian *Rolling Stone* what *Spin* in the United States was to American *Rolling Stone* – an alternative, a slightly ragged vagabond of a competitor. And this was precisely Creswell's aim.

* * *

Craig Mathieson, a music and film writer for Nine papers who got his start writing for fledgling Melbourne street press title *Beat* in the mid-1980s as a seventeen-year-old, came on board as a freelancer for *Juice* quite early. He was one of several writers who wrote for both *Juice* and *Rolling Stone*, his byline also appearing in *Juke* in its final couple of years. But it was *Juice* where he appeared most often.

'It was great for writers, young writers, because Phillip [Keir] brought in Kathy Bail [at *Stone*] and *Juice* started and it was like, wow, they're both using more Australian content; *Juice* had to and Kathy did, she was really good on that front. And so suddenly there were all these bands, there were all these magazines, there were two monthly glossies. It was great. So I started writing for both really quickly.'

This was the era of indie rock, of alternative rock and grunge, of Triple J hitting its straps after beginning its national expansion in 1989. It marked yet another period of Australian musical growth, one no less fertile than earlier spurts. The music was different, but it spoke no less urgently to its audience, young people eager to read as much about these trends, these sounds, these bands as they possibly could.

Juice was 'the upstart, the younger, presumptuous rival', Mathieson remembers. 'And it was the right time for that. American *Rolling Stone* had got pretty moribund in the eighties. A lot of film covers … it'd stayed with the baby boomers all through the eighties. And that influenced the Australian one in the eighties, when the covers coming from the States were Michael Douglas or Dire Straits.'

One thing Toby Creswell did right at the beginning of *Juice*'s life was strike a syndication deal with *Spin*. This was only to last a year or so, the deal falling through, but it was certainly a sign as to where Creswell wanted to take his young, presumptuous rival. According to an article published in *The Sydney Morning Herald* in 2007 (to mark *Rolling Stone*'s thirty-fifth anniversary), *Juice*'s circulation jumped to around 50,000 within its first year, the magazine breaking even after only four issues.

Journalist John O'Donnell defected from *Stone* with Creswell and Furhagen and was installed as deputy editor while *Juice* was in its infancy. 'It was a very messy time, a very painful time,' he told *The Sydney Morning Herald*. 'But looking back it was very exciting, even though it was ultimately a failed venture. We were never trying to hurt *Rolling Stone*, but I think we did hurt it a bit.'[24]

Over its decade-long run, from 1993 until 2003, *Juice* evolved under Creswell and Furhagen. 'I think it became more and more concentrated on new music than previously,' Creswell says. 'I remember looking at one issue, I think it had Lenny Kravitz on the cover, and it had no old people in it, and I thought, *this is kinda good*. So, you know, I think the magazine was a bit ahead of its time in some areas. We tried to explore a lot of dance music and rap, and perhaps the audience wasn't ready for that, but there you go.'

The magazine had found its feet, and it carried on in the niche it'd created alongside *Rolling Stone*. Craig Mathieson was brought on as editor in mid-1994. While the magazine was doing fine, he says, it was never an easy ride.

'Not enough,' he jokes when I ask whether he received a brief from Creswell when he stepped into the editor's chair. '*Juice*'s problem always was that it was trying to be so many things; no one ever said to me, "This is the person we want to buy *Juice*, tailor to this person." It was kind of a freedom on the editorial side cause ... we can put whatever we want in and we were kind of trying to appeal as widely as possible.

'So we kind of pinballed back and forth. There was never a structure. We were ambitious, you know, we put in non-music articles and ... film; we were interested in a lot. So, you know, you've seen it – it's pretty all over the place. Each individual piece is crafted reasonably well. Reviews are comprehensive. We just never had an idea of what we were, and some people might say that's a great freedom in publishing and you're lucky to have that, but I kind of wish we could've just focused and built and crafted an identity. I think we probably should've been a little younger than we were. You know, there were so many teenagers getting excited about Triple J. I think we should've gone more heavily into that world.'

Regardless, *Juice* managed to strike a chord. Until the strings broke completely.

* * *

When the end came for *Juice*, it wasn't subtle. There was no final farewell issue before fading quietly into that good night. It was one of the more high-drama exits in Australian magazine publishing history, certainly in rock press history.

By 1997, Furhagen and Creswell were looking to expand Terraplane, now five years old, by adding more titles to their stable. This was easier said than done, of course, because magazines cost money. '*Juice* never made much money,' Creswell says. While it was breaking even, there was no cash to fund an expansion.

They owed money to their printers, Diamond Press, 'like a lot of publishers did'. Diamond, headed by Sydney business identity John Spira, were invited to invest in Terraplane, which they agreed to do, a deal that on paper looked set to benefit both companies and give Terraplane the option of bringing in more titles. 'Yes, that was the vision,' says Furhagen. Given the dot.com boom was in full swing, soon afterwards it was decided that, in an effort to raise more funds, Terraplanet (as it had been renamed after the merger) would do a float.

Creswell sighs. 'We were a bit naïve. We didn't understand the relationship [with Diamond] very well.' It turned out that Diamond Press 'were in a lot of trouble, and so we didn't realise that they needed this thing more than we did!'

An *Australian Financial Review* article dated 3 April 2001 notes that 'industry insiders' suggest 'Diamond Press is carrying debts of about $80 million'. At this point, Diamond had approximately 7 per cent of market share in the lucrative $1.7 billion commercial printing market, far behind main rivals PMP and the Fairfax and Hannan–owned IPMG. Spira also held a 30 per cent stake in Terraplanet.[25]

Furhagen concedes, 'Yeah, we didn't know the circumstances behind Diamond Press – we were not privy to those – but they were clearly having issues we didn't understand. Combining forces had sounded like a really smart way to grow Terraplanet in a way we could never do, if we never did a public offering.'

But it quickly became apparent that this was not the case. The company, newly flush with cash that had been earmarked for the proposed expansion, but rocking precariously as the dot.com bubble burst and the markets heaved accordingly, became a tense environment, with Creswell and Furhagen on one side and their new partners on the other. 'We went on a buying spree and started to grow,' Furhagen explains. '[They] had different ambitions and objectives, and we found ourselves in this situation, and that was challenging.'

According to the same *AFR* article, Spira placed Diamond into voluntary administration around this time and took a 'leave of absence as chairman of [Terraplanet], handing over to non-executive director Ita Buttrose'. In 'a day of drama at Terraplanet', managing director Lesa Belle Furhagen 'was removed from her executive position' as a Kelvin Atkinson was 'made acting chief executive'.

'So that just fucked it completely,' Creswell says, rolling his eyes. 'And all the money we'd made in the float, which we were going to reinvest in the business, just evaporated. In the meantime we had launched *Recovery Magazine*, which was based on the TV show. And we also bought a teen magazine called *Big Hit* from ACP. And we bought a magazine called *HQ*.' This sequence of events took a toll on Terraplanet and its founders. 'Everything was really damaged by that whole thing,' Creswell says. 'It was all a mess and we just ran out of money.'

Changes in the publishing industry contributed to the woes. 'It [came] at such breakneck speed, this new technology,' says Furhagen. 'Keeping up became really challenging, and although we'd raised enough to grow and develop the magazines, *and* the start of what we envisioned to be the online offerings, it took off at such a pace that we needed really more staff, money, more of everything that we had.'

While the boardroom battles raged and budgets were tight, *Juice* kept running, not missing a beat, along with its stablemates. 'It never stopped.' Creswell smiles. 'The staff were incredible. That last year, at least, it was a nightmare, horrible. You know, the conditions they were under … everyone who worked there was incredible, because there was always this pressure of, what's going on? And this whole corporate fighting going on, it was hard, yeah. But everybody was great. Some of the magazines were really good.'

No money, though, eventually means no magazines. Terraplanet limped along for a while before finally falling over. *Juice* was thrown a lifeline by the Seven Network's Pacific Publications in early 2003, but they closed it due to plummeting circulation figures in July the same year. And so after a decade of running alongside *Rolling Stone*, *Juice* was done. 'It was dreadful,' Creswell says.

'It was a mixture,' Furhagen admits of the eventual demise of the magazine. 'On the one hand, a little bit of relief. But mostly quite a lot of grief. We'd have loved to have done it forever. But when I look back now, I'm really proud of what we did. We started a lot of amazing people's careers. We unearthed amazing writers and photographers; we changed the way advertisers looked at presenting their clients in print media. I think we made a mark.

'And when I go past newsstands today, even though magazines are really no longer a thing, I lament the fact there aren't many really fantastic boutique Australian magazines. And I think that's a shame.'

Juice was one of many magazines that folded during the aftermath of the dot.com crash, and Australia's media landscape was forever left the poorer.

* * *

The year 1992 was a fruitful one for the Australian rock press. Another magazine also began publishing that year. *Rhythms*, often referred to as Australia's roots music bible, is the longest continuously running roots music publication in Australia today. It now publishes bimonthly, and has done since 2013, and it is the true embodiment of a niche publication, easily the most prominent title in the country catering exclusively to a roots music audience.[26]

The magazine first appeared in April 1992, tabloid-size, in black and white, with American blues singer Bonnie Raitt on the cover. It was free, and while short in extent at twenty-four pages, it was obviously fuelled by a passion for roots music – country, blues, soul, gospel, world music, folk. This was before the term 'Americana' was commonly used in Australia, before 'alternative country' became a phenomenon. It was a gamble from the get-go, but over its tenure it has garnered immense respect, not only among its loyal fanbase, but among the music industry and other journalists and publishers.

Rhythms was founded by Brian Wise, an intense lover of the music his new magazine would laud. Wise already had a reputation in the music industry, and in particular the roots music industry, as someone who knew what he was talking about – he'd presented shows on Melbourne community radio station PBS, and by the time he started *Rhythms*, his seminal show *Off the Record* had been running on PBS rival RRR for almost five years. (Wise still presents *Off the Record* on RRR to this day).

Growing up in suburban Melbourne, Wise came to music via the radio, listening in particular to 3KZ presenter Stan Rofe, whose *Go-Set* column he also read religiously. Wise and Rofe became friends, Rofe introducing the young music lover to a whole new avenue of sound. Wise also tuned to the BBC Top 20 and, via shortwave radio, to the American Forces Network radio broadcasting out of Vietnam, where he heard stuff that blew his mind.

As far as print went, he always picked up a copy of *Go-Set*, and he began to devour *Rolling Stone* when it first appeared in Australia. It wasn't until he was in the United Kingdom in the late 1970s, though, that he first begin to see magazines as truly influential – and even though he didn't realise it at the time, he found inspiration there for what would become *Rhythms*.

'When I lived in London there was a great little magazine called *ZigZag*,' he recalls. 'It was more of a fanzine than anything else and I remember they had [American singer-songwriter] Jackson Browne on the cover. They interviewed all the artists that I liked ... and they had long interviews with them, long, sort of interesting interviews with them. The layout wasn't anything fancy, it was very basic. So I always had that in the back of my mind.'

Wise spent most of the 1980s back in Australia, working in radio and reading music magazines veraciously, including *Juke*, which informed his PBS show. He was also a contributor to short-lived but well regarded alternative sheet *VOX*. It was in 1991, though, by which time he was also the music writer for *The Sunday Age*, that the idea of publishing his own magazine became a reality. 'I went to New Orleans in 1991,' he said, and there he encountered two music magazines, *Wavelength* and *OffBeat*. '*Wavelength* went bust a few years later but *OffBeat*'s still going. And I thought, *geez, if they've got two music magazines in the city of 400,000, surely we can have one in a city as big as Melbourne*. And so that's what kind of inspired me to start it, really.'

One day, while on air at RRR, Wise casually mentioned he was keen to do a newsletter, a sort of print version of his show. Shortly afterwards, he received a call from a listener in Williamstown, a bayside Melbourne suburb, who was a graphic designer. 'His name was Mark Jamieson,' Wise says. 'So we started it up, we went into partnership.' *Rhythms* was born.

Given Jamieson's skills, there were no design costs as such, which helped to keep the overheads low, and so issues of the magazine became a regular fixture at record shops and pubs around Melbourne. The first issue's print run was around 3500 copies and cost around $5000. For the first few years, the magazines would turn up on Wise's doorstep, he and a friend would load a station wagon, and off they'd go – true indie distribution.

Characteristic of the genre, the fledgling publication faced some problems. According to Wise, Jamieson wasn't on good terms with the magazine's printers, and it came to a head. 'After a year or so it turned out we were in a bit of a precarious financial position even though we'd been selling advertising, we'd been getting subscriptions,' he explains. 'It was very precarious. And so I had a meeting with [Jamieson] one day and I said I'd like to take it over, I don't want to be a partnership, so we agreed on an amount. I wrote him a cheque for the entire bank balance of $5280. So, that's how I acquired it. Which was probably a good thing, because I think if we'd stayed working together, it would've folded.'

Over the following years, *Rhythms* grew steadily. It was never huge in terms of readership, and it never made bucketloads of money, but it spent the next ten years or so developing a reputation as *the* source of Australian roots music news and information. Wise acquired the subscriber database of short-lived Sydney-based world music magazine *Songlines*, published by Mark Chipperfield, strengthening *Rhythms*' reach, and while the first few years were, in Wise's word, precarious, the magazine kept on going.

It remained a free publication for five years. The thinking was that 'if you could make it free that means that every copy would be picked up, which it was', Wise recalls. 'The way *OffBeat* operated in New Orleans and still does is … it's free in New Orleans, if you live anywhere else you've gotta pay for it. Or subscribe. Great. Simple. And for the first five years of *Rhythms*, that will be it, I thought.'

Wise was eventually dissuaded from this theory, something he regrets, and so today the magazine is available in selected newsagents, with the bulk of its sales being via subscription. *Rhythms* is the epitome of a specialist magazine – its subscribers recognise it as an authority on the music they love, and so they subscribe every year, again and again.[27]

Wise found another graphic designer shortly after Jamison. 'I went to New Orleans in 1995 and I met Mark Ferrie on the tram, on the streetcar,' he says and laughs. 'And we were just having a chat, and I said, "What're you doing?" He said, "I'm a graphic artist." And I said, "Hey! I've got a magazine."'

While still under Wise's control, the magazine's headquarters moved into an ancient office in Swanston Street in the city. Then to the bayside suburb of Port Melbourne, where the magazine was published by Dharma Media (the group who published Melbourne street press publication *Inpress*, and who would go on to form Street Press Australia), before reverting to Wise's full control once more. 'I believe that started in 2001 and went until 2005,' Wise muses. 'Dharma Media's Brian Peacock and Craig Treweek thought it might be a good addition to their stable, but it ended when they decided that publishing a niche magazine wasn't their thing as it was much more difficult to sell advertising, and so they handed it back to me. And they never put any pressure on me to tailor editorial or advertising.' Subscribers continued to flock and the magazine grew in size and scope over the next few years.

Eventually, though, it got to be too much. Wise had too many commitments: he was teaching at a suburban TAFE; he was presenting *Off the Record*; and he was writing for, editing and publishing *Rhythms*, as well as selling ads, arranging printing – the whole nine yards. In 2007, Wise sold out to then *Inpress* music editor Martin Jones, who moved the operation north to Brunswick Heads, on the New South Wales coast. Jones's wife, Verity Bee, was also a designer, and so design costs were kept inhouse once more.

Under Jones, *Rhythms*' scope widened. Americana, an umbrella term that encompassed anything and everything roots-oriented, was huge in the United States, and so over time the magazine grew, slowly, some more. Jones and Bee launched the magazine's website and iPad app, and looked to take the magazine into the twenty-first century. But it was, as it always had been, about the music, and each month the magazine reflected this.

Jones sold after a decade to country musician Catherine Britt and her husband. Given Britt's touring commitments, coupled with a health scare and then the birth of the couple's first child, the magazine plateaued in terms of growth, and after two years they looked to sell. A few buyers thought about it, dithering, until up popped Brian Wise again. *Rhythms* had come full circle, and continues today, fuelled by a pure and unadulterated passion for the music.

* * *

As the 1990s progressed and turned into a new millennium, two of Australia's most successful specialist magazines came out of the same stable, at least for a while, as *Rolling Stone*. *Australian Guitar* and 'hard music' glossy *Blunt* appeared within a couple of years of one another via NextMedia, Phillip Keir's company.

NextMedia had published a number of specialised titles before *Australian Guitar*, mainly internet and gaming publications, but Keir's heart was in music. 'The 1990s were the glory days of music publishing in Australia,' he reminisces. 'Access to retail outlets such as independent newsagents allowed publishers to develop large and diverse audiences. Technological advances through desktop publishing and computer-to-plate printing provided strong cost reductions for short-run titles, allowing niche titles like *Australian Guitar* and *Blunt*, among many others, to be launched. If a title didn't work, it simply closed and was replaced by an another new title. It was possible to react to popular culture audiences in a very immediate way: no market surveys, no corporate strategies, just gut hunches. These were the absolute glory days of magazines in Australia.'

Australian Guitar launched in January 1998, a smart concept given Australia's affinity with all things rock 'n' roll. 'That was a small market, so we just did it quarterly at first,' Keir says, 'but there was a real interest in a local magazine. That was quite durable. It was never a huge seller, didn't have any impact on *Rolling Stone* sales – it was very much aimed towards people who were hobbyists, I guess. It was the most reliable magazine. It was solid. I wouldn't say it had *no* impact what you put on the cover, but by and large it didn't, in the sense that people bought it for the content.'

Australian Guitar still publishes today – it went monthly for a number of years, and currently appears bi-monthly, but it is still a resource for those interested in not only guitar music but also in the techniques and the tech associated with the instrument.

Blunt, which first appeared in 1999 as the emo and nu-metal waves gathered momentum, looked to home in on this alternative-infused slice of the market. American staples such as Slipknot, Blink 182 and The Bronx were featured in its pages, as were local bands like Karnivool and Parkway Drive (who had their first-ever cover story with *Blunt*). Contributors were a mix of local and international, and the features were long and in-depth – certainly the only longform writing on heavy metal and punk that was happening anywhere in Australia at the time.

Then, in 2001, *Blunt* was faced with a surprise competitor. One of only a handful of international offshoots of the legendary British metal weekly, *Kerrang!* saw light in Australia for a brief but fertile period. Allegedly named for the sound of a guitar 'being struck with force', it was a full-blooded heavy metal mag devoted to this niche genre with a uniquely local bent, encapsulating what it was about metal that its local fans so adored.

Helmed for its entire Australian lifespan by Rod Yates, who went on to edit *Rolling Stone*, *Kerrang!* first appeared in late 2001, published by UK multimedia publishing giant EMAP (East Midlands Allied Publishing), which was known for producing a stream of lifestyle and hobby magazines, including the British edition of music magazine *Smash Hits*, celebrity gossip rag *Heat* and men's magazine *FHM*. Its life was short but sharp, running for four years, until 2005. During this limited tenure, it did well, turning a small profit and keeping its loyal readers informed about what was happening in metal worldwide.

Yates had joined the Australian arm of EMAP after a brief stint working for the taxation office. Given he was already across all things heavy metal, when the opportunity arose to edit a new mag brought over from the United Kingdom, he jumped at the gig. 'It was really guerrilla,' Yates recalls of Australian *Kerrang!*'s launch. 'EMAP said, "Right, we're gonna take a chance on a music title. In their stable they had *Q*, *Mojo* and *Kerrang!*, and they said, essentially, "What can we do cheapest, what can we do that'll work but that will also cost less?" And *Kerrang!* was deemed [the winner], Australia obviously being a really big rock market. And *Kerrang!* being a smaller magazine and the fact you'd have four [British] magazines a month to draw content from basically meant they could employ me and have a part-time designer.'

The magazine was an instant success. The first issue went gangbusters, Yates recalls with a laugh. It turned out that there was room for both *Kerrang!* and *Blunt* in this niche market and so each prospered, helped in no small way by the continuation of nu-metal's popularity through the early 2000s.

Yet despite the fact the magazine was making a profit, the end did come quickly, as EMAP changed its editorial focus in 2005. 'Basically they were launching *Zoo* and I think *Grazia* ... [they said] "Let's pour everything into *Zoo*, let's pour everything into ..." – whatever the other title was – so *Kerrang!*, which was making a bit of cash but not a lot, pretty much was just closed.'

Yates felt there was still very much a need and want for the magazine, but the decision had been made. 'I was bummed out that it wasn't going [on], because I think there was definitely a place for it, and I think the scene missed it as well,' he laments. 'It reported on a lot of stuff that was going on that no one else touched.'

Blunt continued printing up until 2017, eventually going wholly online. It still exists today, published digitally by The Complaints Department.

For publications with a limited audience, *Rhythms*, *Australian Guitar*, *Blunt* and *Kerrang!* were all successes. The reason they lasted so long (in the main) is because they kept to their niche, covering only what was of interest to their readers, and they occupied it largely solo. Further, these publications began and were able to develop loyal followings before the internet and social media were to alter media industries.

'We were quite aware, particularly in the music industry, of the potential of the internet,' Keir muses of his company's decision in the late 1990s, as the internet began to stir, to begin producing niche titles. It was a solid move, demonstrating foresight, and served Keir well until he sold out in 2008.

Because the internet was to change everything.

PART THREE

MODERN TIMES

STREET PRESS AND THE SHIFT TO THE INTERNET (1980–2023)

14

FREE FOR ALL

'If it moved, I shot it.'

Tony Mott

No one could have predicted it. A small pamphlet consisting almost entirely of ads for upcoming gigs evolving into a publishing medium like no other, proving impervious to change for decades, snuffing out media behemoths and rendering obsolete a particular mode of magazine production.

Street press: free to the public, funded by numerous cheap ads; appearing weekly, allowing for the most comprehensive gig guides thus seen in the Australian rock press; specific to its particular location, endearing it to the local scene.

The medium, as it came to be known through the 1980s and into the 1990s, was printed on newsprint, eventually with colour on the covers but consistently black-and-white inside. Within its pages, novice and experienced writers alike – but mainly novice – penned inky paeans to what was happening on the ground in cities and regions around the country. Stacks of copies would appear on a Tuesday morning, maybe a Wednesday or Thursday, on the footpath outside record shops, cafés, pubs, anywhere with even a remote connection to the music scene.

And while not unique to Australia, street press proliferated across the nation and became *the* model for the rock press for many years, to the detriment of conventional publications.

Prior to becoming the powerhouse it did, Australia's street press had a disjointed beginning. The tabloid-sized papers that came to define the genre stemmed from the grimy inner-west of Sydney around 1981, but a couple of years before this, two early incarnations of the medium appeared. One acted as a physical blueprint, while the other essentially ignited the tinder that became the free-press bonfire.

Up north, a magazine called *Time Off* appeared in February 1979 amid a steamy Brisbane summer. It was an offshoot of an established university campus newspaper, the University of Queensland's *Semper Floreat*. Helmed by student editors Rob Cameron and Bruce Dickson, *Time Off* wasn't initially a free magazine – unless you were a student at the University of Queensland and picked it up on campus – selling fortnightly from newsagents for 60 cents. 'Initially to be published on a fortnightly basis, it is anticipated that by mid-year the magazine will become weekly, offering even greater services to union members,' reads *Time Off*'s maiden editorial. 'With regard to content, the most important feature of the new-look *Time Off* will be its thirty-page "Living Guide". This regular section of the magazine will provide you with the most complete rundown of cultural and social events available in south-east Queensland.'

Meanwhile, in June of that same year, amid a brisk Melbourne winter, a publication dropped down south that, while it wasn't street press in the sense that term came to be known, certainly pioneered the concept. *TAGG* (*The Alternative Gig Guide*) was a pocket-sized gig-guide magazine created by Mick Pacholli, a band manager with a publishing background who was looking for ways local bands could get gig listings. 'There was nothing around,' Pacholli says. 'You had *The Weekender* in *The Age*, but you had to pay to get a listing in that.'

His father was Jack Pacholli – once dubbed 'Melbourne's most notorious newspaper publisher' for his lax attitude towards defamation[28] – who had begun publishing *The Toorak Times*, an independent newspaper, in 1972. Mick had assisted his father in printing free guides to Melbourne, the production costs for which were funded by advertisers. 'Yeah, we'd do *The Visitor's Guide to Melbourne*, we'd put them in all the bus stops, all the train stations. We didn't charge for them, we sold advertising for them,' he says. It was this same model on which he based *TAGG* – a free music magazine funded by music advertising, to be distributed wherever the music was.

Advertisers at the time included 'Mushroom, Premier, different pubs', Pacholli recalls. 'You name it. Everyone, every pub in the area.' Pacholli ran a music agency, Band Aide, and for a three-monthly fee, bands and outlets associated with the agency could get listed in the extremely thorough directory that dominated the magazine. The money was used towards print costs. 'We also charged 20 cents a copy for outlets to give away,' Pacholli adds.

TAGG was primarily a gig guide, but also contained small (paid) articles and reviews of gigs and live shows by writers such as Al Webb, David Pepperell, Helen Jennings and Cec Cafferey. Released fortnightly, it was more up-to-the-minute than monthly music magazines, and immensely successful in finding a readership – Pacholli says they'd print 5000 copies, all of which would 'fly off the shop benches'. Over the next few years, it branched out to Sydney, where the local edition was edited by Stuart Coupe, 'initially based out of my kitchen in Stanmore'. Coupe explains that 'a *lot* of great people wrote for it', including Clinton Walker, and that it was 'way ahead of its time'. It also inspired a series of short-lived imitators – including *Street Beat* in Adelaide and the tongue-in-cheek *BOGG*, or *Band's Own Gig Guide*, also Melbourne-based, which Pacholli bought from the *Gigs of Our*

Lives comic-strip producer John Taylor and eventually incorporated into *TAGG*. But after only four and half years, *TAGG* collapsed. 'The taxation department came after my father's company,' Pacholli explains. 'I was listed as a director ... so when they got him, they got me and *TAGG* as well. I tried to keep it going for as long as I could ... I'd put a 40 cent cover price on it in 1982 ... but at the end of the day, I got an offer that was too good to refuse in the video industry, and just stopped [producing *TAGG*].'

Pacholli is adamant in claiming he invented the core concept of the Australian street press that sustained the medium over the ensuing decades. Others are less sure: journalist Clinton Walker, for example, recalls a very short-lived title out of Sydney a couple of years prior to *TAGG* called *Town*, which was similar. Unfortunately, any reference to this magazine is lost to history. Yet even if Pacholli's claim is true, *TAGG* wasn't able to scale into a national publication; nor was it produced in the format that came to define this particular genre of publishing. Pacholli was there at the beginning, though – street press certainly owes him a debt, whether anyone associated with it over the years realises this or not.

Sydney is often said to be the city where the Australian street press truly came to be. It too grew from inauspicious beginnings: it also began with a free, ad-filled pamphlet.

'I was in Sydney running [booking agencies] Frontier and Harbour, and I'd seen how the English would promote their shows,' recalls now legendary promoter Michael Chugg on how it all began, back in 1980. A pamphlet seemed a good way to advertise gigs, whether they be under Chugg's banner or someone else's – the form was cheap to print and distribute. 'I think we were charging thirty bucks an ad or something, and I think we called it *On the Street*, because it *was* on the street.'

The pamphlet – which contained, unlike *TAGG*, only ads, no editorial – proved popular among Sydney's gig-going public. Chugg was quickly approached by Patrick Howard, who was publishing a free weekly suburban newspaper called *City Express*, with a view to inserting the guide into the paper. The pamphlet would benefit from the wider reach, while the newspaper would benefit from being associated with the pamphlet's content.

'We bought it, actually, for about $4000, I think, which was a considerable sum of money then,' says Howard, 'on the basis that Frontier would advertise all its gigs, that was the deal. It was a section inside *City Express*, four pages, eight pages, called "On the Street".'

Howard and his partner, Patrick Cusick, had form in community newspapers: they had also published local paper *Sydney Shout*. Under their guidance, *On the Street* expanded. Local journalist Eleanor Boyd was brought on to edit the section, and it evolved considerably over the next couple of years to include articles and reviews, essentially becoming a music magazine in its own right, albeit one running as a section of a bigger publication. Amid a booming music scene, industry advertising increased, and the section was soon making more money than its parent. 'In a *very* short space of time it was making more money than *City Express*,' concurs photographer Tony Mott, who began his career at *On the Street*.

Mott, one of the most prolific shooters of his time – 'If it moved, I shot it' – puts this down to the energy of Sydney's live scene. 'I'd been in Los Angeles, New York and London, I'd lived there, but Australia's music scene in the 1980s was the best in the world,' he recalls. 'Easily. Not best, *easily* the best, there was no second place. You could see quality bands seven nights a week in god knows how many places. One of the great things I always mention about this is that around 1981, '82, The Cure toured Australia … they played Sydney for three months and never played the same suburb twice. That's how great the music scene was.'

This was the era of the residency, where bands would play every Tuesday night for six months. Bands like the Hoodoo Gurus and Midnight Oil played and played, becoming great live acts. Sydney's inner city boasted myriad venues and clubs from which boomed many sounds, the resulting cacophony the soundtrack to an era.

In the mid-1980s, according to Mott, there 'was this left of centre alternative thing'. 'Nick Cave and The Birthday Party and Beasts of Bourbon, all this stuff, and the inner city in particular had this huge new era,' he says. 'And the street press championed that. The fact they had a street press where you could advertise your gig for $25, which is affordable – well, it just boomed.'

Even at this early stage, street press demonstrated a uniquely independent spirit that rang true with the music scene of the time. It was this lockstep with the scene's ethos that helped it to become as popular as it eventually did.

On the Street continued as an insert for a couple of years, helmed by Boyd and publishing writers such as Rob Miller and Mark Mordue, plus giving a leg up to those at the beginning of their careers, like Mott. Also on staff, doing layout, was a young Margaret Cott, whose background was in working on regional papers outside of Sydney. Between them, as Sydney's music scene exploded afresh around them, they grew this section, this musical beast tucked away inside a suburban newspaper.

And a beast it was, soon necessitating a literal split from the paper it'd been a part of since coming under the control of Patricks Howard and Cusick. 'My recollection was that *On the Street* quickly expanded from four to eight, then twelve and sixteen pages per week, and the size was dominating *City Express*, so it was decided that *On the Street* should fly alone,' Patrick Cusick recalls. 'It had its own district street flavour with complimentary design, layout and stories and, importantly, a dedicated readership.' *On the Street* was more than equipped to stand alone, at least financially.

It was around this time that Boyd, on the eve of a deadline, decided she'd had enough, packed her desk and left. 'Eleanor decided overnight, literally in a split second, "I'm out of here,"' Mott remembers. 'There was Mark Mordue and Rob Miller and maybe two others who were obvious choices for editors. And no one could decide … in my humble opinion, it should have been Rob Miller, because he was efficient. So that was the debate going around, and the consequence was, because no one could decide, Margaret Cott said, "Well, I'll run it this week, and then we'll work it all out." And it sorta never got worked out, she just took it over.'

While Cott had no editing experience at that stage, prior to doing layout at *On the Street* she'd been working for her father's newspaper. '*The Southern Highland News* in Bowral. I was coming up on weekends and having the time of my life,' Cott recalls. 'I was probably twenty-two years old, never been involved in the music scene. I was a country girl, but, I mean, really hardworking, so they'd give me this mountain of work to get through and I'd do it.'

Cott jumped into the editing role, and one issue turned into two, then four, and before anyone really knew it, things were continuing along as they had been – selling ads, writing copy, putting out a magazine that was slowly growing in stature in the eyes of the music world.

Then, once again, change. *City Express* was struggling to pay the bills and so a merger of sorts was negotiated with one of the paper's bigger advertisers, Associated Electrics, run by a businessman named Noel Crabbe; essentially, Crabbe was offered a slice and came on board as a part-owner, Crabbe, Howard and Cusick each taking a third of the small empire's worth.

'It was great,' smiles Howard. 'Associated Electrics owned the freehold of their city offices; Noel was a very wealthy guy eventually. So we moved into his offices [in York Street, Sydney] and everything was just hunky-dory. *On the Street* was growing, all that.'

But according to Cusick, this equanimity wasn't to last. 'From the outset it became overwhelmingly clear that Noel believed there was little profit to be made in free city publications and, not being a publisher, writer or editor, Noel's lack of knowledge – along with an unveiled intention to find a quick-sell exit – made our task challenging, if not impossible.'

It all came to a head, and 'Noel threatened to take us to court', Howard explains. 'We were headed to court but settled before it got there, so … Noel won.' Crabbe, according to Howard, said he'd never wanted it to come to this.

The three negotiated a settlement whereby Crabbe took 51 per cent of the company, the two Patricks 49 per cent. 'And that drove Patrick absolutely fucking bananas,' Howard alleges. 'Fifty-one per cent, you own the thing. A minority shareholding in publishing is worth nothing, absolutely nothing.'

Cusick, having had enough of the in-fighting, left the company, and shortly afterwards Howard ended up in hospital, with ailments he believes were brought on by the stress of running a small publishing empire in the mid-1980s. And so he too pulled the pin. Howard, who can lay claim to being one of the first street press publishers in the country (albeit perhaps accidentally), was done, his association with the rapidly growing *On the Street* over. The magazine, now under the publishing control of Noel Crabbe and Associated Electrics, continued unabated.[29]

According to Margaret Cott, who most likely was unaware of all this background upheaval, Crabbe was generous towards the staff. 'He said, "It's fine, we'll continue printing it … you have 20 per cent, Marg, and he gave the accountant 10 per cent and someone else [too]. So away we went.' It wasn't long before the team had turned the financial situation, caused by breakdown of the management partnership, around. 'We went from being $20,000 in the red to being $40,000 in the black, and it was starting to really be a bit of a force,' Cott says. 'And we were printing more and more newspapers, and you know, people really respected what we were doing.'

At this stage, as the 1980s hit its halfway mark, *On the Street* was the only free mag in town, if not the country. From their base up in The Cross, they presided over and existed alongside a strong and eclectic music scene – each fed off the other.

The paper was, at least to Cott's mind, grungy and esoteric, a true grassroots publication that spoke as much for the young, first-time band looking to advertise a maiden gig as it did to the promoters and managers and bigger bands of the time. The continuing proliferation of fanzines, however, fostered a sense among some that *On the Street* was far too 'establishment', not edgy enough.

'We were up against it,' Cott says, smiling. 'It was grassroots, [but] it wasn't grassroots enough for a lot of people. We were still grungy and esoteric and seminal and all those wonderful words ... but we always knew we had to pander a bit to the promoters and the record companies. We were criticised because we weren't edgy enough. But we were.'

The paper continued to grow in both size and stature under Cott. Its pages were filled with words from talented writers such as Mark Mordue, Jack Marx, David Brearly and poet Steven Herrick. 'There were lots of people from the ABC [who contributed], a lot of people who had other jobs who were just bored,' says Cott. 'People who were lawyers who needed to write something other than reports. We were promoting young bands, but we were also promoting young writers.'

Mott also considers the promotion of a new generation of critics a valuable aspect of the publication at the time. 'The editorial was always minor at first ... it was all about advertising and gigs, and that's what it was, a gig guide. But of course, as it grew, it grew the editorial – some fine journalists have written in street press. It was like having a school for rock journalism. Fuck, it taught you how to write, how to write on a deadline ... going to work for Fairfax after that would be a doddle.'

According to Stuart Coupe, however, the degree of editorial attention given to the writers was nothing like at *RAM* and *Juke*. 'I've always been on record as being a long way from being a fan of street press, because once street press came along, the role of the editor, for music publications in this country, changed dramatically,' he asserts. 'Because there was no one there who had the training. Not to say they were bad people, but they weren't editors in the traditional sense of editing.'

The craft of editing might have been starting to fall by the wayside, to the detriment of the contributors and the industry as a whole, but no one at *On the Street* appeared to be losing sleep over this when the publication was doing so well on every other measure – particularly financial.

'When you consider that *On the Street* was completely free, it was making money because there was that much advertising, not to mention all the little things at the back of the paper, classifieds – $20 [and] you can say what you want,' says Mott. 'In *RAM*, a quarter-page ad was $300, which was out of your budget when these bands are being paid so little.

'It was very bad for *RAM* and *Juke*, they must have seen it, they would have seen it and been like, "Fuck." *RAM* were very good, they cared about their journalistic integrity, so they did get the best of the writers. And when they did a feature on New Order, it'd be two pages of quality journalism. The New Order piece in [*On the Street*] was probably done an hour after [the show] in real time, but ultimately ... it's free. Even though it's obvious the *RAM* article would be a better read.'

* * *

Time Off wasn't technically a street press publication during the period in which it was associated with the University of Queensland, though it shared a newspaper format and tabloid size with *On the Street*. Its use of a graphic logo, along with its 'Living Guide', an early attempt at an incredibly detailed gig guide, were the types of features that would become a hallmark of street press for years to come.[30]

However, it wasn't to last overly long through the university, as in the early 1980s it was bought by mining magnate Denis Reinhardt's publishing company, Fortescue Media. Under this umbrella it was transformed into a free street press publication, but it never really reached its potential – in terms of both finances and readership – through the early to middle part of the decade. It would eventually flourish, but that would come later.

Yet Australia's street press – a small network of publications that were free to all and championed the scene from the ground up – was off and running. At this early stage, around 1985, street press had yet to catch on nationally as a publication model, but there was no reason why it wouldn't or shouldn't. Melbourne's inner city and Brisbane's Fortitude Valley were breeding the same hectic scenes as Sydney's inner west, as were Perth on the west coast and Adelaide down south. All these micro-scenes needed support, coverage and criticism in equal measure, and this new form of press, despite its guerrilla approach to publishing and symbiosis with advertisers, was all the while building a presence among the fans, shifting more copies, pulling in more ads. As the 1980s progressed, the writing on the wall for *RAM* and *Juke* was becoming all the more clear.

15

WEST, EAST AND DOWN

'Obviously the bourbon was talking, but we decided it'd be great idea to start our own magazine.'

Andrew Watt

The seemingly limitless potential that *On the Street* was exhibiting in Sydney was bound to spark interest elsewhere in the country. The connection street press was forging with the music scene at all levels already showed signs of bringing opportunities to an industry so fertile. *Time Off* in Brisbane was on its way to emulating *On the Street*'s success, but perhaps surprisingly, it was on the western side of the country, in Perth, where street press next took hold.

Five O'Clock News appeared on the streets in the Western Australian capital in July 1983, as a direct competitor to the entertainment section of local afternoon newspaper *The Daily News*. Spearheaded by printer Joe Cipriani, whose company Addco Productions was involved with the entertainment industry, 'providing graphics and a range of printed materials including rock posters for hundreds of Perth bands, venues, promoters and touring events', the magazine was an attempt to ensure some sort of grassroots control over industry coverage, along with providing more affordable advertising opportunities.

'The idea of a street press came out of our art department, as at the time we were setting the entertainment ads for *The Daily News,* the go-to for local entertainment,' Cipriani explains. 'The industry at large was disgruntled with this medium, though, as the editorial coverage was poor and the paper wasn't cheap to advertise in. So in July 1983, I called a meeting of the industry at the Raffles Hotel, to gain a vote and general consensus of support for the launch of *Five O'Clock News*, a weekly entertainment newspaper. The vote was unanimous, so we went ahead and launched into a major operation to combat *The Daily News'* entertainment pages.'

Cipriani says, 'We put our balls on the line and employed fifteen staff, photographers, et cetera, plus the deputy editor of the *Western Mail* newspaper's lifestyle section.' While this fledgling attempt at a western street press was well received by those in the industry, 'unfortunately, seventeen weeks later *Five O'Clock News* and our production company was placed in receivership ... that is, we went under. We simply went too big, too quick. On day one, we carried major operating expenses with nil income, and the sales income was simply slow coming. The receivership also encompassed Addco Productions, the head printing company.'

Five O'Clock News was a boisterous publication, its only aim being to support the Perth music industry – an industry that was small compared to its eastern counterparts, but no less important; far more important than the local dailies had pegged it as. Cipriani and his fellow industry members would no doubt have been stung by the failure, but to their credit, while they might have lost a battle, they considered the war far from over.

'With the support of private loans from the industry, we managed to buy back the production assets at a creditor's meeting, where we gained great support to continue,' Cipriani tells. 'The idea and dream of a street press was still there, so in July 1985 we worked up the guts to launch a small A5-size magazine to be named *X-Press Magazine*, on a fortnightly basis produced and printed by our company, where there were minimal costs and risks attached.'

This time they were more successful. From the get-go, Cipriani went all in. The magazine employed an editor, four staff writers, an ad department of five, plus a production manager and a distribution manager. It seemed to work, as word quickly spread and reader numbers grew. 'By 1986,' he enthuses, 'we increased the magazine size to tabloid and printed on the newspaper presses in a serious attempt to take down the competition, *Daily News*, again. This marked the beginning of the history of *X-Press*.'

The Daily News was already facing turmoil and, like many embattled publications before it, was not to last. Four years on, in September 1990, Cipriani and the rest of the city was witness to its demise.

X-Press, meanwhile, seemed here to stay. 'As the publisher we ran a tight ship,' Cipriani says, demonstrating his determination to build a sustainable enterprise. Nevertheless, as operations expanded there was the need for more hands on deck. Over the ensuing three to four years, the publication's staff grew to twenty-three, along with a host of freelance contributors. *X-Press*, which had its own small market to itself for now, was on its way to becoming one of the longest-lasting, most resilient and most respected street press titles in the country.

* * *

In the mid-1980s, Melbourne's music scene was of course as big and vibrant as Sydney's, if not more so, and the medium of the free press was bound to catch on. Indeed, one could have bet the farm on it, given that *TAGG* had already had a short, sharp lifespan in Melbourne. There had also been a smaller (though no less important) paper in *A–Z*, a street press–style publication that began in 1985 and ran for approximately three years, providing another gig guide.[31]

It was a young entrepreneur named Rob Furst who, in the wake of these smaller papers, and witness to the success of *On the Street* up north and *X-Press* in Perth, made a move. Furst had worked in sales for *Juke* and so was no stranger to Melbourne's rock 'n' roll press, but he knew that selling ads for a magazine published by a multinational likely wasn't going to make him the money he would have been chasing.

As long-term street press editor Andrew Mast speculates, in Melbourne, street press first appeared in the form of pamphlets and flyers, as it had in Sydney. 'I think St Kilda was the impetus because we'd all go to the Seaview Ballroom, the Prince of Wales and The Venue on a Thursday night, all three,' Mast remembers with a laugh. 'The Prince and Seaview were free, three bands at each, so you'd walk back and forth and you'd see six bands, and then you'd go round to The Venue and it was maybe a $3 door charge and you'd see a bigger band … so you'd have seen six lesser-known bands and then walk around and see, maybe, the Hoodoo Gurus or something. They called it the Thursday Night Crawl. So we're talking the healthiest I'd ever seen Melbourne's music scene. I've never seen it like that before. This is '83, '84.'

He recalls that 'you'd walk out, and all the cars in the area would be plastered with flyers' for upcoming gigs. 'So the council started getting pissed off with all the flyers, so someone … came up with the idea to take all the flyers, put them into a plastic bag and stick them under the windscreen wipers. So that lasted for a while, then I think that got banned, and after that, I'm pretty sure it was Rob who said, "Well, why don't I do this?" And basically *Beat* was a response to this ban of all the band flyers. So that's where [I think] it came from – it came from the council banning these flyers.'

Beat, first published in 1986 by Furst Media, was Melbourne's first street press in the tabloid-sized format that quickly became popular. It appeared a couple of years after *TAGG* had folded, and existed alongside the short-lived *A–Z*, quickly beginning to make inroads within Melbourne's tightknit music community.

Two of *Beat*'s first employees were Andrew Watt and Rowena Webber. Watt, who had just completed his law degree and had been writing for *Lot's Wife* at Monash University, came on board as a staff writer at the outset. Webber, a recruit from the University of Melbourne, where she'd been editing student paper *Farrago*, was then hired as editor.

According to Watt, *Beat* didn't immediately hit its straps. Not long after Webber was hired, 'Rob jumped on a plane and went overseas on a buying trip, as he also owned a knitwear company, so he went overseas and left her in charge,' Watt says. 'And this was long before email and mobile phones, so he was gonna be uncontactable, so poor Rowena was left in charge of *Beat*, not knowing anyone, and really not knowing much about the business. So naturally, she would turn to me, as someone who had been with *Beat* since the beginning. She'd say, "What are we supposed to do about this – we've got an advertiser who just pulled their ad out because I didn't put their press release in last week?", or something. So she'd have all these crises that she was left to deal with, and she'd turn to me.'

Watt was concerned that Furst did not have the time to devote to the fledging magazine.[32] 'Rob was an entrepreneur – he had a knitwear company, he ran nightclubs, he bought a pub and he started *Beat*.' He felt that, with an owner whose time was so divided, the publication was not geared to realise its potential. Over time, this became a source of discontent. 'I thought *Beat* had a lot more potential, that it should have been at the level that *On the Street* was in Sydney, which was thirty-six, maybe forty pages. *Beat* came out at twenty-four pages, and it stayed at twenty-four pages for months.' With the free press, the number of pages is determined by how much advertising has been sold – the more ads you have, the more pages you have. And the more pages you have, the more content you can fit in. 'And I thought, *This bloody thing, it's just not growing. And it's not growing because he doesn't seem to care about it.* I thought that *Beat* was not fulfilling its potential, and so another thing should be made available.'

Watt and Webber quickly defected from *Beat* and started a rival, *Inpress*. Arriving a little over a year after *Beat*, in 1988, *Inpress* immediately began to demonstrate the level of success that Watt had envisioned for *Beat* in its early days. By this point, he'd had some experience in the fledgling medium and so had an idea of how quickly it could grow; to his mind, street press had serious potential. Within months of launching, then, *Beat* had a serious competitor.

It began partly as Webber and Watt 'became really close', Watt recalls. 'I'd go in there on the Monday night and help her put *Beat* together, you know, we became really close mates,' Watt recalls on the beginnings of *Inpress*. 'And late one night we were complaining about this guy Rob, leaving her in charge and going off on his overseas trip. Obviously the bourbon was talking, but we decided it'd be great idea to start our own magazine – "That'll fix him, that'll teach this bloke for leaving you in charge of his business and not giving a shit about his business." Time would tell Rob obviously did give a big shit about his business, he cares a lot about it, but that was our perception at the time.'

As with many small publishing ventures, *Inpress* was made possible by naivety of youth. 'We were young,' he says with a laugh. 'I was twenty-six, she was twenty-four. It was a pretty brave thing to do to start your own business, in retrospect. It didn't feel brave at the time, though; it just felt like the natural thing to do.'

So as not to tip Furst off about their plans, Watt and Webber had to map out the first issue of *Inpress* in secret. 'By this stage I'd stopped being a lawyer and was working for [music promoter] Paul Dainty,' Watt says. 'So I spent half the day doing what I was supposed to do for Paul, which was work, and half the day on the phone to Rowena hatching our secret plot.'

There was a lot to work through in starting a new publication. The pair had to find offices, incorporate a name for the company they'd created, source computers ('We had one computer,' Watt laughs), gather writers, find an ad salesperson. It was no mean feat to do all this in secret, in an industry still so relatively small.

Watt had by this time developed a decent-sized list of industry contacts, and he worked through it in a frenzy as the pair attempted to make their dream a reality. 'I had relationships with people through the club scene, so we would talk to potential advertisers and say, "Between you and me, we're going to start our own music magazine, and when we start it, we want you to advertise." So we had the Metro nightclub, we had Chasers, we had Mushroom Records – which was sneaky because Amanda Pellman [who worked for Mushroom and had brought Watt onto *Beat* in the first place] was Rob's friend, that was difficult – ready to advertise in the first edition, so we sort of came out blazing with that first edition in that we already had full-page advertising.'

All of this, no matter how clandestine it seemed, had to be done in advance of the publication's launch because street press, as everyone knew by this point, requires ad money, lots of ad money; without it, you can't give anything away for free, and therefore, there is no magazine.

'It cost money, that first edition had to get printed.' Watt smiles. 'Forget paying people's wages – people were prepared to wait for a week to get paid, but cashflow-wise, the printer didn't want to wait for a week. We were a start-up business and he wanted to get paid before he printed the magazine. So we got a $10,000 overdraft from a bank, which I personally guaranteed – which was interesting, as I had no assets. Rumour at the time was that Paul Dainty was actually funding me, because I was working for him … which was a *long* way from the truth. In fact, he didn't even know I was doing it. I was using his office to make my phone calls and getting a wage from him, so poor old Paul had no idea I was moonlighting.'

On 13 July 1988, the first issue of *Inpress* finally hit the streets. Its maiden cover featured television presenter Richard Wilkins, who had not long before become the host of the newly launched (in Australia) MTV. The strapline read (Watt paraphrases): 'Does This Guy Have the Best Job in the World?'

The print run of that first issue was 12,000 copies, an impressive number by any measure. 'We printed 12,000 and told the advertisers we were doing 16,000. So I think we basically lied about our circulation initially, which most publications probably do.'

Nevertheless, the significance of *Inpress's* entry into the market was clear. Melbourne, in the space of a little under two years, had gone from having no street press to having two competing titles.

'He hated it!' Watt laughs when asked what Furst thought of it all once he found out. 'He was absolutely ropable that one of his trusted lieutenants, me, [had left], he felt like I was disloyal. And even worse, I'd taken Rowena away from him, this girl that he'd given an opportunity to. We didn't regard it as being disloyal, we felt he was wasting the opportunity with *Beat* to turn it into something that was really good. So I genuinely didn't feel disloyal, we felt that he almost had it coming. And of course he was angry, because he had a monopoly and in any market, having a monopoly is a much more attractive position, and the monopolist likes to keep that position. So of course he didn't want a competitor.'

As it turned out, though, this competition would work for both parties, not to mention the industry in Melbourne, which now had two papers in which to advertise and garner press for their artists. It became a battle that played out in page extents. 'We put out our first edition and we were twenty-eight pages. They were twenty-four,' Watt explains. 'The next week, Rob had twenty-eight.' Watt laughs. 'The following week, we went up to thirty-two pages, and the week after, he went to thirty-six. Then we went to forty. And so suddenly – because there was this war on the streets, with us both actively getting out there and selling ads and really pushing – suddenly all the advertisers around town were like, "This street press thing is really happening, we need to get involved." So where he seemed quite complacent with *Beat* stumbling along at twenty-four pages a week and not growing, within two months we were both over forty pages a week. We were making a little bit of money, and he was making a little bit of money as well. Whereas previously, he wasn't making any.'

According to Watt, Furst quickly came to the realisation that this was the best thing that could have happened. 'He didn't say that publicly and I didn't say it publicly. Publicly, we hated each other's guts … we'd go to a record launch or something, and people would be like, "Oh my god, Rob's over there and Andrew's over there, I hope they don't punch on or something" – which there was never any prospect of, but people thought there was absolute hatred. But beneath the surface, we both knew we were good for each other.'

So while street press was ticking along in Sydney, it was in Melbourne where it began to really bloom. Ads were cheap, compared to *RAM*, *Juke* and the daily papers, and discounts were offered for bands. Classifieds thrived, bringing in more money as the 1980s neared their end. This street war fuelled the medium, and led to street press spreading to other parts of the country as the music industry began to see how powerful it could be.

Both *Beat* and *Inpress* grew through the remainder of the 1980s and into the 1990s. And in a very short time they became a part of Melbourne, as *On the Street* was in the process of doing in Sydney, *X-Press* in Perth, and *Time Off* in Brisbane would slowly do too.

As Andrew Mast says, remembering his days working for both *Beat* and *Inpress*: 'Back when it started, there was almost a religious vibe – it was a *part* of your week. In Melbourne, you *had* to grab the street press before you went out on a Thursday night. Then you had to get the *EG* (from *The Age*) on the Friday. And they went hand in hand with the particular radio shows you're listening to, you know, Friday afternoons on PBS, then you'd switch to RRR on Friday night … so street press was part of that almost religiosity of how a music fan went about their week. There is no doubt about that.

'And the record stores were a part of that too,' he adds. 'You'd hit Gaslight or Missing Link or something like that after whenever your payday was, and you were usually buying stuff you'd read about the day before.' Street press, in its early days, was a boon to retailers as much as it was to the music industry and to fans.

* * *

Even though *Inpress* was flourishing, according to Watt these were still not easy times. As he tells it, there was never a period during his almost ten years of owning *Inpress* 'when I was able to sit back and go, "Gee, this is a comfortable little business, this is running itself. I don't need to come to work or collect debts, there's plenty of money in the bank, I can take a holiday from this."' There was never even a week where he felt that way. 'In retrospect, it really did wear you down. I was lying in bed awake at night, going, *Jesus, the print bill is getting up*. It was constantly a financial battle, right up until I was lucky enough to sell it. Someone bought it and I used the sale of the magazine to pay the debts we had, with a little bit left over for Rowena and me, but yeah, a constant battle to keep the doors open.'

The sale came out of the blue, just as Watt was beginning to wonder how he and Webber would keep everything together. On top of running the paper, he was also acting as a manager to a few musicians, while Webber had gotten married and was expecting her first child.

In 1997, Watt was in New Orleans producing demos with the artist Julia Darling. He rang Rowena, who was running the business alone in his absence. 'And she said, "Something weird just happened. A guy from Perth just rang saying he wants to talk to us about buying *Inpress*."'

This 'guy from Perth' was Joe Cipriani, whose company Columbia Press was publishing *X-Press* in the western capital. 'He was backed by Rural Press, which is a division of Fairfax,' Watt explains. 'He was given some money by them with the [directive] "You need to go forward and make some acquisitions in the street press space." And he targeted us. Which I was extremely thankful for.'

Since the advent of *X-Press* in 1985, Cipriani had looked to set a plan in motion. 'We always wanted to run *X-Press* as you would a proper newspaper, because in Western Australia the competition [for us] was with the newspaper industry and not necessarily at street level. So I looked for ways to break into the national market as a professional media group – we brokered a deal with Rural Press, who became 50 per cent shareholders in the newly formed Columbia Press.' It was during this fruitful fifteen-year relationship that Cipriani came to buy *Inpress*.

After the sale, Watt's and Webber's association with street press came to an end, but their legacy was to live on in *Inpress*, which by this stage had been taken to the collective bosom of industry and punters alike in Melbourne.

* * *

In 1989, a year after *Inpress* had begun its journey, another title joined Australia's street press, this one in Adelaide. Like Perth, the South Australian capital fosters its own cottage industry, its music and art scenes readily banding together in order to grow the whole. Street press was proving viable, which meant it was only a matter of time before it went national.

Through the late 1980s, publisher Margie Budich had been running a cover-priced monthly called *Network Magazine* out of Adelaide, which catered to the club, pub and film scene, but it wasn't particularly sustainable. The clubs and pubs Budich was working with needed a more frequent vehicle in which to advertise. *Network* petered off and she replaced it with a new, free weekly: *Rip It Up*, which went on to become one of Australia's key street press titles.[33]

An eight-page fold-over tabloid printed in black and white, *Rip It Up* hit the spot with local readers and music afficionados. 'It was a great thing,' remembers Robert Dunstan, who began as a freelancer not long after it started, moving up to co-editor in late 1994. 'I used to go and pick it up at a record store called Muses every Thursday. Every second Thursday was payday so I'd go there to buy a record and a grab a copy of *Rip It Up* to see who was coming to town that week.'

Budich, when she began the magazine, wasn't terribly aware of the growing street press scene that was beginning to boom on the east coast. She and her partner released the magazine for free due to the large amount of advertising they sourced straight up, given their existing connections. 'Well, I think the record companies saw the power of it, and it just became massive,' Budich surmises.

As Adelaide's music scene was small compared to Sydney's and Melbourne's, *Rip It Up* needed to account for that. Budich gave coverage over to theatre and food, aware that specialising in music in such a small market wouldn't have been sustainable. She viewed *Rip It Up* as part of the city's cottage music industry, in which everyone was close-knit and relied, to an extent, on everyone else. 'Yeah, we wanted to create a business, number one, but we were pretty close with a lot of the club owners and then we became very close with a lot of bands, musicians, and really it was to help them to create a business as well, make them successful,' she says. 'So we were having a ball, it was fun, and it was working. The whole industry just exploded overnight.'

As such, the magazine grew at a rapid clip. According to Robert Dunstan, 'Margie started the magazine, and her partner got involved, and all of a sudden she thought, *I need a salesperson.*' He laughs. 'And then, *I need an office, I can't work from home.* So she got an office in the city. And then she needed a receptionist. Now, *I need a graphic designer to put this thing together because it's getting too big.* Now, *I need two sales people.* And it just grew from there. And she needed an editor: *I can't be doing all this myself!* So it was me and another guy, we were co-editors, and there was also an assistant editor as well. I mean, back in the early days she'd deliver it herself, drive around the city with the mags and drop them off at the pubs. And that got too much, so … we had uni students delivering it, for $50 a [batch].'

Rip It Up was riding the street press wave, quickly becoming an important part of the small yet fertile scene Adelaide was fostering. For Budich, it was a heady time, a period not just of financial success, but of good times born of being a part of it all, covering it all, not wanting to stop being immersed in all that was going on. Budich and her partner also started a publication focused on dance music and one on fashion, both free, in the same vein as *Rip It Up*. 'There were two big nightclubs, Planet and Heaven. They wanted to start a dance magazine, so we started a fortnightly dance magazine called *Onion*. And then we started a monthly fashion mag called *Attitude*. And they all just went through the roof, it was crazy.' Budich laughs.

It was this passion and energy that would see *Rip It Up* continue for many years to come, ensuring that Adelaide wasn't ever lacking cultural coverage.

As street press spread around the country, having now been in existence for almost a decade, it caused flow-on effects. Its proliferation finally spelled the end for *RAM*, the magazine fading out in 1989, gasping for ad money as it went. *RAM* had met its match, and that match was street press, which, it had to be acknowledged by even the most ardent of detractors, was now more than a collection of inky, low-rent rags; it was a cultural force.

16

BOOM TOWN

'We were constantly reviving people
and calling the police.'

Margaret Cott

Margaret Cott simmered with anger. She sat in her Surrey Hills office late on a Thursday afternoon in September 1990 and took a deep breath, trying to keep calm.

The past few years had taken their toll. *On the Street* was thriving – having survived the market crash and subsequent recession of the late 1980s, *On the Street* had prospered, becoming the best-regarded street press title in the country. With Margaret's sister Jenny running the sales department, the Cotts had put in the work, and it had paid off – from humble beginnings as a literal pamphlet tucked into local news rag *City Express*, *On the Street* was now a trusted, independent weekly chronicle of Sydney's ever-growing music scene.

And yet despite the prosperity, the past couple of years had presented a problem, and this problem was about to become the catalyst for a major upheaval, not just in Cott's world, but across the Australian rock press as a whole. That problem? *On the Street*'s majority shareholder, Noel Crabbe.

Until the late 1980s, Crabbe had been content, as *On the Street*'s associate editor Michael Smith says, to be 'the ghost publisher': 'Margaret and Jenny would pay him his slice of the pie every half year or whatever.'

According to Smith, Crabbe had little to do with the running of the title in the first years of its life; yet several of his other business ventures had suffered in the market crash, and so seeing this venture growing, with the potential to grow even further, he changed his focus. 'Noel comes in and decides he's going to run the paper properly,' Smith remembers. 'His background is in accountancy, so he's just looking at the figures. Knows nothing about music, knows less about the scene.'

'You have to understand that we came from a background where if we took a pen out of the stationery cupboard, the accountant would come and say, "Who took a pen," you know?' says Margaret Cott. 'We really lived on the smell of an oily rag. So when the business started to turn into a positive, the silent partner, who was Noel Crabbe, started to get noisy. That's the best description. Noel had lots of business in America, and he really suffered from the exchange rate. And he basically,' she pauses to laugh, 'used to take the money that we so carefully squirrelled away … and he had every right to, he was the majority shareholder, he had every right to do it … he put it down to dividends.'

Smith recalls that Crabbe 'started instituting this, prompting that, and essentially was making all these really weird decisions, unnecessary decisions that had nothing to do with the magazine or the direction of the magazine or the music scene or anything else. He was trying to figure out how to make more money out of it.'

'He should have just left the bloody thing alone,' opines Tony Mott, who started as a freelancer for *On the Street* in 1983. 'It was working fine. I don't know why he thought he needed to get involved.'

Cott, Smith and Mott do not seem to bear any ill will toward Crabbe these days, but at the time, as Cott says, despite whether he was entitled to the money, 'it just didn't sit well with us'. And so tensions built, not that the public would know it – the staff continued to produce the highest quality weekly product they could, a strong mix of editorial and advertising. The latter of course was where the money was coming from: the root of the impending upheaval.

The breaking point came when Crabbe allegedly began making arbitrary staffing decisions. 'When he started summarily dismissing people because he didn't like them, that was it,' Smith says ruefully.

Late on a Thursday in early September 1990, Crabbe had allegedly threatened to fire the publication's accountant, Maggie Scott. Cott's simmering anger came to the boil, and she stormed out of her office and into Crabbe's. 'I said, "If you fire the accountant, I'm walking out."' says Cott. 'And so by the time I'd said, "I've had enough, I'm going, you all know what you're doing, you don't need me anyway, if you're gonna fire poor old Maggie the accountant, I'm gone," by the time I'd walked downstairs, Michael Smith was there, Jack Marx – there was a whole team standing down there saying, "We're going too."'

And so, on Thursday 6 September 1990, the day after issue number 505 had hit the street, every member of the editorial staff walked out of *On the Street*'s office, never to return.

* * *

As the immediate future of *On the Street* hung in the balance, up north in Brisbane, things were looking up. *Time Off*, from university beginnings on the leafy University of Queensland campus, hadn't managed to achieve the same success throughout the 1980s as *On the Street* in Sydney and *Inpress* and *Beat* in Melbourne. It had managed to survive as part of Fortescue Media, mainly as a culture magazine, and while it slowly began to add more music to its coverage towards the end of the decade, under a number of early editors who were career journalists, as opposed to afficionados of the bustling Brisbane rock scene, it stayed the course but did not grow exponentially.[34]

However, in 1987, a young freelancer had made his debut for the magazine: one Sean Sennett. Sennett's first published work as a freelance writer was a review of a book by one of his university lecturers, Ross Fitzgerald, which ran in *The Age* and garnered him $100. His first foray into *Time Off*, later that same year, was a review of a Cockroaches show at Dreamworld, where he worked part-time. 'I went to meet the [*Time Off*] guy to get a cheque, he put it in my hand, and as I was walking out I thought, *Great, another $100!* I opened it up and it was $15.' Street press, as Sennett found out, paid a lot less than the metro dailies.

Sennett, an avid music fan, made himself indispensable to *Time Off* over the next couple of years, writing on anything and everything, cashing in on the music boom associated with World Expo 88, which ran in Brisbane that year. By 1989, he was sitting in the deputy editor's chair, effectively running the magazine.

The market crash affected Fortescue Media as well, and so come 1990, around the time the staff of *On the Street* staged their legendary walk-out, *Time Off* entered receivership, and its days looked numbered. For Sennett, this presented an opportunity. The receivers 'wanted to sell it, and me and another person put in a bid to get it, didn't get it, then me and two other guys put a bid in and we got it,' Sennett explains. His two partners quite quickly 'fell off the twig', and so Sennett, three years on from joining *Time Off* as a young, music-obsessed rock-journo wannabe, now owned the paper. This was the kick the magazine needed to enter the big time.

Time Off grew over the next few years, in part due to the fact that Sennett was an unabashed music fanatic. 'I think what happened was … it was the only mag around Australia that was owned by an editorial person and not an advertising person,' Sennett opines.

'We did our best, and it would probably have been a bit amateur compared to today's standards, but it was just a really, really great, fun time. It was like we were given the key to the city.'

What also helped *Time Off* find its feet was the growth of the Brisbane music scene itself in the early 1990s. Long regarded as a 'large country town' by those from Sydney and Melbourne, Brisbane was starting to throw off the yokel tag bestowed upon their local record companies, media groups and bands. 'There was a real drive in Brisbane at the time with the record guys in particular, they didn't want to be an outpost,' Sennett explains. 'They wanted to get bands signed [in Brisbane] and start getting interviews exclusively. These guys really wanted to see stuff in *Time Off*, so we were in a situation where we'd often be getting the drop on *The Courier-Mail* on an interview, because [the local record companies] thought if we do *Time Off* to [20,000] people who really care about what's in it, it's gotta be better than being in *The Courier-Mail*, stuck on page 57.'

And so street press had properly arrived in Brisbane, and for Sennett, it was intoxicating. 'We'd go to gigs every night, or there'd be a movie preview on,' he enthuses. 'I used to keep a journal of the movies I saw, and there were three years straight that I saw 100 films at the cinema! Twice a week, go to the movies. Plus the amount of gigs was fantastic. And, you know, what it's like to speak to someone for the first time, like, you get to talk to someone like Tim Finn or Steven Cummings – wow, these people are legends!'

Sennett was in his element, and as the 1990s rolled on, *Time Off* was becoming the publishing power Brisbane deserved.

* * *

The irony was not lost on the staff of *On the Street* that many found themselves exactly where they had been nine years earlier, after all that time spent building the publication into a force. By this point, 1990, street press had killed off *RAM*; *Juke* was flailing, continuing only because it had some financial clout behind it in the form of Fairfax.

The *On the Street* staff milled about out the front of the paper's offices for a few minutes before drifting in the general direction of the pub – a natural decision for a clutch of journalists, particularly ones without a job, and indeed for many, without any prospects of one. 'We all went down to the Excelsior and grizzled and groaned for a couple of hours and then said, "Oh shit, we're all unemployed, what are we going to do?"' laughs Michael Smith.

There were around a dozen of them – members of the art department, advertising and sales, Jenny and Margaret Cott, photographer Tony Mott, writer Jack Marx. A family, as Smith calls them more than once. The group was pondering a financial climate not exactly sympathetic to those wanting to find quick work. According to Cott, it was simple: 'Okay, we're all unemployed, we've all got rent to pay in two weeks' time, next week, you know, what are we gonna do? So we thought, *Okay, we'll put a newspaper out.*'

At the time, in the front bar at the local pub, a few schooners downed, lamenting on the knowledge and passion they had in spades, this would have gone down a treat. In hindsight, it was a ludicrous project to embark on, full of logistical challenges, and yet, with that rather blasé statement, the idea for a paper was birthed. And not just any paper. For the result of this front bar session was *Drum Media*, the free paper that was to become the best of them all.

The idea was solidified several days after the pub session, as Cott fronted a rally outside Sydney Town Hall, protesting the imminent 'rationalisation of Triple J', where 'under new management playlists had become stricter, current affairs programmes were axed and staff were set to lose jobs', explains Cott of the Free the Jays event. 'I'm going, "Well, we're gonna start a new paper,"' she says, 'and people are going, "What's it called?" Well, I don't know! Anyway, we hadn't even registered a name, we thought we'd better go down and do that.

'We wanted to call it *The Drum*,' she continues, 'and they said, no you can't do that ... because of the rollie tobacco and this and that, so we just whacked a 'media' on it, and thought, *that sounds great, how about* The Drum Media? Okay, that's good. Anyway, so that took a good fifteen minutes of thought!'

Of course, nothing much could be done without money. As Smith remembers it, the Cott sisters had some money saved that they were going to put towards a house. Independent publisher and music industry heavyweight Phil Tripp lent them $10,000,[35] and the Cotts' aunt, herself a successful businesswoman in her time, remortgaged her house to make up the rest, such was her belief in her nieces. 'To this day, I don't think I've met a more generous person, really,' Cott says with a smile. 'Such a lot of faith in us.' From there, by all accounts, it all fell relatively easily into place.

It all came together incredibly fast – within twelve days from idea to printed issue. Smith says the Cott sisters marshalled their relationships. 'They had been doing it for half a dozen years so knew the mechanics of it, and thankfully they had a good enough name and reputation for doing the right thing by people, and that's all it is,' he says. 'Same as any other business, if you're looking after your advertisers, they'll come with you, and that's what happened, they came with us.'

'How did we do it? I think we just knew what to do, it was too easy.' Cott smiles. 'The hardest bit was we had absolutely no furniture! We ended up in the Roosevelt building up at Orwell Street, which was a goldfish bowl right up there at the Cross, and people were constantly overdosing outside the window.' She laughs at the gruesome memory of it all. 'We were constantly reviving people and calling the police.'

As far as Smith was concerned, once they'd secured premises and found enough chairs and tables, it was as though nothing had changed. *On the Street* had built up a solid reputation within the industry over the past decade, its staff cultivating strong relationships, and so starting a magazine of the ilk of *Drum*[36] was as relatively simple as making dozens of phone calls and then filling pages – as they'd been doing the previous week, but now for themselves. 'Literally just turning up to the office, having a look at everything that was around, phoning people up, you know, chasing stuff, getting onto record companies, business as usual essentially,' Smith remembers. 'I'd read a book, so I wrote a review – it ended up being 1000 words long. Filled a bit of the magazine.'

On Tuesday 18 September, the first issue of *Drum Media* hit the streets, appearing as if from nowhere. Adorning the maiden cover was Midnight Oil, still riding high on the release of *Blue Sky Mining* seven months earlier. In big, bold print at the top of the page was 'Issue No. 1', and underneath it a very ambitious 'Distribution: 40,000' – ambitious in that with its first issue, *Drum* had printed 25 per cent more copies than *On the Street* ever shifted, even when it was the only game in town.

'Yeah, I think we were a bit optimistic.' Cott laughs. 'I think we may have overreached.'

That first issue was no lightweight. At forty-eight pages, it was shorter than the concurrent issues of *On the Street*, which miraculously continued to appear in the following weeks, but by year's end it had hit seventy-two pages, thanks to a solid classifieds section and a slew of advertising and editorial, for the most part provided by freelancers who'd followed the team over from their now-competitor. The fact it appeared on a Tuesday too, a full day before *On the Street*, was a small but effective dig.

A triumphant editorial appeared on page 2 of the first issue under the title 'Welcome to *The Drum Media* – the New Kids on the Block!':

> Everything from this point in time is focused on the future. *The Drum Media* brings excitement back to publishing this week and every week. *The Drum* will bring you the latest beats on the Arts, entertainment, the sciences, social issues, travel, health, video, books, dance events, restaurants, overseas music but above all a commitment to the independent music scene. We are here both for the advertiser and the reader. With a circulation of 40,000 we want to reach further than publications have reached before whilst taking a serious stand on social issues like our front cover feature artists, Midnight Oil. We intend to 'Publish or be damned'! *The Drum* offers a bright, new hope in the media maelstrom that is the nineties. With your support, *The Drum* will become the back beat of Sydney life – no formulae, no favouritism, no bullshit. The time for change has arrived, and we will be delivering it each and every Tuesday.

The similarities between this editorial and the one written by Tony Schauble back in 1966 to herald the arrival of *Go-Set* are amusingly obvious. The time-for-change motifs; the 'no bullshit' sentiment; power-to-the-people phrases such as 'We intend to "Publish or be damned!"' – both magazines saw themselves as The Alternative, the one to take notice of. *Look out you squares, here comes the real shit*, they were saying.

The test of the team's resolve in following a dictate of 'Publish or be damned' came sooner than thought. Noel Crabbe applied to the Supreme Court for an injunction to stop *The Drum* being published, alleging that Jennifer Cott had stolen advertising contacts, an action which ultimately failed.[37] As Margaret Cott says, 'We went into a legal battle with Noel. He said that because I was a director of the company I had my fiduciary duties, I hadn't resigned as a director. [The court] initially put interlocutory control on us, but within a week the court had lifted [it] and said you can now publish.' She smiles, adding, 'And we said, that's good, because we'd already, you know, essentially we'd already done it.'

The legal action went on 'for probably a year and a half', according to Cott. 'And it was really expensive, as you can imagine, we were in and out of court ... But we had good legal counsel.'

One of the hardest aspects for the team early on was coming to terms with what they were doing. They'd started a paper as a direct competitor to a publication they'd all built up together; as Cott says, it was challenging. 'We knew how good they were because we'd built it to that point, so it was like we were fighting ourselves,' she says. It was some time before that feeling faded.

Support came thick and fast, however. The Cotts, and by association *Drum*, had an 'amazing' support network. At the time, the independent operators in the music industry readily banded together to support one another, be they publications, labels, clothing lines, record shops. *Drum* carried weight from that very first issue.

In fact, in the first issue were testimonials and messages of support from various industry peers. Scott Pullen from Free Style Promotions wrote, 'Congratulations Everyone!!! See, there is strength in unity.'

'Congratulations on your new magazine!!!' echoed publicist Miranda Brown.

A slew of congratulatory messages printed in the second issue confirmed what the staff had hoped – 'We Think They Like US!' read the small headline. On the opposite page was a Quote of the Week (which became a regular feature) from Michael Smith: 'Never have so many had to put up with so much for so little ... AND WON!' The jubilant tone was for good reason: now they marched to the beat of their own drum.

From issue number two a week later – which featured on the cover Jon Marsh and Steve Waddington of British electronic music group

The Beloved, decked out in newly minted *Drum Media* t-shirts, shot by Tony Mott – the publication's circulation figure (not CAB-audited at that point)[38] dropped to 10,000. This conservative number was as there were still so many copies of issue 1 lying about. 'By the third issue sanity prevailed and we settled to a weekly print run of around 30,000,' Cott says, which is where it stayed for some time. But the numbers hardly mattered. The point was that *Drum* had hit the streets successfully, coming together in under a fortnight, born in the front bar of a pub in Surry Hills as a clutch of music journos and ad staff contemplated their futures.

* * *

By the early 1990s, the rock 'n' roll media landscape had well and truly changed. *RAM* was gone, and in late 1993 *Juke* followed suit, unable to compete with the numerous grassroots free press publications. *Rolling Stone*, whose readership and production values were more sophisticated than street press, was going strong, and had attracted a like-minded competitor in *Juice*. *Rhythms* magazine was just getting off the ground, and specialist publications such as *Australian Guitar* were soon to be occupying their own niche.

But street press was reigning supreme. A little over a decade since the appearance of *On the Street*, the medium was now regarded as powerful. These were the papers those in the music industry clamoured to advertise in because they knew that the publications were being picked up in their thousands every single week, all around the country. Street press was booming, and the industry, the bands, the punters, all were benefiting.

It wasn't just the larger cities to which street press was now confined. *Forte* appeared in Geelong in 1991; *Rip It Up* picked up a competitor in Adelaide in *dB* the same year; *BMA* launched in Canberra in 1992; and *Mixdown* (more aimed more at musicians than fans with its reviews of equipment and gear) came out of Furst Media, and was distributed nationally, in 1993.[39]

This was now the age of street press.

* * *

Only a year and a half after Sean Sennett wrested control of *Time Off* from the receivers and began to revive it in 1990, over on the other side of Brisbane's Fortitude Valley a competing title emerged, looking to cash in on the strength of this form of publishing.

Rave appeared on streets in October 1991, spearheaded by Linda Woodhead, who had begun her street press career in the ad sales department at *Time Off* in 1987, when Fortescue Media were publishing the magazine, along with a string of other papers. 'We had our own printing press, which is quite unique,' Woodhead remembers, adding with a laugh, 'it was an awful press, it had come out of a fire from Papua New Guinea. It was just terrible.'

Not long after she joined the company, however, the stock market crash of 1988 took a heavy toll on Fortescue Media. 'So literally within a day, the receivers came in and closed up shop,' Woodhead recalls. Woodhead, the manager of sales for all titles under the publishing umbrella, was asked to stay on to keep sales turning while the receivers looked for a new owner. This eventually ended up being Sean Sennett, along with his partners Russell Hunter (who'd been with *Time Off* for some time) and Godfrey Scoullar. Woodhead then left, only to be asked by Hunter to come back for a spell in order to help with sales.

'I'd just had a baby, actually,' she says. 'He said, "Can you come back and help us with some sales?" And so I went back for probably only a few months, but just didn't really love the direction or what was happening, it just didn't gel. So I left ... Sean had stepped in as editor, everybody had kind of left, it was the new guys, so I just didn't want to be there.'

Woodhead began thinking. And she decided to get 'the band back together', assembling a good number of the crew she'd been working with prior to the magazine being sold and got down to the business of starting her own competing title. This, predictably, didn't sit too well with *Time Off*'s new owners, Russell Hunter in particular. 'Back then, they would have had all the ad contacts, so [*Time Off*] initiated taking them to court to put [an injunction] on them for six months, because they were salespeople, they sold the ads,' Sennett says, laughing. 'They were ambitious, they wanted to own the magazine, which I understand.'

'They did take me to court to try to stop me launching, which was funny,' Woodhead says. 'They just felt I had an unfair advantage in the marketplace because I knew everybody. The court case went for a couple of days, and what was handed down was basically ... we had an injunction, so for the first four weeks there was a list they came up with of about twenty or thirty people that we weren't allowed to approach for advertising. It was a bit silly, because we *could* speak to them about editorial.' And so *Rave* was off and running.

Woodhead's vision for the magazine was essentially to tap deep into the local music scene, an idea that was close to her heart, having worked for small music papers back in the United Kingdom before moving to Australia. 'Something that was a voice for music in Brisbane,' she sums up her ambition for *Rave*. 'Gavin Sawford was the driving force as the editor, and I certainly allowed that and welcomed that; he was very in tune with the Brisbane scene. It was really about supporting the local band scene, and it wasn't just Brisbane, it was Brisbane and the Gold Coast, the Sunshine Coast and out to Toowoomba.

'We were very much about the music,' she continues. 'We did have a section within the magazine for the arts – theatre and cinema and stuff – but generally *Rave* was more about the music [than *Time*

Off], because I think we just had better inroads with some of the record companies, some of the touring and publicity people. We were probably a bit more on the alternative side.' Brisbane's music-going public readily embraced the new kid on the block, the fact there were now two papers a bonus for punters and industry alike. 'Yes, 100 per cent,' Woodhead agrees.

'I guess Brisbane supported two for a while, and it was kind of interesting. They were very good salespeople, they had that down,' says Sennett. 'We had very good editorial … they used to play the underdog card: "We're struggling, *Time Off* is the big, iconic thing." So occasionally we'd really suffer because people would say, "You can do an REM story, but we'll take out the ad with *Rave*, because they're struggling." We're like, "No, no, can you please put the money in our account, we have to pay people as well!"'

Rave's run under Woodhead was sweet but short. Having created a viable alternative to *Time Off*, family circumstances led to her selling the title in 1996 to her printers, who coincidentally were on 'a bit of an acquisition trail' at the time. 'They asked if we were interested in selling, I said make me an offer, they did. It was hard work. I'd had three kids in that time – I'd say goodbye to them on a Monday and hello on a Wednesday because we'd work until four or five o'clock in the morning on a Tuesday!'

Woodhead happily gave away the weekly street press grind, a job well done behind her to show for it. *Rave*'s printers, no doubt buoyed by the fact they owned one of only two street press papers in Brisbane, saw an opportunity to knock *Time Off* its perch. Sennett recalls that they came to him and said, 'We're going to crush you, we're going to undercut all your ads, we're going to print double the copies you print, we're just going to obliterate *Time Off*.' 'I thought, *Wow, that's really serious*. Because they wanted to be the only game in town.'

It was tough talk, but Sennett wasn't shaken by it, and history proved his approach the right one. *Time Off* prospered under his control, growing steadily through the 1990s as street press blossomed throughout the city, and the country.

* * *

Brisbane, with its engaged live music scene, was such fertile ground for street press that in 1993 yet another free paper emerged. The new title, *Scene*, joined *Time Off* and *Rave*.

No other Australian capital had three street press titles. To an outsider it would have seemed like overkill – indeed, utterly unsustainable. And yet despite the fact that no one would have predicted it at the time, these three titles would co-exist in Brisbane for decades, highlighting how strong that city's music scene and industry are.

Scene began as *Club Scene*, founded by graphic artist Rohan Duggan. Duggan asked his brother, Howard, to come on board to sell ads; as Howard was quoted as saying in *Scene*'s 1000th issue though, 'he nicked off and I'm still here'. The name change to *Scene* happened within a few months, but the magazine's involvement with the burgeoning club scene was to stick for years, and became the paper's point of difference – whereas *Rave* was all across punk rock, and *Time Off* was very much a rock 'n' roll paper, *Scene* attached itself in the main to the growing rave culture. All three titles, then, found the readership to flourish in the northern capital – even when a fourth South East Queensland street press paper, *Tsunami*, based on the Sunshine Coast, popped up in 1999.

'We were unaware that street press even existed,' Howard Duggan says on the brothers' decision to launch another paper onto Brisbane's streets in 1993. 'If we had, we probably wouldn't have started it. I don't know what was in Rohan's mind – this was very much his idea.' They stuck with it though, and it began to grow. 'The rave scene was just blowing up. It'd been going in Europe for five or six years, but it was just blowing up here in Brisbane … so we were clubbing, fashion. We kicked off with a gay column, which of course no one bats an eyelid [about] now, but it was not your standard fare in *Drum Media* or *Time Off* in 1993, I can assure you.'

Howard Duggan placed stock in innovation, and was not content to rely on a single street press title to sustain what he saw as a growing company. He and his group opened Café Scene – an internet café on the bustling corner of Brunswick and Ann, right in the heart of Brisbane's throbbing Fortitude Valley. 'In the nineties, our star was rising very rapidly insofar as we had started Café Scene, that was two or three years old, and we were pioneers in this,' Duggan says. 'We traded twenty-four hours a day, 364 days a year ('cos Mum wouldn't let us open on Easter). We were an internet café, we were a ticket outlet, we were very avant-garde … [*Scene*] had commitments to the arts, we had a full-time arts editor, we had the gay column, we were the first to get a gloss cover. So I didn't feel competition. I felt we were racing past everybody; our competitors didn't have colour on every page. Didn't have gloss, didn't have a café that traded 24/7 right in the heart of everything.'

It's often said within the music industry that you need to be a certain type of person to be a festival promoter – calculated, canny, uncompromising. The same can be said for publishers of print papers, and Howard Duggan is no exception. A tall, lanky Englishman, balding, with dark penetrating eyes, he does not fuck around. If he doesn't like something, he will tell you to your face. If he wants to do something he thinks will benefit his business (and, to be fair, the Brisbane music scene), he will move mountains to make it happen.

It doesn't always work and, often, it will put people offside; there are many in the industry who are of the opinion that Howard Duggan is not a gentleman. Everyone is entitled to their opinion, of course, and he could not care less: as the 1990s entered its second half, he was busy hustling, building Brisbane's third free paper. From the outside, everyone was benefiting.

* * *

Nothing blooms forever, though, and the free press was no exception. Street press's first casualty was its oldest member. The demise of *On the Street* perhaps seemed inevitable once its staff walked out in September 1990, but despite what many predicted at the time, it didn't immediately fade into obscurity. The first issue following the walk-out appeared on the Wednesday morning as usual, and while it had less pages than previous editions, it was of reasonable quality nonetheless.

The masthead listed no one other than Tony Mott (who was very loyal to the Cott sisters and who was also listed in *Drum*), and yet it was advertising as usual, editorial as usual, largely because the bulk of the content had already been locked in prior to the exodus. From the 26 September issue, though, the editor-in-chief was listed as Scott Howlett, recruited from *X-Press* in Perth, a young journalist who wrote the bulk of the magazine's features for some time. For a while it seemed *On the Street* had survived and Sydney now had two competing street press titles.

Yet while it may not have been evident from a reader's point of view, the publication was anything but stable. Howlett was the first of an estimated twenty editors from September 1990 until the publication's demise in late 1996, one of whom, for a short stint, was publisher Noel Crabbe himself. An article that appeared in the Spectrum section of *The Sydney Morning Herald* in June 1996 written by Malcolm Knox quoted an *On the Street* staffer as saying the previous two years were 'total chaos'.

Crabbe eventually disappeared from view, his last mention in *On the Street* being as part of the advertising team. This came in the 9 September 1996 issue, an edition notable for having no other staff listed on the masthead. A new publisher, Lisa Walton, was listed in the following issue, along with a new editor, Alvin Stone, replacing editor Andrew Hunter and managing editor Mark Cushway. This team remained unchanged until the final issue on 11 December that same year.

Stone believes that Crabbe didn't really understand how important distribution was to street press and so, in order to save money, had been cutting back on copies. By this stage as well, the magazine's reputation had plummeted, in part due to its instability. Stone and Walton decided to walk; the magazine was 'going nowhere' in their eyes. And in fact it was true. *On the Street* wound up when they left. Today it exists only in personal collections and on dusty shelves in the storage facilities of the New South Wales State Library. And yet its impact had been profound, and changed the course of Australian street press forever.

17

LET'S GET NATIONAL

'They'd lost enough clients,
they'd been made to look stupid.'

Howard Duggan

By the turn of the millennium, street press wasn't just a powerful publishing medium, it was a vital part of the music industry. It's like it had always been there. It was unthinkable for a music fan to head out on a Friday night not having picked up one of myriad titles occupying space on record-store countertops, on top of cigarette machines in front bars or on the pavement outside the local café in order to see who was playing where.

Rob Furst in Melbourne, the Cott sisters in Sydney, Sean Sennett in Brisbane and Joe Cipriani in Perth were all publishing leading titles. Howard Duggan was also operating in Brisbane, Margaret Budich in Adelaide, others dotted around the smaller cities and regional centres, with titles including *dB*, *BMA*, *Forte*, *Mixdown*, *Tsunami*, *3D World*. The streets were littered with words and everyone was thriving. This was their time.

In Melbourne, this was not going unnoticed. Craig and Leigh Treweek, both in the restaurant business, had an eye on this still-growing publishing medium, and as keen businessmen, they wanted a piece. Craig made the leap first, moving over to *Inpress* (then being published in a fifty-fifty split by Cipriani's Columbia Press in Perth and Rural Press in Melbourne) as sales manager in August 1998. He came into 'the most disastrous businesses I've ever walked into'. Both Treweeks are natural businessmen, though, and so within eight weeks, Craig had the magazine breaking even. 'It was a bit of a basket case,' Leigh Treweek says, laughing, 'but Craig started to turn it around.'

Rural Press were looking to unload the struggling Melbourne title, while Cipriani's Columbia Press had plans to expand up the east coast. And so *Inpress's* business manager, Brian Peacock, stepped in to buy it, offering Craig a slice of the action. '[Peacock] was looking at buying the magazine and saw that Craig was turning it around and said to Craig, "Do you want to come in and buy the magazine?"' Leigh says. This was all in the first months of Craig making the switch from hospitality to publishing.

'I fell in love with publishing,' Craig confirms. 'Not with street press, but I fell in love with publishing. Weekly deadlines, the thrill of it. All that kind of stuff.'

Peacock, who was already known within the industry as a musician and later manager of Perth band Eurogliders, among other acts, approached Craig to buy *Inpress* with him via a vendor agreement. Craig didn't have the money at the time, so Peacock said he'd put up what was required, and Craig took control of 45 per cent, he and Peacock operating as Dharma Media.

Leigh Treweek then came on board in sales, selling ads for the magazine's dance insert 'Zebra'. 'I grew the sales in the first year; I took it over and it tripled or quadrupled,' he recalls. 'So from there we built a magazine that had been doing thirty-six to forty-four pages up to fifty-two pages at times in 'Zebra' alone. And then in *Inpress*, the rock side, we were doing 100 pages [between] each magazine. We built it solidly, created the relationships and took it back. I think the biggest thing that was done was the change in backing good people. Basically Craig gave the responsibilities to people like Myf [Warhurst, the editor at the time] on the editorial side, and said, "So we've got a sales team that sells ads, an editorial team that creates great editorial. If you're creating great editorial then people will read it and then people will want to advertise." And we got rid of all the selling of cheap ads and all that, and really went for content.'

Herein, however, lies a double-edged sword, one which has sparked its fair share of detractors of the medium. Street press is, and always has been, a breeding ground for new writers. The small amounts of money paid for articles, relative to the major metro dailies, *Rolling Stone* and a slew of other higher-echelon titles, meant writers who progressed their careers ultimately spent less time writing for street press. The bulk of the words, then, were penned by up-and-comers, and it's fair to say a lot of this content was far from brilliant.

Street press, though, is about passion. Whether a writer is unseasoned or a pro, he or she writes for this medium because they love music, love writing, love the music scene. This is why contributors such as Jeff Jenkins, Anthony Carew, Cyclone and many others continued writing for street press for a long time.

'I think we create opportunities for young journalists to come in, but we don't expect them to be with us forever, we expect them to move on to bigger and better things,' Leigh Treweek reasons. But 'the passion for [music journalism] means we have people writing for us who get their $1000 or $1200 writing for *The Age* but are still gonna do the $50 story with us, because it's that passion, they love it. That's what makes street press so good, no matter who's coming through it … we've always invested in the people, because that's what makes what we do work.'

Inpress had been floundering, having left Andrew Watt's hands some time before and coming under control of a joint company, half of which was based on the other side of the country. The Treweeks turned that around, and with Brian Peacock, the paper began to flourish once more, taking its place alongside *Beat* as part of Melbourne's grimy street scene. And the Treweeks were far from finished; acquiring a stake in *Inpress* was one thing, but these two had plans. Big, big plans.

* * *

The majority of street press publishers, whether they published for a couple of years or a couple of decades, worked on a single title. Their focus was on one paper, one town or region. Yet as the new century dawned, the idea of a national network of magazines became the reality, and even the norm – papers in multiple cities run by one publishing group, offering a coast's worth of coverage to advertisers.

These publishers were businesspeople, after all, and no matter how many of them professed to love music (and most did and still do), the endgame was making money. The more titles you have, the greater the potential to add to the bottom line. Such is the logic of capitalism.

In 2002, Howard Duggan, still at the helm of Brisbane-based *Scene*, decided the time was ripe for expansion. He was ready to take this magazine, which had been a part of Brisbane's cultural make-up for almost a decade, national. And why not? To his mind, *Scene* was *the* street press publication, so why not share it with more readers?

'I don't know whether it's true or not – I wouldn't testify to it in court – but I am certainly aware of being the first publisher with ideas of being genuinely national,' he says. 'I mean, it was a case of which city first. I had a good-faith belief that we were the market leader by a country mile here [in Brisbane]. *Rave* were doing the punk scene and doing it very well, much better than we were. And I think *Time Off* were doing very well with the old six-string, middle-of-the-road [rock 'n' roll]; the most dangerous thing that I recall them getting was Powderfinger. Perhaps I just wasn't looking hard enough and perhaps they were doing great things. What I do know is that our distribution was brilliant. We had more page numbers, we had more advertisers and we were booking the business.'

Howard Duggan is nothing if not confident, and so the decision was made to bring out a title in Melbourne, expanding Duggan's media empire, as he saw it. This wasn't done lightly, of course; it wasn't a quick decision. But to many who were aware of the influence of Melbourne titles *Beat* and *Inpress* – how utterly entrenched within the grey-skied southern capital they were – this seemed an odd move, and one destined to fail. Both *Beat* and *Inpress* had been running for almost twenty years, twice as long as *Scene*.

Duggan re-mortgaged his house to fund the venture, so sure was he that he could do down south what he'd accomplished in Brisbane. He viewed both *Beat* and *Inpress* as vibrant, but certainly no better than his own magazine. Both these titles were very focused on rock 'n' roll – naturally enough, given the strength at that time of Melbourne's live rock scene – and while *Scene* did cover that aspect of the industry, it was better known for covering club music and the arts, which Duggan felt would stand them in good stead in Victoria.

'They did both have [club sections] at the time, and they had loyalty,' Duggan recalls, referencing 'Zebra' in *Inpress* and '100%' in *Beat*. 'My recollection is that *Beat* was more gauche and mainstream with its clubbing, not very sophisticated, whereas *Inpress* had the cooler clubs and the better-branded clubs. But at the end of the day, they were inserts, they were an afterthought. There was no 'God is a DJ' on the front cover [a cover story on Welsh DJ Sasha, named for the Faithless song], which is what the rave scene was pushing out in the late 1990s and the early 2000s.'

To Duggan's mind, *Scene* would fit right in, find its niche straight away and prosper. He describes his way of thinking as a combination of the 'bravado of youth' and the fact 'that I'm a balls-out publisher and I have been like that, it's in my DNA'.

And so in early 2003 *Scene* set up offices in Johnson Street, in the working-class inner-north Melbourne suburb of Collingwood. The first issue of the Melbourne edition of *Scene* hit the street in March that year, and while initial reader reception might be hard to gauge, the reception from 'clubs, our Queensland advertisers who operated nationally, national clients such as HMV and local clients looking for an alternative' was terrific, according to Duggan.

But ultimately, Melbourne is a rock 'n' roll town, a stubborn and shadowy city, one much more inclined to favour sticky carpet and six scruffy strings over a DJ, despite how strong its club scene might have been. *Scene* lasted in Melbourne for around a year before Duggan pulled the plug and headed back north. Other pundits tell that he just couldn't make it work, that Melbourne was too hard a market to crack, and there's an element of truth to this – *Scene* just couldn't compete with *Inpress* and *Beat*, although you'd be hard-pressed to get Duggan to agree.

'I had planned on taking Melbourne. There is evidence that I probably could've done, based on how I am, how I brand, how I work, how I network. It must be said at the time, Rob Furst and the Treweeks had got pretty sick of a guy from Brisbane,' Duggan opines. 'They'd lost enough clients, they'd been made to look stupid. Sorry, my word. By that I mean Rob had taken out posters all around Johnston St saying '100%' Number One. And I mean, that's outrageous! No one in street press has ever seen fit to take posters around someone else's office. You do that when you've got a pom from Brisbane in your grill, taking your business.

'So we were definitely affecting them. While I was there with my gloss and my club and everything, [the Treweeks] had been putting out a newsprint newspaper! That's it! And colour wasn't available on every page until they too found religion. And they too got some gloss in a hurry. So in the space of three months, pretty well from November to January, guys that may be telling you there's nothing to see here, they were moving very, very quickly, trying to plug holes left, right and centre.' He smiles. 'I love that sort of stuff. That's not the first time that someone's gotten sick of Howard coming in and showing them up.'

Regardless, *Scene* was done in Melbourne, outgunned and outlasted by these two Melbourne mainstays and their loyal readers. No doubt a fair number of Duggan's detractors smiled snarkily at this turn of events, the words 'told you so' not even needing to be uttered.

There is, however, a personal side to this story. Right at the end of 2003, Duggan's first son was born and diagnosed with severe cerebral palsy. The following few months proved to be taxing, and as hard a businessman as Howard Duggan may be, his heart lies with his family. And so he made the tough decision to pull out of Melbourne, *Scene* quickly becoming all but a memory on the southern capital's bluestone streets.

'If *Scene* magazine had gone to Melbourne and won the war and kicked the house down in nine months, which was never gonna happen, then I would've been able to put a manager in, retire, all the rest of it,' he says. 'That certainly didn't happen.' *Scene* published its fifty-second Melbourne issue in March 2004 (fifty-two issues is no mean feat, to be fair), then left town and headed home.

* * *

While Howard Duggan's initial foray into taking street press national had failed, Furst Media had already made inroads. *Mixdown*, the stable's muso-oriented street press title, had been publishing for almost a decade by the time Duggan had looked southward, and was the only national title in the country, being distributed in all capital cities. As well, Furst Media had made moves into Sydney specifically. They began publishing a Sydney version of *Beat* from early 1994, according to Adam Zammit, who began as head of sales, before moving across to managing editor seven months after its launch. 'It was, like, a little A5 listings guide,' Zammit says of Sydney *Beat*. 'And there was *Drum Media, On the Street, 3D World* – there were a lot of papers out there – which is why Rob [Furst] took that format, that listings approach ... They struggled. They were doing okay, but they were definitely the third-stringer in the competitive set there.'

Zammit became restive over the next couple of years. 'I was running it and I wanted to move to a gloss cover to get a competitive advantage, but Rob didn't want to, and then he wanted to leave our printers, Theo Scalkos at Foreign Language Publications,' he explains. According to Zammit, Furst sent him over to tell Scalkos they were leaving for a cheaper printer. Scalkos replied with a laugh and made him a counter-offer: 'No, you're not. You're going to leave *Beat*, come here, start a new magazine, I'll give you 50 per cent of it. Call it what you want, bring over all the staff from *Beat*. So that's what I did.'

And so Sydney, out of the blue, gained another street press publication in *Revolver*. Zammit had created a competitor to the struggling *Beat* and taken some staff with him, a move that ended any amicable relationship he would have had with Furst. *Revolver* ran for six years (Sydney *Beat* folded eight or nine months after Zammit defected), a time in which it did well. 'In Theo I had a pretty aggressive partner, and we owned the printing presses so we were able to produce pretty effectively,' Zammit says. 'Our tone was pretty cutting and acerbic, we weren't constrained, we gave ourselves a wider remit [than *Drum*]. I got a lot of support from labels and things, so we got a lot of advertising, and people just seemed to like it – we were kinda more like a well-funded fanzine than we were a traditional street press.'

However, a major upheaval occurred in 2003: Zammit, who had by then stepped away from the day-to-day running of *Revolver* and was overseeing a dot.com start-up and an entertainment and marketing agency called Peer Group Media, got wind that the printer was in financial trouble, just before 'his whole business went into liquidation'. Zammit offered to buy the magazine back for a dollar, and when rebuffed, made the first of two phone calls, this one to the *Revolver* offices on the Thursday before the Friday print deadline. In a ballsy move, he told them to 'bring over all the files' as 'you've got a job here' and 'they all did', putting out the magazine under the name *Evolver*. This moniker lasted two weeks until, with the aid of 'a nine-hour brainstorming session', he and his team came up with '*The Brag* magazine in an effort to rename it', Zammit says.

The other phone call he made on that Thursday was to Rob Furst. 'I hadn't spoken to Rob in six years, since I'd taken his staff and left,' Zammit remembers. 'So I called him and said I know we hadn't spoken for six years and I was sorry at how it ended … but do you want to own this new magazine with me fify-fifty? So he got on a plane and flew up and we did the handshake deal to co-own *The Brag*.'

By this point, *On the Street* was long gone, so Sydney returned to some sense of publishing normalcy in that it was now host to only two street press magazines in *The Brag* and *Drum Media* – as the ensuing years showed, there was easily room for both titles.

Steph Harmon, today culture editor for the Australian edition of *The Guardian*, edited *The Brag* for three years from 2010. She had come from a digital background, having founded arts and pop culture site *Throw Shapes*. She embraced the role, learning as much as she could.

The salary was very low but she threw herself into it 'with that arrogance of youth, and it was fucking amazing, it was such a fun job'. 'I was at gigs most nights a week,' she says. 'I could not sustain that lifestyle now. Sometimes I would pop from venue to venue. So much live music, reviewing and interviewing at the same time as editing, and pushing out this magazine.'

There were challenges, of course, and Harmon didn't escape a brush with misogyny in what is sometimes a blokey industry. 'I remember very vividly our rock news writer at the time, Nathan Jolly, wrote a Soundwave lineup announcement that was like, "Get Ready to Go Back to the 90s, Kids!"' Harmon says. 'And it was quite tongue-in-cheek, but I got a call from a promoter, like, literally calling me a child: "I don't know who the fuck you are, little girl, I'm on the phone with your boss." I remember that really vividly.'

Harmon moved on from *The Brag* in 2013 and went on to co-found music and culture site *Junkee*, while behind her, Furst Media quietly looked to expand its reach around the country.

* * *

Over at *Inpress*, the Treweek brothers had the drive to expand. It's fair to say that they're not people to do anything slowly – which isn't to say they don't think about things, make calculated decisions, but they act quickly. The idea of what became their company, Street Press Australia, was birthed early, and once the wheels began to turn, they turned fast.

'The inefficiencies of the street press networks,' Craig Treweek says on why a national network was such an alluring idea. 'We were missing out on major advertising, missing out on brand advertising, because we were so confined to a certain market and a certain region. The inclusivity of a multiple booking? We just saw that nationalisation would be a huge opportunity. I kinda wrote the SPA plan a couple of weeks after

I started at *Inpress*. It seemed to me to be such a great business to be in, a lot of fun, it seemed a logical step.'

'Every title would initially have to retain its own localisation [because] 60 per cent of the ads came from local venues, so you needed that,' he adds. 'The initial plan was to just have a single booking point.' Essentially a one-stop shop – make a call, buy an ad in every market in the country.

There is some contention over the brainchild of a national street press network. Howard Duggan says he had the idea of going national first, which can be seen in his 2002 plan to expand *Scene* into Melbourne. 'This is long before Street Press Australia. Long before,' he says. Yet 'the day I took over [*Inpress*], I pretty well wrote the business grant plan for Street Press Australia', Craig Treweek says with a laugh. 'And I wrote that plan and the first part of the plan was to buy *Drum Media*.' This was in 1998. And of course Furst Media had been publishing titles in multiple cities since the early 1990s.

The idea in place, what the Treweeks needed now were the magazines themselves. The first step was to buy *Inpress* outright, which they did in 2005. 'Basically what happened there is we borrowed a certain amount of money, and Brian Peacock agreed to vendor terms for the rest of it,' Craig Treweek says. Then they set their sights north, on *Drum*.

'I was watching Rob [Furst] make plays into the Sydney market, and the only way you could create what we [wanted to create] was to own *Drum Media*,' he says. 'It was the key, number-one brand in the country, the most profitable street press in the country, and it was required to do anything. And no one was going to battle it … it wasn't like *Inpress* recovering against *Beat*, where we've shared the market pretty well since that day. That wasn't gonna happen in Sydney, there wasn't a competitor that was going to compete. I could have brought *Inpress* up there and … it wouldn't have made a difference. *Drum* was the key brand in the country.'

Craig Treweek had been working towards buying *Drum Media* for some time. 'It took me eight years. I used to fly up here every year, go out for dinner with the Cott sisters and ask them if I could buy it,' Treweek says with a laugh.

Margaret Cott remembers one entreaty in particular: 'It was at a party, and [Craig] came up and said, "I'm gonna buy *Drum*." And I was like, "Oh god, you're just a kid. Go away, don't bother us!"'

But by 2005, the Cotts were moving towards entertaining an offer from Treweek. 'By that stage, I'd been doing it for years, I'd married, had a kid, got myself a mortgage, and I was getting older,' Margaret Cott says on effectively selling off her life's work. 'And Jenny was getting older as well. She just said, when Craig approached us, she said basically, "Marg, I'm not sure I want to be fifty and running a rock paper … I don't think I have an input anymore, I think we're redundant."' Cott laughs again at the memory, although it was still another year before the sisters agreed to sell.

'Basically, we had nothing to invest in until we had the impetus of expansion,' Treweek explains on the brothers' vision for nationalisation. 'With my plan being that we can only expand by owning *Drum Media*, it wasn't until [the Cotts] said yes, we're willing to negotiate, that I seriously went looking for investors. Because I needed someone to fund that purchase. Me and Leigh were fine with *Inpress* on our own, moving along slowly there, [but] funding expansions where we needed the money, that's when we went and found the Larobina family.'

The Larobina family, based in Melbourne, run the Italian Media Company, publishing Italian-language newspapers *Il Globo* and *La Fiamma*, as well as hosting radio station Rete Italia. It was to them that the Treweeks turned for the capital to realise their dream. 'I found the Larobinas through a mate of mine,' confirms Craig Treweek. 'So they introduced us and I presented the plan of a national street press.'

The Larobinas were convinced and came on board. The Treweeks created a new company called Street Press Australia (of which they owned 45 per cent) and into this new company they sold *Inpress* for 'a combination of shares and cash', Craig Treweek says. 'And then there was cash and loans into that to go and buy *Drum Media*. So it all happened within a couple of days. Without *Drum* there, the Larobinas wouldn't have just bought into *Inpress*. It was about that expansion, which led us on our way to acquiring *Time Off* and creating *Drum Perth* and all those kind of things.'

The purchase of *Drum Media*, which occurred in 2006 and was rumoured to involve a substantial amount, happened fairly seamlessly once the Cotts had agreed to sell, although the deal wasn't without emotion on their end. 'We knew a lot, and we still loved it, but I guess when you lose that fire in your belly, it's time to step aside,' Cott muses. 'And the night that we finally met the Larobinas and we went out for dinner and [managing director Julius Larobina] shook my hand, and he said, "You've done a really good job with this newspaper," and he turned around to the boys and said, "Don't change a single thing," I think I got home that night and just howled ... It was almost primal, I was so upset ... I could not believe I'd done it. I could not believe I'd sold *Drum*.'

* * *

Shortly after the acquisition of its crown jewel, Street Press Australia created *Drum Perth* in September 2006. The logic was that Joe Cipriani's *X-Press* had the market all to itself (as it had done for two decades, in the main) and so there was room for a competitor. '*Drum Perth* was simply because *X-Press* was never going to sell and *X-Press* had no competition in the marketplace – every other state had two street press titles, even Adelaide had two. So it was kind of important we went down that path,' says Craig Treweek.

Where to next then? Adelaide, of course, although the acquisition of Margie Budich's *Rip It Up* didn't quite go to plan. 'Well, Javier Moll is a very influential newspaper man out of Spain,' Budich explains with a smile. 'He came to Adelaide and fell in love with it … and anyway, two designer friends of mine happened to live in the same building as him, and so one evening I found myself having dinner with Javier and his wife. He had come to Australia and wanted to take on Murdoch.

'So we got on really well and he bought half my business, we went into partnership,' she says, adding with a laugh, 'Unbelievably, a month after I met Javier, Craig Treweek flew into Adelaide and I met Craig and he wanted to link all the magazines … but he was a month late, I said "I'm in due diligence with this Spanish guy!"'

'Yeah, I went to buy off Margie Budich,' Treweek says wryly. 'I went to take her out to lunch to make her an offer for *Rip It Up*, and she'd just sold it the day prior! And she goes, "I sold it to a billionaire," and I'm like, "Okay, well, I don't want to fight with him, let's do a deal."' This deal ended up being an agency agreement whereby *Rip It Up* was essentially part of the Street Press Australia network, just not owned by the Treweeks.

Within the space of twelve months, the Treweeks had gone from owning half a paper to owning three and a half. This was rapid expansion even in street press's fast terms, and there was more to come. Their stable was filling up, their national tour almost complete, and the resulting network was now almost a reality.

* * *

On 8 March 2006, in issue 631, Brisbane's *Scene* magazine launched a new column, 'Fight Club'. Tucked right down the back, on the long-running paper's last page, the column was a short space set aside for, essentially, reader rants. A reader would email in a rant on something

– anything – and it'd be printed, the idea being that the following week another reader's reply would run, usually of a differing opinion, hence the column's name.

Scene readers were obviously pissed off at a range of things, as the column stayed on and looked to become a fixture. Drugs in the Valley, smoking laws, alcohol taxes, 'scumbags' in New Farm, emos – you name it and readers of *Scene* had a gripe with it. Some of the rants, and the replies, were articulate and made decent points. Others were vitriol for vitriol's sake.

Two months into the column's tenure, something happened that *Scene* publisher Howard Duggan says was 'a game-changer'. In issue 641, 17 May 2006, a letter was printed under the pseudonym 'Funked Off'. This person's gripe was with 'door bitches', the colloquial and not-so-endearing name for those, usually females, who stand outside clubs and decide who to let in. It read, in part:

> I am writing to express my angst about a certain skank bitch who positions herself at the entrance to one of Brisbane's most happening nightclubs, that manages to pull the best international and interstate DJs when it comes to house, breaks and hard dance. I have been a regular punter at this venue now for three years, and I'm FED UP with having my night ruined, ego shattered and my plans diverted all because this mole decides that I'm not 'FUNKY ENOUGH' for her club.

Funked Off goes on to express his or her displeasure with the vagaries of club door policy, whereby people get knocked back for no set reason. He or she uses some very colourful language in the short piece, which, aside from the denigration of this particular woman, is about as bad as it gets. At least on the face of it. The following week, someone calling themselves Backslap Joe replied saying they'd worked in clubs and there was indeed no set policy, but whatever decision was made on the night was designed to keep the right people out, as well as the right people in – 'Like it or not, that door policy is doing you a favour,' they wrote, and that, it seemed, was that.

Not so. *Scene* under Duggan's tenure had some lucrative advertising contracts in the Brisbane club world, the biggest being Family, a world-renowned superclub owned by a group called Katarzyna (who, at time of writing, also own Fortitude Valley venues Cloudland, The Warehouse, The Empire Hotel and Press Club). As Duggan tells it, the club at which Funked Off's 'skank bitch' worked was quite obviously Family, and this did not sit well with *Scene*'s long-time advertisers. 'This not-funny letter got published and [the owners] called me and said, "Howard, this thing's on the street, what the fuck is going on with it?"' Duggan recalls. 'I called back and tried to patch it up. Not interested. They'd seen red. They picked up their campaign … walked over the road to *Time Off*, and a plonker like Sean [Sennett] is sitting there having no idea what to do, [because] he's getting beaten up every week, and he has this $2000-a-week campaign walk through the door.

'And those sorts of things are game-changers. We were kicking butt, [but] that's when we really started to struggle.'

A $2000-a-week advertising contract was big money to a music magazine in the mid-2000s. This was a period when the internet was beginning to dominate and print magazines and newspapers were starting to feel the sand shift beneath their feet. Losing a regular slice of income like this would have rocked anyone.

To Duggan's mind, it was this advertising contract that bolstered *Time Off*'s worth, enabling them to start printing glossy covers, and making them a desirable acquisition for the Treweeks as they looked to expand their street press empire. 'They hadn't bought *Time Off*,' he explains, 'because Howard was the winner and you don't want to buy a lemon.'

Duggan's assertion that Street Press Australia hadn't bought *Time Off* because it was inferior to his own publication wasn't entirely correct. The Treweeks had, in fact, made enquiries as early as 2006 regarding a *Time Off* buy, but Sean Sennett just wasn't looking to sell at that point. 'Every year, someone would ring me and say they wanted to buy *Time Off*,' Sennett says. 'I'd always hang up on them. I had no interest at all.' The Treweeks' offer '*was* interesting though'. 'They would try to squeeze in by offering to sell ads for us … They put a lot of business our way, because they were selling something to someone in Sydney and they'd say, "Oh, we can put that in *Time Off* too for you." … And we'd say, "Well, don't do that, we kinda want our guys to do that because we want to maintain the relationship with the person." But sometimes, they'd ring up on a Tuesday afternoon when you were low and say, "We've got a full-page for you for such and such," and you'd say "Thank you" and stick it in.'

But Sennett let the offer drift, content to continue publishing a title that was doing fine. 'We kinda hit a nice little stream there for a while where we were doing good magazines, we were doing well, everyone was getting paid, people were making money.'

Sometime in 2007, he changed his mind. It happened as he walked out of a band rehearsal. 'I came outside and there were five guys from different bands standing there around a car, all looking at their phones,' he remembers, adding with a laugh, 'And I thought, *It's over*.' The first rumblings of the global financial crisis were being felt around the world, and 'I just thought, *It's gonna happen, it's just gonna change*,' Sennett says. 'I still believed in street press at that particular time, but, you know, they made me a really good offer. And I thought, I've done it for twenty years, would it feel any different to do it for another twenty? Would it feel like the same experiences? I was already doing a lot of freelance stuff for people around Australia anyway … so I just thought, you know, *You're not gonna have any financial worries*, and it kinda felt like it was the right time.'

It turns out it was. 'At the time you think, *Fuck, what if I sell the magazine and then in years to come it's like that house at the beach which is now worth 12 million dollars?*' He laughs. But in hindsight, 'sadly, global warming has arrived, and the house at the beach isn't there anymore'.

And so the deal went through. There was some back-and-forth, some bullish behaviour from the Street Press Australia lawyer that Sennett didn't appreciate, but ultimately, after eighteen years as owner, he pulled the trigger and sold the magazine he'd bought out of receivership and turned into a thriving title.

The day the Treweeks handed over the cheque was a good one. 'When the Treweeks left the room, I remember being on my own in the office, after twenty years, and I did something I'd never been able to do before, which was a fist pump to have a cheque that freakin' big. That is just a once-in-a-lifetime sort of thing,' he says. 'And then after that, I would have felt a bit flat because, you know, I'd been associated with the magazine my entire working life, and, you know, yeah … it was disappointing.'

Sean Sennett had, whether by design or pure luck, one of the best runs in street press – he bought for a song just before the boom began, and sold for a bomb just before the steady decline (the actual sale amount is bound by a confidentiality agreement, and remains unknown outside the negotiating circle). And while the Treweeks now had the national network they'd been dreaming of since 1998, street press mags hanging from it like Christmas ornaments, it was becoming obvious to many that the very medium was in danger of collapsing.

Like *RAM* and *Juke* before it, street press was staring down the barrel of its own demise.

18

RIGHT PLACE, WRONG TIME

'You put the ten top US athletes together, LeBron James and all that kind of stuff, they've got a bigger audience than NBC.'

Craig Treweek

Through the late 1990s and into the 2000s, electronic dance music (EDM) was huge. Jonathan Morris had started the country's first dance-specific street press, *3D World*, in 1999 out of Sydney, and it was booming. The rock papers too had their own dance inserts – 'Zebra' in *Inpress* and '100%' in *Beat* being the notables – and as Craig Treweek says, they were paying for everything.

'You've gotta realise, "Zebra" was what drove us to gain market share off *Beat* and to [get] the mag to be turning over multiple millions of dollars a year,' he says, referencing the early 2000s as he and brother Leigh fought to turn *Inpress* around. 'And our biggest struggle in the early 2000s was to keep the dance section smaller than the rock section. Because the rock 'n' roll brand was where, I guess, the credibility stood, even at that point. But "Zebra" was doing twice the revenues of anything else; [its] smaller pages were supporting the rock pages every week. I'd set the magazines, and if

I did it straight on revenues, "Zebra" would have been seventy pages and the rock section thirty.'

Yet in the mid-2000s, the EDM scene appeared to fracture and shrink. Advertising revenue started to drop off, which presented a fairly serious problem. Add to this the steady rise of the internet and the slow but inevitable growth of online publishing, and it would have seemed a bigger problem still. At this point, everyone in the street press realm was still printing but everyone was thinking of establishing an online presence (if they hadn't already). It was business as usual, but with one eye on the online world, the other on the bank balance.

Except EDM wasn't actually dying, shrinking or fracturing. It was merely shifting its focus elsewhere.

'No, I don't think we were ever nervous. We had faith in what we were doing,' says Craig Treweek thoughtfully when asked if this gathering storm gave him or his investors pause. Despite falling revenue from the dance pages of his magazines, despite the rise of the internet, Street Press Australia were still banking on their people, on their products. But this shift in focus, this was the killer.

'We saw the internet,' sighs Treweek, 'but we didn't see Facebook.'

The impact of social media, then in its infancy, was to be devastating. The internet, while it has created havoc within all echelons of print media, didn't have the same effect on street press that social media was to have. Social media allowed individuals to create and curate their own audiences, and it proved to be the death knell of many publications. 'Oh, big time,' Treweek says, pausing and laughing ruefully. 'Yeah, that was the start of what I would almost call the street press crash.

'We didn't see the building of audiences, whereby promoters could have a fanbase they could almost invite to a festival or a gig,' he goes on. 'That's what we missed, just how much that would impact it all. EDM wasn't dying off, EDM was the just the first to grow their own audience and say, "Hang on, we only need 800 people to walk into the club on Friday night, and we've got 10,000 people on our Facebook page. We don't need anything." If you've got a large, dedicated audience via your social media channels, why bother spending money on an ad in a printed newspaper?

'The internet killed the printed word, but it didn't kill the revenues initially. Facebook was massive,' Treweek reflects. 'So whether with printed word in its physical format or its digital format, we were still disseminating a crapload of editorial about bands and music and all that kind of thing, and all that was really exciting. [But] we were losing advertising because people were creating their own audiences.'

Much like the town hall dances of the early 1960s, the clubs and parties and bush doofs were all in full swing. The difference was, they now had control of their own means of advertising, and it was free. The irony would not have been lost on many in the street press community.

* * *

Street Press Australia bought *3D World* in 2009, as the publication teetered on the cusp of receivership, looking to add it to their Sydney stable. They had acquired *Drum Media* in 2006, so the idea was that then they'd have the best rock and dance papers in New South Wales. This they did, but they couldn't save it. The advent of social media killed off the dance-specific titles, and so Street Press Australia closed *3D World* shortly afterwards.

The silver lining was that from the ashes of *3D World* rose the short-lived but acclaimed *Three*. The first magazine created entirely for iPad (no other digital presence, no print mate), *Three* was the brainchild of the Treweeks, Group Managing Editor Andrew Mast and another Street Press Australia editor, Kris Swales. It only lasted six issues in 2010, covering countercultural trends, emerging art, aspiring designers, burgeoning brands and adventurous pop culture, but during its short run was listed as one of the Top 20 best iPad magazines in the world, in the inaugural awards, alongside such publications as *National Geographic* and *Vanity Fair*. Both Craig Treweek and Mast list the creation of *Three* as one of the highlights of their career.

'It was so much fuckin' fun.' Treweek laughs. 'I seriously can remember at 4.00am copping a text saying, *You've just been voted in the top twenty magazines in the world!* And as a publisher ... I was just like, *what the fuck?* Nothing, nothing in my publishing career will ever top what I think we did with *Three* magazine. We were at the start of what, at the time, looked like the future of publishing and experimenting with new technologies to enhance magazine content. And we got to present the work of another great editor in Kris Swales, alongside Masty's genius, one of the top writers/editors that this country has produced. Most of all it was a "blank page" magazine: we started with a whiteboard with nothing on it and anything could fill the pages – literally no idea was unwelcome, hence the fun!'

'*Three* was one of my favourite things we ever did,' concurs Mast. 'We were the first stand-alone title for iPad, the first free stand-alone title.'

According to both men, *Three* was ahead of its time, and so after a short, sharp run covering anything and everything, it had to fold. 'We couldn't make it work. We were literally too far ahead of the curve and no one wanted to advertise, and that's your disruption – when people stop advertising, the end is near,' Mast says.

'It was just the ultimate passion project,' Treweek agrees. 'What we learned with *Three* was you can't be too far ahead of it. Unless you've got a massive funder behind you, if you're a little old street press like us with no fucking cash, you can't be too far ahead of the curve.'

* * *

As the 2010s kicked off, some in the street press community had an inkling they were in for a brutal decade. These were the years that saw street press finally fade, this unique medium that grew from obscurity and morphed into a form of publishing that lived in the same space as the music, that was grassroots, grungy, a training ground and a reassuring presence in equal measure. It was inevitable, perhaps – nothing lasts forever – and while many street press titles seemed inviolable, so too did *RAM* and *Juke* before them. It was a bitter lesson in publishing: the boom times are often followed by a fallow period where many cannot continue to produce.

Publications began to call time, mainly because they could not compete with social media in any meaningful way with their dwindling resources. *Rave*, by now being published by Colin Rankin, pulled the pin in June 2012, after 1047 issues. Rankin announced in a press release: '*Rave* Magazine has now ceased publication of the weekly print edition of its magazines. Currently our financial advisors are investigating options with regard to the sale of the magazine and its associated digital assets.'

Newcastle and Central Coast mainstay *Reverb*, which began life in 2006, appeared monthly until September 2012, when it stopped printing (after seventy-three issues) and became an online-only publication, *Reverb Online*.

It was a similar story for many street press publications around this time. Printing is typically the biggest expense, so it made financial sense to cut the print bill and move solely online. This of course raised a question: if a street press magazine is not on the street anymore, is it in fact even a street press publication?

For many publications, the answer was no. It soon became clear that their identity was integrally tied to their existence as print products; ceasing to print and existing purely online meant they became just another music and culture website, their brand and reputation fading.

And so the masthead was relegated to one among a million, existing among the silent cacophony that is the internet.

Rip It Up suffered this fate. The print version was shuttered in 2014 and the publication moved purely online. Readers scattered and so it was terminated altogether in 2016, ending twenty-seven years of free press publishing in Adelaide. 'I had small kids, so I'd left. It was the right time for me,' says founding publisher Margie Budich on walking away from *Rip It Up* a few years before it folded. 'But the writing was on the wall when I left. The whole industry was changing.'

Also in Adelaide, *dB* magazine called it quits the same year *Rip It Up* ceased printing, pulling their digital presence as they did so. The magazine's URL has now been co-opted by another *dB* magazine, this one specialising in sustainable architecture. *dB*'s last Facebook post, spruiking a Mark of Cain national tour, was in October 2014.

Other titles died quietly, as the day-to-day running of them fell to fewer and fewer people, the publications existing on barely a cent, then on pure passion, then on nothing, long since ceased printing, website domains left to lapse, little trace left other than unattended social media sites acting as digital tombstones.

Tsunami, out of the Sunshine Coast, was one such example. On the magazine's Facebook page, their About section still exists:

> *Tsunami Mag* is far more than just a street press – it is a cutting-edge music, fashion and pop culture publication deeply ingrained into QLD iconography. We doggedly reject cliche and mediocrity in our pursuit of innocation [*sic*: innovation][40] and individuality. This pursuit has brought *Tsunami Mag* to where it is today – a proud magazine standing apart from the crowd. Every two weeks *Tsunami* hits the Sunshine Coast, Brisbane, the Gold Coast as far east as Toowoomba, as far south as Coffs and as far north as Cairns.

Tsunami Mag has been around since '99, so we know what we're doing.

Their final Facebook post was late September 2012.

Yet while many of its contemporaries around the country were expiring, Melbourne's *Beat* was still going strong. And it still publishes today – in print. According to Patrick Carr, Furst Media's managing director, *Beat* continues to survive, if not flourish, because of the people. 'Yes, it serves its purpose and it's ingrained within the culture and everything, but *Beat* is there because it's bigger than the name or the mag – people are invested in it. People come in every day to work, and they fight hard for it, that's what it is. We've had some bloody tough times, and we've had to reinvent and go with everything … but we're still here because of the people; the people make it.'

* * *

In 2013, Street Press Australia made the decision to rebrand all their titles. This wasn't done on a whim. By this point, advertisers were leaving, social media was well engrained, and the balance sheets of most of its printed papers were dire. As Craig Treweek says, 'We had to look at making changes.'

The shift was monumental. *Inpress* ceased to exist. *Drum Media* ceased to exist. *Time Off* ceased to exist. *Drum Media Perth* ceased to exist. All these titles, bar *Drum Perth*, had been running under those names for decades, *Time Off* since 1979, *Inpress* since 1988. All were rebranded to *The Music*, followed by their specific city: *Inpress* became *The Music – Melbourne*, for example. For titles as iconic as those Street Press Australia had custodianship over, this wasn't a decision made easily, but Treweek was correct: times had changed, and street press needed to move with them.

'Basically, one of the things with social media and online meant we could see and understand a little bit more about our readership and get feedback,' says Leigh Treweek. 'One of the biggest points was we were getting lumped together with newspapers and newsprint. You know, newspapers are dead, so people were bundling us up in the lot. So I think for us, it was a matter of making sure that we basically looked at what our readers were doing, what they were after, what our distributors wanted … the change in *The Music* was to give it a single brand and link back to our online, so people knew there was a source there that was able to give them what they wanted online, able to give them what they wanted in print, what they wanted in an article … [the aim was to] bring that all together, and in doing so, make it easier for people to go, "I trust that brand, and that's the brand here."'

As Street Press Australia transitioned into a new era, they made other changes, too. Perhaps the biggest of these was the size of these newly rebranded magazines. For the first time, these titles moved from tabloid size to A4. Smaller magazines with a new name and logo, an easy link to themusic.com.au: this was the plan, a shakeup designed to refresh the whole enterprise.

'It simplified things,' Leigh Treweek says. 'It didn't change any of our staffing levels at any of our offices, it didn't change anything we did – the local content was still there as much as it was before – but it was just from a brand point of view, and especially from an online point of view, it helped bring everything together. And changing format to an easier format to read, an easier format to take home … that was the way to go.'

'It was the smart business thing to do,' Craig Treweek concurs. 'It was done for simplicity for advertisers. So, yeah, it was driven by financial reality at a time when the magazine revenues were beginning to fall off a cliff.'

As it turned out, the refresh of the physical magazines did very little to bolster their circulation, to stop the decline. The magazines were smaller not only in size but in editorial content, with as much space as possible given over to advertising. 'The honest truth? Wrong decision. Because we did it for business reasons and not for the reader,' Craig Treweek admits.

Rebranding all the titles they'd acquired in their portfolio over the years, titles that had over a much longer period gained the trust of readers in fickle local markets, caused surprisingly little stir among readers. The loyalty *Time Off*, *Drum Media* and *Inpress* had inspired during their heyday was not much in evidence, which Treweek was very disappointed about. To his mind, radio silence was one of the worst things that could have happened. 'I think for me that probably made me think not that the decision was wrong, but kind of that every decision we've made for quite a while was wrong.'

The Music, and indeed SPA as a whole, stagnated. The refreshed magazines didn't hold the cachet of their former incarnations, and while they were still picked up in pubs and record stores, mainly for the gig guide,[41] it was in smaller and smaller numbers.

* * *

While *Beat* was quietly doing its own thing down in Melbourne – as was *BMA* in Canberra and *Forte* in Geelong – up in Brisbane the only competitor to *Time Off* (now *The Music – Brisbane*) was Howard Duggan's *Scene*. And it was tough for them too. Duggan still felt that losing at least one lucrative ad deal to their rivals had been a turning point.

'It took nine months of Sean [Sennett] agonising, not wanting to sell up his life's work, for the Treweeks to spend someone else's money,' Duggan says on the period around 2008, as Street Press Australia bought *Time Off*, 'and they did. And that's when we really struggled.

I was telling you about how we were kicking butt. That's when we really started to struggle.

'We felt the pain of Street Press Australia for the first time in 2009, when our sales went backwards for the first time ever,' he laments. 'Between 2007 and 2012, they had a five-year run where this brand, Street Press Australia, mesmerised record labels [with that] idea of one-stop-shopping. They just mesmerised Sony, the promoters. I had clients apologising to me: "Howard, I've gotta do it … it's just too good to be true." Bearing in mind that it wasn't the creation of anyone. It was the result of just buying other people's work and paying way over the odds for it. And you just can't fight that. If someone wants to come in and buy that building next to us and just turn it into a nightclub and just throw Branson money at it year after year, they will eventually destroy the next nightclub.'

He sighs. 'Up until 2009, we'd always done year-on-year better. And then it started to go backwards. [The years] 2009 to 2012, that was very tough. And not just for me. It was tough for everyone.'

Much like his main competitor, Street Press Australia, Duggan needed to affect change to assure the survival of his title. He was again looking at nationalisation, no doubt taking notes on what was and wasn't working at Street Press Australia. But it was the immediate future that needed his focus, and so he too looked to rebrand. '[I'd started] *Scenestr*, which was to be a national, digital-only, website,' Duggan says. 'Which it was. And it was more of the usual stuff, fashion, arts, trying to work ourselves into a brand where we would be just as happy covering a metal concert as we would the opera. And I think we've been quite successful at doing that and it's difficult to do.

'So *Scene* continues to be in trouble,' he goes on. 'And I also wanted to align the national digital brand, which we'd built up a few years earlier with *Scenester*, with the magazine. So a simple way was …

changing *Scene* to *Scenestr*. So that's how *Scenestr* was born; I needed to be national and *Scene* by itself wouldn't cut it. So in one action, in July 2014, we changed *Scene* magazine to *Scenestr* and made it monthly. That all happened in the one shot.'

Scene published 1054 issues before rebranding to *Scenestr*, the new incarnation picking up exactly where its predecessor left off, branded as issue 1055. This done, seamlessly according to Duggan, the old nationalisation chestnut again became his *raison d'etre*, and from here Duggan and his publishing company, Eyeball Media, moved quite quickly, despite the ongoing uncertainty that was now part of life as a print publisher.

'We launched in South Australia in June 2015 after *dB* and *Rip It Up* had vacated the market,' Duggan says, referencing his first move out of Queensland, only a year after rebranding his title and turning it into a monthly publication. A little over a year later, in August 2016, *Scenestr* launch its New South Wales edition. A Perth edition followed in May 2017, 'After *X-Press* and *The Music* had vacated the market', and Melbourne in September 2018, some fifteen years after they'd first attempted to set up in the Victorian capital.

So *Scenestr* was doing what Street Press Australia had done, but by this point, as the end of the 2010s neared, were no longer able to sustain. Duggan had his national network, which to him meant he had 'won', although whether anyone else knew they were playing remains unclear. *Scenestr* was on the street, all around the country, and not merely doing a standard twelve issues a year – each state had 'special issues' at various points during the year (for Adelaide Fringe, for example), and a Christmas/New Year special issue, in addition to the December issue.

It's fair to say that neither *Scene* nor *Scenestr* ever commanded the degree of loyalty or cultural cache of titles like *Drum Media* or *Inpress*, but Duggan's publications were all over the country, championing the local arts and music scenes, and so they continue. It's a legacy of which to be proud.

* * *

After 1527 issues, *X-Press* in Perth wound up in 2016, Joe Cipriani having seen the writing on the wall for a couple of years. '[The year] 2014 began the decline of the newspaper industry due to the digital revolution as we know it, where Facebook and Google had a negative effect on advertising revenue,' he confirms, adding that this was what began to erode the magazine's print numbers. 'Digital sales conversion from print would not have been 10 per cent of revenue, which could not sustain the same level of operation.'

In the magazine's twenty-fifth anniversary issue, August 2010, Cipriani is interviewed at length on his time in free press publishing. 'I suppose it's just the disease,' he muses when asked what it is about the industry that excites him. 'Being addicted to the entertainment industry, and also you get addicted to ink on paper. People that are in the print industry stay in that industry; they just like the idea of producing something. I was always an entrepreneurial type, I've always run any of the bands that I was in, even at the age of fifteen … music and print were the two things I've always liked, and I've never really wanted to venture out of that.'

As the magazine eventually shuttered, Cipriani's company Columbia Press revamped its digital presence (which still runs to this day), along with, in more recent years, 'the introduction of digital assets including the website, app, newsletter [and] Facebook, forming part of [our] weekly publishing to the Perth market audience'.

'*X-Press* lived and breathed the local music industry, by supporting and sponsoring many annual events not only in music, but the arts and fashion as well,' Cipriani says, looking back on it all. 'The front covers of *X-Press* published many new artists we felt were headed for fame and great success on a local, national and international level.'

When asked at the end of the twenty-fifth anniversary interview if he can be interviewed in another twenty-five years and whether the magazine will still be there, Cipriani replies, 'I don't know about me, but I think the publication will.' Unfortunately, this isn't the case, but *X-Press* can lay claim to being one of the longest-running and most trusted of all among Australia's free music press.

* * *

In November 2018, Street Press Australia attempted a final roll of the dice. Their rebranded titles – smaller in size and stature since 2013, low on editorial and altogether bereft of much of what had made them what they'd once been – hadn't done what the Treweeks and long-term Group Managing Editor Andrew Mast had hoped. And so, in the face of prolific competition via the internet, still being ground down by social media (although now also using it to their advantage, as best as any publisher could), they gambled, as they'd done so many times before.

The Music 2.0 was, it must be said, a very strong magazine. B3 in size, full gloss throughout, pages and pages of ads[42] while still leaving room for editorial – and not just the short pieces that had become the tired and almost pointless fodder of other street press, but longer, more in-depth feature writing, of the sort not seen in street press for decades. It was ambitious, and it was of a quality that perhaps should have made an appearance four and a half years prior. Regardless, it had done so now, and it looked good.

A year prior to this relaunch, I'd asked Craig Treweek how important he regarded *Go-Set* as being to the rock press as it existed today, half a century later. He hadn't even paused before extolling its virtues. 'I think the next two to five years will show how important it was,' he'd said then, in 2017. 'Because one of two things will happen: we'll find the *Go-Set* for the modern age, the cross-platform, multimedia *Go-Set* will be discovered, [or] street press will die. In two to five years, we're all dead, or one of us has found the holy grail, which is the *Go-Set* for now.'

Go-Set was so popular in the 1960s because it filled a need – even more, the collected needs of a generation looking for information and opinions pertinent to them and their burgeoning values. Pop music, of course, was one of those needs, perhaps the most important. *Go-Set*'s editors realised this and catered accordingly, evolving (or, as co-founder Phillip Frazer has posited, *devolving*) with its audience over the years, capturing as best it could what its readers were after.

It stands to reason, then, that the same sort of model would work today, hence Treweek's forecast of a modern *Go-Set*. This was the hope – not just for the Treweeks, but for everyone publishing street press in 2018: *The Music*, *Scenestr*, *BMA*, *Beat*, *Mixdown*, *The Brag*, *Forte*. Would anyone find the new *Go-Set*? Only time would tell.

19

THE PAPER HIGHWAY IS LITTERED WITH CORPSES

'We were always arrogant or stupid enough to believe that we can drag ourselves out of stuff.'

Craig Treweek

In June 2015, I sat down with Matt Coyte, then editor-in-chief of Australian *Rolling Stone*, at his office in Newtown, Sydney. We spoke about the state of the press as it was and as it had been, and where we saw it going. We also, as you would expect, talked about music and its place within an ever-changing world. A theory I'd been musing on was that music today is no longer revolutionary, at least not in the same way it was in the 1960s, and so doesn't hold the same power to drive social change as it did when rock 'n' roll was in its infancy and offered a perceived alternative set of values for a youth looking to escape the parental yoke.

Coyte suggested that young people today listen to music differently; it's far more about an experience than it is about the music itself. 'I feel like that's the endgame now,' he reflected. 'Kids want to know how the music relates to their lives; they're not interested in Anthony Kiedis as a character, they're interested in a Red Hot Chili Peppers song as a soundtrack to their life.

'It's like, "Remember when we went on that road trip and we listened to Mumford & Sons over and over again? Fuck, that was sick!" They're not talking about Mumford & Sons, they're talking about their road trip. And it's social to them, it's marking something about them; it's always about them and their experience. That's what I've gotten from talking to kids … It's always like, "Oh, man, this songs reminds me of when I did this," or whatever. And it makes sense. It's almost like journalling everything that happens in your life, putting a soundtrack to it.'

Perhaps this correlates with the 'death of the album' as a concept, where due to the advent of music streaming services it's now more about individual songs (which you're more likely to listen to in the car with your mates than solo on a record player through headphones). These songs can be preselected for any situation, surrounded by other song selections in a user-curated playlist, their intended sonic context forever lost within the miasma of advancing technology and changing social norms.

The advent of services like Spotify[43] make this approach all the easier. Almost every song ever conceived contained on a device people carry in their pockets, granting the ability to cherry-pick and create endless playlists for as little as $12 a month – this has completely and irrevocably changed how music is consumed. The same goes with information in general: the internet is hardly new – there are millennials who were born after its advent – but the speed with which it and social media evolve, the pure and unfettered accessibility it gives, that's new. Most everything in today's world is immediate, and an entire generation have grown up to take this for granted.

The result is change on a global scale, rendering much of the media previous generations grew up with obsolete. The Australian rock press in 2023 is vastly different to what it once was, a difference not just in form but in philosophy. There are only a handful of magazines still printing; music coverage in newspapers is thin and often seems designed to cater to a broad, non-specialist readership; street press as a publishing medium adhering to the three tenets that once made it so compelling – free, weekly and location-specific – is essentially dead. The bulk of Australia's coverage of music today is online, which raises the question, is it really the rock 'n' roll *press*?[44]

'I think "rock press" is an antiquated term,' muses Poppy Reid, award-winning editor-in-chief of The Brag Media's suite of online music titles. 'I don't think the future is around genre-focused publications, I think it's around covering everything for a certain demographic.'

The truth is there is still much energy in music journalism in Australia – you just need to know where to look. Online portals such as *Music Feeds*, *Tone Deaf*, *X-Press*, *Reverb Online*, *The Music* and a host of others all exist as purveyors of information and opinion targeted to a certain demographic, just as *Go-Set* or *RAM* did during their respective heydays, even if they lack the romanticism of print.[45] Other sites like The Brag Media (a host of sites, as opposed to just one), *Junkee* and *Pedestrian TV* act, in the vein of *Go-Set*, as cultural nodes aiming at a younger audience and provide news, analysis and critique not only on music but on all aspects of youth culture, the data they collect enabling them to do so.

'When it comes to our music publications, people look to us for two things,' says Reid. 'They want to know what's happening around the artists that they like, and they want to be sent new music or new content from artists they've never heard of that they'd probably like. And we'd never be able to do that with the access to the data that we have.'

Music information, and indeed information in general, is ingested differently today. A longform article on a band, intricately researched and painstakingly edited, isn't for the most part how young people engage with music journalism anymore. Many music sites present information in small, quick, easy-to-read fragments, short items in a stream constantly in motion, as each item is usurped, gone and lost among the digital detritus.

This isn't bad. It's merely change. Australia's rock press history is vibrant, a direct reflection of how strong its music scene has been. This scene today is no less vibrant – it's boisterous and real and alive – and music journalists, no matter where they publish, will no doubt continue covering it all with the same passion and energy as generations before.

You can, of course, still hold a magazine in your hands. *Rolling Stone*, which went into receivership in January 2018, was relaunched in print by The Brag Media on 4 May 2020 and appears these days as a quarterly. *Rhythms* prints every second month; *Trad&Now* produces eight issues a year; *Australian Guitar* appears in newsagents, as do various titles from overseas, including the relatively new local edition of UK stalwart *NME*.

When it comes to street press, as the pandemic finally waned and people were allowed back on the streets once more, a small but lively pool was in evidence. *Scenestr* is still printing monthly across five states (they did put various titles on hiatus through the pandemic, and publisher Howard Duggen notes that the government's JobKeeper initiative did save them from folding). *BMA* in Canberra, *Forte* in Geelong, *Beat* in Melbourne (after its own Covid hiatus) and *Blank* on the Gold Coast are all printing, although none more often than fortnightly. There's even a new addition in *Harbour*, which comes out of the Coffs region and began in 2021.

The Music no longer prints. Its B3 format, which proved solid for a couple of years, was unable to survive the global pandemic. 'We had a good run right through to Covid,' Craig Treweek recalls. 'Lot of the same team, lot of new faces, expanded the digital presence, stuff like that. But then, like every other business in music, we sat down when we heard about Covid and the first lockdown, and we worked out we had one month to survive. Lots of tears.'

They didn't tell their staff at that stage as 'we were always arrogant or stupid enough to believe that we can drag ourselves out of stuff', but they quickly realised it was over. The magazine shuttered, and a host of new initiatives took their place (some in conjunction with the Victorian Government), like live-streaming gigs, aiming to 'put some money into the artists' pockets', Treweek says.

The Music was sold to SGC Media, a company based out of Brisbane, who are in the process of digitising a slew of Street Press Australia's back issues. It's with SGC, along with much bigger The Brag Media, where perhaps the future of online media in general, and the rock 'n' roll media specifically, lies.

SGC describes itself as 'a full-service PR, radio plugging, digital and strategic marketing company'. It publishes online titles *The Music*; *Purple Sneakers*, 'Australia's leading electronic, urban and indie community'; *Countrytown*, 'Australia's biggest online home of country music'; *Kill Your Stereo*, 'Australia's home of heavy music'; and *Radio Monitor*, a global monitoring service dubbed 'the world leader in airplay intelligence'.

The Brag Media aims to be 'the most ubiquitous presence in Australian culture; with its people, its artists and brands'. It claims the titles in its publishing arm – which include *The Brag*, *Rolling Stone*, *Tone Deaf*, *The Music Network* and *Variety Australia* – reach 20 per cent of the Australian population every month. It has an events business, a talent business, a 'creative team'. Sitting with CEO Luke Girgis at industry conference BigSound in 2019, I was struck by how forward-looking the company was, despite the history a lot, if not all, of their magazine 'brands' carry.

Girgis, who comes from a band management background, is a canny digital afficionado. As he watched what was happening online in the publishing realm while a manager, he saw potential to grow the industry. 'Publishers now either don't know how to find an audience, because they're from print and they don't know how to go to digital, or the ones that are really good at digital are just chasing traffic, they don't actually have an audience or fanbase themselves,' he said to me at the time.

Realising this was a penny-drop moment for Girgis. And so once he finished working with the various bands he'd been managing, he teamed up with Seventh Street Ventures, a venture capital firm, to form Seventh Street Media (which then became The Brag Media). His first moves were to buy *Tone Deaf* (online) and then *The Brag* (still printing at the time) from Furst Media. '*The Brag* was a Sydney publication in a suite of stuff they were doing in Melbourne, so we got that,' he explains. 'It barely had an online presence, it was on this terrible digital platform, almost no traffic … a dinosaur online. So we grew it and changed it a lot, actually.' The company then started The Industry Observer, an industry B2B tip sheet, followed by Gen Z music publication *Don't Bore Us*. *The Brag* is now online only, which is where the vast majority of The Brag Media's business lies – and there's a lot of it.

Across its websites, The Brag Media claims to have nine million monthly active users; 40 million monthly page views; 320,000 subscribers to their digital newsletters (which include The Industry Observer, Entertainment Biz Observer and The Music Network, which they purchased in February 2022); 18.7 million global social media followers across its channels; and 100,000 podcast downloads a month. Have The Brag Media found that fabled '*Go-Set* for the new age'?

* * *

One of my favourite Australian magazines, of all that have sprung up over the fifty-odd years this country has been fostering its own dedicated rock press, was one that managed to successfully meld its print and online presences before anyone truly realised how necessary this would become.

Mess+Noise, a monthly almost underground publication out of Melbourne that first appeared in print in April 2005, was conceived by designer and web developer Danny Bos and photographer and artist Kristy Milliken. It was actually the website that came first, Bos being a gifted coder; the magazine sprang from the site. The magazine was never a commercial success, but it became a record of Melbourne's incredibly fertile indie scene in particular, showcasing some of the best longform music writing on offer via writers like Kate Hennessy, Anwen Crawford, Adam D. Mills and Shaun Prescott.

What made *Mess+Noise* unique, what bonded its very passionate readership, was its online forums. The magazine was consumed rabidly, but it was online where fans of both the music and the magazine gathered. There has never been anything like the *Mess+Noise* forums in Australia: the passion and the comradery, the shouts and the whispers; indeed, the mess and the noise.

'It was such an exciting time, pre-Facebook, so discussions about music, that's where they lived,' says Darren Levin, who was editor-in-chief of *Mess+Noise* for five years, of the forums. 'So the magazine fed off that. Articles would go straight into the forum, and you'd have 600 comments on a Royal Headache review. You see Facebook comments on music writing and they're just like, "This is shit," just pithy, pathetic one-liners … it's not a conversation. And that's one great thing about the *Mess+Noise* forum – it was a real conversation about the review, or the feature, that actually added something *to* the conversation.'

'There wasn't much money in it at the start … it's a tough world to be in because [we were] so indie, you know?' remembers Craig Mathieson, who edited the physical magazine, having edited *Juice* through the mid-1990s. 'We published some great stuff every issue – there'd be at least one great thing in every issue. I mean, I thought we'd gone past the street press pretty quickly; I thought we were a great alternative.'

It was a gritty publication dedicated entirely to Australian music, but as so often happens, it wouldn't last. Mathieson says the team was able to sell enough ads to pay themselves a small part-time wage by the end, but print costs became prohibitive. And so the physical magazine came to an end in 2007, after fifteen issues. It existed online for a number of years before being sold to Sound Alliance, who rebranded as Junkee Media, and while they kept the *Mess+Noise* website for a while, it was eventually whittled down to little more than the odd news piece, plans for longform (albeit sporadic) features not eventuating.

Another aspect of the Australian rock press, and one often overlooked, is the major daily newspapers. Through the 1980s, 1990s and into the 2000s, before print came up against the internet, these papers had strong and well-respected music coverage – staff writers who focused purely on music, such as Bernard Zuel (*The Sydney Morning Herald*), Patrick Donovan (*The Age*), Iain Shedden (*The Australian*) and Noel Mengel (*The Courier-Mail*) became trusted household names.

Today, Kathy McCabe is still writing about music for *The Daily Telegraph*, while Andrew McMillen,[46] who filled Shedden's chair at *The Australian* after Shedden's death in 2017, is arguably the most prolific music journalist in the country. *The Guardian*'s culture section, which has been helmed for some years by Steph Harmon, while it is solely online, has become a trusted source for music information, albeit constrained by budgetary restrictions. Add to this pool the less-frequent music coverage in Schwartz Media titles *The Monthly* and *The Saturday Paper*, which provide sporadic space to longform music writing courtesy of some of the best in the game, such as Robert Forster (who was part of seminal Brisbane band The Go-Betweens), Anwen Crawford and

Shaad D'Souza. Longform music writing doesn't appear often anymore, and so it is an exquisite pleasure when it is encountered.

Together, every one of these magazines, newspapers and online publications have made up over half a century of Australia's rock 'n' roll press, a press which has churned alongside our strong and vibrant music scene in a unique way. From pop-tinged beginnings in the mid-1960s to today's digital frontier, our rock 'n' roll press has recorded all that's happened in music – the changes and innovations, the sounds, sights and sensations that have melded together to create what's been.

There's no denying that over the course of this half-century, the rock 'n' roll press in Australia has changed drastically. But it began changing almost from the moment it began, *Go-Set* even in its early years consistently evolving in order to meet the needs of its changing audience. At the same time, as the music scene grew, new trends and sounds and ideals and motives entered the frame, sparking reinvention and, sometimes, revolution.

I wonder sometimes if today there is the same religiosity in the consumption of music journalism there was when one's fingers would become ink-stained by delving into a street press paper before heading out on a Thursday night. I wonder if there's room in the online cacophony for the aspiring music writer, the music critic, the rock journo, 'the enemy' to truly thrive. Instead of waiting for Wednesday morning to grab a magazine from a newsstand on your way to work, you've got it on your phone, and maybe too much of a good thing dulls the excitement.

Maybe, or maybe not. It probably depends in part on who you ask. Things have changed, which is simply just how it goes. The music is still here, though, still pounding and thumping, provoking, inspiring, and whether you're a music fan or a music writer, it will stay with you your entire life. I've had countless moments over the past twenty years where I've had to pinch myself: I can't believe I'm speaking to Gillian

Welch or Dave Mustaine or The Black Keys or The Dandy Warhols … I can't believe George Clinton looked at me askance through a smoky haze, rounded up his funky troops and led them out the door towards another plane of existence.

Music may not have the power to affect change anymore, at least not en masse as it once did, when for a new generation everything seemed new and exciting and possible, but it still has the power to inspire passionate feelings, memorable experiences, and to transport us to other worlds. As long as we have music, there'll be a rock press attempting to capture it, creating a chronicle of our lives as it does so.

ACKNOWLEDGEMENTS

In researching and writing *Full Coverage*, a process that took the better part of a decade, I came into contact with a great many people.

Some of them I already knew, others I knew of. Still more I met along the way. Each and every one gave of their time and knowledge openly and, for the vast majority, with a degree of enthusiasm and excitement that often left me humbled; so happy were they to recount times gone by, and to someone who was in many cases was an absolute stranger to them. My favourite part of this process were the interviews that, mere minutes in, ceased being formal journalistic exchanges and became conversations; the majority fit into this category.

I interviewed around 100 people for *Full Coverage*, and to every single one, whether I quoted them directly or used their input as background, I would like to extend my heartfelt thanks. There were a few individuals in particular who indulged me on more than one occasion in the flesh, as well as fielding numerous emails, texts and phone calls during the writing and editing processes: Phillip Frazer, Stuart Coupe and Craig Treweek, founts of knowledge all.

I'd also like to extend a very large thank-you to my publisher/editor, Julia Carlomagno. The role of editor in these situations is often left unacknowledged, but without the tireless efforts of Julia and her team at Monash University Publishing, not to mention their belief in the project as a whole, this book would never have seen the light of day.

Finally, and by no means least of all, I would like to acknowledge the incredible amount of love and support offered me by my wife, Claire, and our daughter, Adeline – often was the time, particularly during deadlines and edits, when I'd be wandering about purporting to be a good husband and father, when in reality I was a million miles away, lost among tales of inky times long gone. Their patience, first and foremost, was incredible, and without them I would certainly not have made it to the finish line.

NOTES

1 Sheldon also edited and published a short-lived magazine entitled *The Popular Musician* around the same period.
2 These stories included the likes of 'Black Mass in Color: Shock Witchcraft Pictures', 'The World's Most Topless City', 'Those Nude Films' and 'Jayne Mansfield Tells All: Those Lewd Film Star Orgies'. Jeffrey Turnbull, 'Melbourne Music in Print – Go-Set Magazine – February 1966 to August 1974', Go-Set Charts, date unknown.
3 'Rebel with a Cause', Monash University, www.monash.edu/giving/ways-to-give/leave-a-bequest/bequest-stories/rebel-with-a-cause
4 Lot's Wife Editors, 'An Explanation', *Lot's Wife*, 14 January 2015, https://lotswife.com.au/an-explanation/
5 In hindsight, Waverley Offset Press, 'straight types' as Frazer calls them, were remarkably open-minded to take the risks they did with *Lot's Wife* and then *Go-Set.*
6 Browning went on to co-found management agency Consolidated Rock with Michael Gudinski in 1970. He also, along with Bill Joseph and Rodney de Gruchy in 1973, opened Melbourne's original Hard Rock Cafe, which is where he discovered AC/DC, becoming their manager for many years.
7 *Go-Set* was for its entire lifespan in debt to its printer. The debt would lessen over time but never be fully paid.
8 It seems this title was his in name only, as even though Barker saw it as his role to control how the magazine came out, the editorial content would have been at the discretion of whoever was editing it.
9 This date and final line clearly had significance to Jiva, but it is not clear whether anyone else was in on the joke – if indeed it was a joke.
10 Barker wouldn't stay up north for long – the following year, he received a call from Gudinski, asking him to return to Melbourne to work as a label manager at the newly formed Mushroom Records.
11 When it finally folded in January 2018 (after numerous ownership changes), the Australian *Rolling Stone* was the longest continuously running version of the magazine outside of the United States. It was revived in March 2020 by The Brag Media, and today prints quarterly.

12 *Nation Review* was a self-proclaimed 'lean and nosey' politics and culture magazine first appearing in 1972 as a binding of *Nation* and *Sunday Review*, from publisher Gordon Barton.

13 Philip Mason, who would go on to become quite a publishing name in Australian rock circles, was at this time working as marketing director at Sungravure, and he has no recollection of this ever being a policy.

14 A short while into *RAM*'s existence, an old friend of Philip Mason's, Barry Stewart, came on board to sell ads, having worked as the sales director at Channel 9. He had a share in Soundtracts, which later on became Mason Stewart.

15 'We had a terrace on Glebe Point Road,' Coupe recalls, 'and downstairs was *Tracks*, the surfing mag – also published by Philip Mason by then. Those guys would spend four feverish, speed-fuelled days putting together [their] mag then go off surfing, that's what they did.'

16 'Jeez man, it just pissed me off' was the thought bubble in the cartoon that accompanied the article on the dole. The article itself was entitled 'Get on the Dole – Live The Good Life Ha! Ha!'.

17 The origins of the publication's title are unclear. 'Juke' may have been a play on 'jukebox', or evoking the slang meaning to make a move intended to deceive an opponent, or something else entirely, but no one seems to know for sure.

18 Newspress, which later became Syme Magazines according to Eliezer, was headed by Leonard J. Shaw, who by default became editor-in-chief of *Juke*.

19 The Australian version of *Smash Hits* birthed from the UK original in late 1984, published initially by Fairfax's magazine arm, before being purchased by Mason Stewart. It ran as a fortnightly at first, syndicating material from England mixed with some local content, before morphing to a monthly, then a bi-monthly, folding in 2007 due to low circulation numbers.

20 'Paul Gardner had kind of said maybe we should do this cover, maybe not… it was a whole thing,' Creswell recalls. 'He wanted just Michael, and I was quite close to the MMA people who were INXS's management, [they] wanted the whole band. And they wanted this and that and I kind of felt I didn't cope very well with the tension of that. So they ended up getting the cover, it was a Michael Hutchence cover. It did really well, and that was kind of what broke the drought with *Rolling Stone* on Australian covers. That was my first one. That was exciting.'

21 'The plan was for *Age* management to go to *RAM*'s office on a Wednesday and tell them they were under new ownership,' Eliezer clarifies. 'I arranged with a big-name freelance photographer to be at their offices and take photos of their shocked faces which we could publish in *Juke*. Alas, the announcement was put forward by two days and we missed our chance.'

22 Creswell wrote a biography of Cold Chisel's lead singer, Jimmy Barnes, which was published by Random House's Vintage imprint in September 1993.

23 Cultural influencer Annie Flanders was the founding editor-in-chief of *Details*, established in 1982 and published by Condé Nast. It ceased production in late 2015.

24 O'Donnell went on to become a music-industry executive, holding senior roles with Sony Music Australia and EMI Music Australia and launching artists such as Silverchair, Jebediah, Something for Kate and Missy Higgins.

25 Luke Collins, 'Spira Finds that Diamonds Aren't Forever', *Australian Financial Review*, 3 April 2001.
26 *Trad&Now*, a magazine covering a similar range of music, appeared in 2002, and while it still prints eight issues a year, it has never had the influence or reach *Rhythms* has commanded over its thirty-plus years.
27 I've been involved with the magazine in one capacity or another since 2001 (including as assistant editor between 2010 and 2015), and through staffing the *Rhythms* stall at the Byron Bay Bluesfest for a number of years, I came to know a good number of the magazine's subscribers, as they'd always come back to extend their subscription. This is one reason the magazine still survives today.
28 'The Colourful Career of Jack Pacholli', *Crikey*, 4 December 2004.
29 Despite repeated efforts, Noel Crabbe could not be located for comment.
30 While not overly music-specific (it was a uni campus magazine, after all), *Time Off* contained small pieces of student news, profiles on various staff, a note from the union president, ads for calculators and short features on things like new venues in the western suburbs ('Beer & Loathing'). Music-wise, in the first issue, there was a Q&A with Brian Wilson, and a full-page feature on The Stranglers ahead of their Feb/Mar tour.
31 'Trevor Young started *A–Z* with financing from the bloke who owned Blackmores health products, they went into partnership,' says Mick Pacholli, who'd worked with Young previously on *TAGG*. 'He employed three or four of my key ex-*TAGG* people. *TAGG* was very much an alternative magazine, and they [copied that] but tried to corporatise it.'
32 Despite repeated invitations to go on the record, along with offers of a right of reply, Rob Furst chose not to be interviewed for *Full Coverage*.
33 'She called it *Rip It Up*, which I think she stole from the New Zealand street press mag,' long-running editor Robert Dunstan laughs. 'How she got away with that, I don't know.'
34 Thanks to writers and editors including Shar Adams, Brent Hampstead and Gavin Sawford.
35 'Which we paid back with interest,' Cott laughs, 'put that down, for goodness' sake.'
36 Initially the legal entity and title of the publication was *The Drum Media*, but as Cott says, 'Aussies love a nickname, so it went from *The Drum Media* to *Drum Media*.'
37 *On the Street PTY Ltd vs Cott*, Supreme Court of New South Wales, 24 September 1990.
38 The Circulation Audit Board (CAB), under the auspices of the Audit Bureau of Circulations (ABC), verifies distribution data on behalf of the media industry. Street press titles were audited by the CAB in order to prove to advertisers that the print and distribution numbers quoted by publications were accurate.
39 '*Mixdown* is a promotional tool for distributors, [a trade mag], it really is, and that's where it sits,' says Patrick Carr, who edited the title in 2010, and who is now Managing Director of Furst Media. 'And then the beautiful thing is, that's how it lives, and then you can bring the beautiful stuff on top – the features on different artists, how to make the sound, interviewing producers, all sorts of stuff.'

40 This typo indicates that at this late point in the magazine's lifespan, mediocrity was, unfortunately, not being as doggedly rejected as whoever was left in charge would have liked.

41 And given the magazines were now monthly, the gig guide, which had always been king, was no longer the weekly deep dive into what was happening. And this was true with any street press paper that changed from weekly to monthly – the gig guide, so long a vital part of street press's makeup, lost its potency without that regularity, and as a result, street press lost a lot of its relevance.

42 In the second issue of the relaunched *The Music*, December 2018, there were seventeen pages of ads before the masthead alone.

43 Spotify was founded in 2006 in Sweden – it took a little while to catch on, taking five years to reach one million paying subscribers, but in June 2016 the company reached 100 million users, 40 per cent of them paid subscribers. In 2022, Spotify reported 188 million paying customers, and 433 million in total.

44 By the term 'press', which I have used throughout this book, I mean printed media, excluding radio and television, which have their own, unique history.

45 Other great online magazines have included *Addicted to Noise*, a pioneer that started in 1997 and was edited by *Rhythms* magazine boss Brian Wise, and *The Vine*, published by Fairfax, which ran for a number of years through the 2000s and was edited for part of this time by respected journalist Marcus Teague.

46 Not the Andrew McMill*a*n who wrote for *RAM*. McMillen the second, as Clinton Walker calls him.